Mass Media Policies
in Changing Cultures

Mass Media Policies
in Changing Cultures

Edited by

GEORGE GERBNER
The Annenberg School of Communications
University of Pennsylvania

A WILEY-INTERSCIENCE PUBLICATION

JOHN WILEY & SONS,   New York · London · Sydney · Toronto

Copyright © 1977 by John Wiley & Sons, Inc.

All rights reserved. Published simultaneously in Canada.

No part of this book may be reproduced by any means, nor transmitted, nor translated into a machine language without the written permission of the publisher.

Library of Congress Cataloging in Publication Data
Main entry under title:
Mass media policies in changing cultures.

"A Wiley-Interscience publication."
Includes bibliographies and index.
1.   Mass media—Addresses, essays, lectures.
2.   Intercultural communication—Addresses, essays, lectures.   I.   Gerbner, George.

P91.M343   301.16'1   77-2399
ISBN 0-471-01514-8

Printed in the United States of America

10 9 8 7 6 5 4 3 2 1

CONTRIBUTORS

IRVING LEWIS ALLEN
Department of Sociology, University of Connecticut

JAY G. BLUMLER
Centre for Television Research, University of Leeds

OLIVER BOYD-BARRETT
Department of Social Sciences and Humanities, The City University, London

ELIZABETH DE CARDONA
International Development Research Center, Bogota

ALEX EDELSTEIN
School of Communications, University of Washington

PAUL EKMAN
Laboratory for the Study of Human Interaction and Conflict, University of California, San Francisco

GEORGE GERBNER
The Annenberg School of Communications, University of Pennsylvania

THOMAS H. GUBACK
Institute of Communications Research, University of Illinois

DONALD L. GUIMARY
Department of Journalism, Portland State University

MICHAEL GUREVITCH
Faculty of Social Science, The Open University, Bucks, England

RANDALL HARRISON
Laboratory for the Study of Human Interaction and Conflict, University of California, San Francisco

SYDNEY W. HEAD
School of Journalism, Temple University

IVAR IVRE
Audience and Programme Research Department, Sveriges Radio, Stockholm

DIANA LANCASTER
Croftways, Kerikeri, New Zealand

HAMID MOWLANA
School of International Service, The American University

KAARLE NORDENSTRENG
Institute of Journalism and Mass Communication, University of Tampere, Finland

HELI E. DE SAGASTI PERRETT
Academy for Educational Development, Washington, D.C.

O. W. RIEGEL
Washington and Lee University

HERBERT I. SCHILLER
Communications Program, Third College, University of California, San Diego

ROBERT LEWIS SHAYON
The Annenberg School of Communications, University of Pennsylvania

KUSUM H. SINGH
Administrative Staff, College of India, Hyderabad, India

TAMÁS SZECSKŐ
Hungarian Radio and Television, Budapest

JEREMY TUNSTALL
Department of Social Science, The City University, London

FRANK OKWU UGBOAJAH
Department of Mass Communication, University of Lagos, Yaba, Nigeria

JORGE WERTHEIN
São Paulo, Brazil

PREFACE

Critical communications policy problems confront all countries with far-reaching decisions. The need for research and planning is becoming evident (1–5). One requirement is the development of a multinational comparative perspective in which to study trends, examine new directions, and consider alternative conceptual frameworks for analysis and interpretation. This book is a contribution toward such a perspective.

The world is our laboratory. Scholars from many countries contributed reports on trends, directions, and theoretical approaches. Part I is a survey of international trends; the authors briefly describe early Western leadership and the more recent shifts in the balance of powers. Part II is an exploration of new directions in communications policy in traditional, transitional, and revolutionary societies; some issues involved in conflicts and controversies such as have occurred in Sweden, India, and South Africa are illuminated. In Part III we present developments in theory and research that can be useful in considering different approaches to cross-cultural comparative media studies.

This volume is for students, social scientists, and policymakers in the mass media and for those in all countries who wish to take an informed part in the shaping of communications policy.

I am indebted to many persons who have assisted in the preparation of this volume; in particular, Nurit Guttman, Valerie Jaworski, Walter Lupan, Kiki Schiller, Marsha Siefert, Tucker Sweitzer, and Jane L. Wilson.

GEORGE GERBNER

Philadelphia, Pennsylvania
February 1977

REFERENCES

1. "Cultural Exchange—or Invasion? A Symposium," *Journal of Communication* (Spring 1974), 89–117.
2. "Forms of Cultural Dependency: A Symposium," *Journal of Communication* (Spring 1975), 121–193.

3. Golding, Peter. "Media Role in National Development: Critique of Theoretical Ortho-
    doxy," *Journal of Communication* (Summer 1974), 39–53.
4. Parker, Edwin B. "Technology Assessment or Institutional Change?" in George Gerbner,
    Larry Gross, and William H. Melody (eds.), *Communications Technology and Social Policy.* New
    York: Wiley, 1973, pp. 533–545.
5. Pool, Ithiel de Sola. "The Rise of Communications Policy Research," *Journal of Communication*
    (Spring 1974), 31–42.

CONTENTS

Mass Media Policies
in Changing Cultures

PART I

International Trends

CHAPTER 1

The American Role
in Worldwide
Mass Communication

JEREMY TUNSTALL

Each of the major mass media—newspapers, magazines, films, records, radio, and television—originally emerged from different countries. But each of these media was first given its characteristic large market shape within a single nation—the United States. All other nations in the world were then exposed either directly to the American media product or to homestyle imitations.

Several scholars in recent years (5, 8, 12, 16, 18) have contributed valuable studies of the spread of American film and telefilm in various parts of the world since 1945. This chapter extends their work.

AMERICA INNOVATES. THE WORLD FOLLOWS

Since the early days in the United States the federal government has always encouraged the mass media, primarily by creating a favorable legal situation for existing media enterprises. While European governments taxed and censored the press, the American government traditionally subsidized it. European governments established state monopolies in radio and television; the American government awarded privileged licenses to commercial enterprises. This pattern has encouraged rapid early growth of new media in the United States.

Within this encouraging environment American media have sought revenue from the market, whereas in Europe and elsewhere media have relied much more heavily on political party and direct government subsidy. "Free enterprise" media at the American national level led to limited competition;

A version of this chapter appears in Jeremy Tunstall, *The Media are American* (London: Constable, 1976).

the few surviving national firms entered the world arena with an aggressive marketing orientation, combined quite often with cartel behavior.

Rapid American expansion in the early stages of a new medium was accompanied by technological developments. Commercial, political, and legal battles focused on patents, lawsuits, industry-supported legislation, and industry-lobbied technical decisions by federal regulating agencies. For example, *most* of the major technical innovations in the nineteenth-century press—Hoe rotary presses, linotype machines, and many other—were American and were then exported to Europe. This was also true in other media: Americans developed records, FM radio, and sound and color for film. Once innovated, the technology was quickly standardized.

The American marketing orientation saw the media audiences as the basis of the media enterprise. When American media products and marketing techniques were used, they quickly captured sizable slices of the European working-class audience.

Accordingly, American media entrepreneurs aimed at a large slice of the total available audience—a "middle market" which was often operationally defined at about 75 percent of the American population (blacks and the poorest whites have until recently been relatively ignored as lacking sufficient revenue prospects). Compared with Europe, American media reached farther down and on a bigger scale in the (especially urban) working class, and most American media were much less concerned with the top 5 percent in terms of income and education.

In addition to standardizing technology and adapting marketing techniques, early American developments in a new mass medium involved standardization of content. Each medium developed a characteristic one. For example, magazines focused on stories and features, records and radio on popular tunes, films on the fictional drama; television in due course focused on various kinds of serial drama and adaptations of the standard contents of all the other media. These American formats have been exported to the world.

In the American media a dominant new type of communicator has appeared. Whether journalist, director or producer, he differs from earlier European models in that he sees himself primarily as a value-neutral "professional," stressing technical and presentation skills; typical European loyalties to political party and artistic reference groups were downgraded. The "professional" orientation has been influential among communicators around the world; this ensures that even in a country where few American media products are imported, communicators—especially in a major national media— look toward New York or Los Angeles (or London) for leadership and ideas.

The pattern of diffusion of American media influence appears to follow the classic S-shaped curve, rising to an early peak, then declining and finally leveling out. Important in the early stages is a phase when the American market for each new mass medium exceeds the market in the rest of the world. From 1850 to 1880 and probably longer, more than half the world's daily newspaper sale was in the United States. In the early-1920s the United States probably had more than half the world's radios; in 1930 the United States still had 43 percent and now has 13 percent of the world's radio sets (3). In 1954 only 16.8 percent of the world's TV sets were *not* in the United States, and of these over half (10.6 percent) of the remaining world total were in the United States (13).

During this early period of American dominance other nations looked to the United States for leadership in every aspect of the new medium. The leadership has in recent decades been assisted by military conquest and quasi-military media activities, but there are three other ways in which leadership has been exerted:

1. Direct exports of media content—most common in the early stage
2. Imitative competition in which American formulae are given local expression (e.g., the wholesale borrowing of film plots, or TV quiz shows)
3. Less specific imitation of American formulae via American orientation of local communicator occupations

The three types of leadership also broadly describe chronological changes over time as a new medium becomes established internationally.

During later stages of this diffusion the more indirect nature of influence makes the identification of specific examples difficult. Although in some countries, such as China, previous substantial American influence may appear to have ceased, in most of the world's countries influence appears to flatten out at a lower but still substantial level. The continuing importance of all the major American media on a world scale means that one medium reinforces another at the organizational level. For example, leadership in electronic media is supported by American dominance in the distribution of world news and its still expanding share of the world's advertising.

This reinforcement process also occurs at the level of content and stars; the same U.S. superstar appears in films, television, records, newsfilm, news agency stories, syndicated gossip columns, and radio interviews, with each medium reinforcing and publicizing the others. This in turn reinforces the widespread belief around the world that the American media are *the* media.

AMERICAN NEWS VALUES AND THE WORLD

In 1850 sales of newspapers per population in the United States were probably about five times as high as those in England (4, 17); and if the main American cities were compared with England, the disproportion was much higher. In England "the taxes on knowledge" were being disbanded, but other European countries were far behind. The rapid growth of the American press was widely known in Europe; for example, in his *American Notes* Charles Dickens fiercely attacked American newspapers.

American newspapers, magazines, and news agencies have profoundly influenced world journalism since about 1840. This influence has never been widely acknowledged nor systematically studied, yet biographies of major European press "innovators" such as Northcliffe (11), August Scherl, founder of the *Berliner Lokalanzeiger* (6) or Luigi Albertini, founder of *Corriera della Sera of Milan* (1) reveal much quiet borrowing: "He [Northcliffe] owed much to American journalism. The first issue of *Answers* had drawn freely on American newspapers and magazines for articles and paragraphs. They continued to be a fertile source of editorial ideas" (11, p. 161). This quotation suggests at least four reasons for the failure to acknowledge American influence. Much of the "borrowing" was so brazen that European "innovators" preferred to conceal it from their readers. Some influence reached newspapers via magazines; some American influence reached Europe and especially Italy and France via London; influence reached Europe in general and Germany in particular via the American foreign language press.

After 1900 the influence of American magazines in Europe was considerable. This grew in the 1930s and of course remains strong today. In the 1970s the presence of American journalism in other countries is especially strong in news and glossy magazines and syndication of columns, features, and comic strips by agencies and American prestige newspapers. Two large American news agencies dominate the distribution of foreign news to newspapers, radio, and television and monopolize the world wirephoto market.

American influence is, perhaps, especially potent in magazines and in "prestige" and "tabloid" newspapers. Many prestige or elite newspapers around the world model themselves on the *New York Times* and use large quantities of American syndicated and agency material. Tabloid newspapers were first developed in Britain but were fully exploited in New York; they remain strongly influenced by current American magazine formats.

Journalists in much of the world have to a greater or lesser extent adopted American news values, styles of newswriting and presentation, and definitions of the role of the journalist. Examples of news values include stress on personalities, human interest, conflict, "bad" news and the "Who? What? When? Where?" approach. Examples of styles include the summary first sentence, the inverted pyramid structure of writing that allows a story to be cut off at any point, and the use of bold headlines and pictures. Examples from the journalist's role include the notion of political neutrality, a substantial degree of occupational autonomy, the protection of confidential news sources, and an ability to produce a specified number of words for a specified deadline.

All of these "neutral" news values and modes of operation reflect American political values. However, outside the United States these political values may be more or less alien. For example, the values imply a degree of journalists' independence from politicians and media controllers that may conflict with local mass communication institutions.

AMERICAN ENTERTAINMENT VALUES AND THE WORLD

The American marketing orientation does not seem to allow for a sharp distinction between news and entertainment, and the electronic media have become primarily equated with entertainment. The definition of radio as primarily an entertainment medium had worldwide implications. But even more important was the definition of television as not merely another entertainment medium but as a visual version of radio. The American radio networks, especially NBC and CBS, dominated the development of television, and after 1945 Britain also resumed television broadcasting inside the state radio monopoly. In short, no nation in the world divorced TV from radio, although a priori it would have been at least as sensible to see television as a national offshoot of the film industry rather than of radio.

Whereas much of the external influence of American radio was exerted via sheet music and later records, the external influence of television was exerted by direct program sales. Typically, imports of U.S. telefilm started high but then fell. Nevertheless Varis (16) found that in 1970–1971 at least 50 percent of television programming was imported by one or more TV channels in Chile, Dominican Republic, Guatemala, Uruguay, Iceland, Ireland, Australia, Malaysia, New Zealand, Singapore, Iraq, Israel, Kuwait, Yemen, Nigeria, and Zambia. Countries with channels importing at least one-third of their programming included Canada, Colombia, Mexico, Finland, Norway, Portugal, Sweden, Bulgaria, Hungary, Hong Kong, Pakistan, Egypt, Lebanon. With the exception of Bulgaria and Hungary, these imports were dominated by American and British products (15).

United States exports of films for theatre showing are more profitable, however. Total theatre film export earnings by American companies for 1973 were running at a rate of about $400 million (15), although Varis (16) found total export sales to television, including feature films, to be about $100 million. The reason for this disparity is obvious. In feature films a monopoly seller (the U.S. Motion Picture Export Association) sells to weak buyers who have inadequate supplies of locally made feature films; in television the typical situation is of a monopoly buyer (the state TV network) confronting many sellers, all of whom are prepared to cut prices and some of whom may supply telefilm free.

What social values does this flood of electronic entertainment promote? At different times American magazines have focused upon different kinds of heroes for biographical treatment: at the turn of the century Napoleonic self-made men, during World War I the industrial "organization man" (7), and during the inter-war years entertainers and other "consumption" hero figures (9). A number of well-known studies deal with such topics as the portrayal of romantic love in songs (10), the "good-bad girl" in Hollywood films (19), and the portrayal of middle-class heroines triumphing through their personal qualities in daytime radio soap operas (2).

One common theme in American mass media products is the emphasis given to individual actions and qualities and personal relationships. Nearly all of the content studies report findings that show the American media consistently project a view of social inequality that stresses status and consensus rather than class or caste and fundamental social conflict.

This consensual and status view of social inequality must, however, be less common in Europe and other parts of the world. These values may well account for some of the audience appeal of American entertainment. Presumably, American marketing has arrived by commercial trial and error at these formulae because they enable the media to appeal successfully to large sectors of the potential audience such as youths, women, and men with roughly average incomes. However, the stress on the young in film and pop songs and on women in most media content may be heady stuff in other countries.

THE MARKET ORIENTATION

By the early-1920s the United States was far ahead of the rest of the world in the quantity of its advertising, market research, and public relations and was being heavily copied in all fields in Europe. Direct involvement of U.S. advertising agencies in other countries began before 1939, but the major development occurred between 1955 and 1965. By 1965 American advertising agencies were playing a prominent part in domestic advertising especially in Britain, West Germany, and Latin America. Since 1965 there has been further expansion in France, Italy, and many other countries. These developments have accompanied the continued international expansion of American consumer goods companies and of television advertising in Europe and elsewhere.

Related to this has been a large expansion in the direct activities of American market research and public relations agencies. By 1970 the international strength of American advertising agencies had succeeded Hollywood as the single most remarkable aspect of the American media presence. The influence of these agencies is illustrated by their preference for television. The kind of American company, such as Proctor and Gamble, that favors TV advertising inside the United States is often prominent internationally. As a result, in many countries in the world advertising men see television (as compared with press media) as less partisan, more American, more researched, and requiring more of the professional expertise advertising agencies claim to offer. This preference for television advertising favors commercial against noncommercial TV.

However, to think of American marketing influence as operating only in television would be erroneous. The enormous commercial marketing character of the U.S. press is illustrated by newsprint statistics. North American per capita consumption of newsprint in 1969 was 11 times that of the U.S.S.R. and 70 times that of Africa and South Asia (13). Well over half of the newsprint used in the United States was for advertising or public relations materials. Because North America alone consumed 47 percent of the world's newsprint, the assumption can be made that American companies were responsible either for using or placing advertising on the majority of the world's total consumption of newsprint.

THE KEY MARKET: BRITAIN AND THE COMMONWEALTH

Historically Britain has long been both the best single foreign market for American mass media and the *entrepot* through which they reached the rest of the world. The American press has influenced English books and magazines since the late-nineteenth century, and the whole history of the BBC can be seen as a long slow defensive action against American styles in radio and television. Major steps in this retreat included competition from European-based American-style commercial radio in the 1930s and from wartime American fare during 1939–1945. The appearance of a commercial television channel in 1955 and the recent appearance of commercial radio complete this pattern.

British concessions to American media products and influence were important because they opened the British Commonwealth market. The Indian subcontinent was early penetrated by Hollywood films; in 1970 India, Pakistan, Bangladesh, Sri-Lanka, and Burma had a population of 700 million. American media products have similarly gained access to much of the African market. The "white Commonwealth" countries—Canada, Australia, New Zealand—have probably the three most American-influenced mass media systems in the world.

English has become the language of international mass communications. For example, Agence-France Presse is forced in much of the world to distribute its news in English, not French. The leadership of America and Britain in the media partly results from and contributes to this position of the English language. More people in Europe now speak English than speak French, and this is especially marked among young adults (14).

European mass media have long been influenced both by the British example directly and by American influence arriving via London. For about 100 years London was the world's telecommunications capital; today it is still the first or the "first equal" center in Europe for each of the mass media. It is also still the leading world *entrepot* for foreign and financial news of all kinds and for television news film (Visnews and UPITN).

Seen from Bombay or Bogota, one can hardly distinguish between American and British mass media. In the nineteenth century and in more recent times the American media have drawn much more heavily on British experience than upon that of any other country. Britain is also the only foreign nation with more than a nominal level of media exports to the United States. British Reuters now operates within the United States as a domestic news agency, and American TV imports come mainly from Britain (mostly ATV and BBC).

LATIN AMERICA, AFRICA, ASIA

In Latin America U.S. mass media influence first became important in the 1920s. Hollywood films dominated, and radio was widely adopted on an American pattern (many local stations, commercial ownership, advertising). During 1939–1945 the American news agencies became powerful and remain so. Brazil and Argentina began television broadcasting early and by 1954 were ahead of most of the European countries in TV sets per capita (14, pp. 77–82). The pattern followed that of their own radio and American TV. Because the many stations, long hours of output, and low revenue left the Latin Americans short of programming they quickly turned to cheap imports of American series. Mexico has played a key role in influencing the rest of Latin America, and their mass media display strong American influence.

Disregarding China and the U.S.S.R., the 11 next most populous nations of Asia—India, Indonesia, Pakistan, Bangladesh, Japan, Philippines, Turkey, Thailand, South Korea, Burma, and Iran—all show substantial Anglo-American influence on their mass media. Each of the following is found in over half of these 11 Asian nations: foreign advertising agencies; commercial television; the main national news agency relying heavily on one or more of Reuters, AP, UPI; a primarily privately owned press; American and British imported films with a substantial share of the domestic market; and substantial imports of American magazines. In 1970 all 11 nations had some English language *domestic* media, usually daily newspapers.

In Africa there is still probably more British than American influence, but the latter is growing. French colonization also shaped African media.

Although differences both among and within Latin America, Asia, and Africa are enormous, one can note some common patterns.

1.   A heavy stress on daily newspapers based on cities and modeled on the prestige papers of the West, including sizable proportions of foreign news

2.   A low emphasis on rural media in general and rural or weekly newspapers in particular

3.   Heavy emphasis on the cinema, which is also a primarily urban medium

4.   A tendency to introduce television to the major cities before radio has reached most of the rural population

5.   A substantial element of government influence or control in the media

6.   A tacit (or formal) bargain struck between the national government and the international (especially Anglo-American) purveyors of media products by which substantial media imports are allowed to enter under strict government control and censorship

All of these common factors are likely to ensure the continuing presence and influence of Anglo-American media. One can speculate on reasons for the relative success of Anglo-American government media efforts in the world compared with those of the Soviet Union:

1.   The international flow of mass media is dominated by Anglo-American commercial efforts, and to swim with this flow is much easier than to try to swim against it.

2.   English is the language of international communication. Russian and Chinese are not world languages in the same sense.

3.   The western governments' media make greater use of local personnel and give them more freedom in deciding what to write or to broadcast.

4.   Western news values that emphasize speed of response enable Anglo-American broadcasters to provide "up-to-the-minute" news and comment; communist media are often delayed by their need for political guidance.

5.   Western market-oriented news values and entertainment values are more flexible and more universally acceptable than nonmarket communist news and entertainment values.

Has Marshall McLuhan's global village arrived? A more useful image might be of a "global city." In much of the world the mass media are still heavily concentrated in the cities, and Anglo-American media products and influence are most evident there. To think in terms of a common agenda shared via the mass media by urban residents throughout the world may not be too farfetched.

Insofar as there is a common worldwide reality, it is a reality constructed mostly by organizations based in New York, Los Angeles, and London.

REFERENCES

1. Albertini, Alberto. *Vita de Luigi Albertini.* Rome: Mondadori, 1945.
2. Arnheim, Randolph. "The World of the Daytime Serial," in Paul F. Lazarsfeld and Frank Stanton (eds.), *Radio Research, 1942–43.* New York: Duell, Sloan and Pearce, 1944.
3. Batson, Lawrence D. *Radio Markets of the World, 1930.* Washington: Government Printing Office, 1930.
4. De Fleur, Melvin L. *Theories of Mass Communication.* New York: McKay, 1970.
5. Dizard, Wilson P. *Television: A World View.* Syracuse: Syracuse University Press, 1966.
6. Erman, H. *August Scherl.* Berlin: Universitas Verlag, 1954.
7. Greene, Theodore P. *America's Heroes: The Changing Models of Success in American Magazines.* New York: Oxford University Press, 1970.
8. Guback, Thomas H. *The International Film Industry.* Bloomington: Indiana University Press, 1969.
9. Horton, Donald. "The Dialogue of Courtship in Popular Songs," *American Journal of Sociology, 62* (1957), 569–578.
10. Lowenthal, Leo. "Bibliographies in Popular Magazines," in Paul F. Lazarsfeld and Frank Stanton (eds.), *Radio Research, 1942–43.* New York: Duell, Sloan and Pearce, 1944.
11. Pound, Reginald, and Geoffrey Harmsworth. *Northcliffe.* London: Cassell, 1959.
12. Schiller, Herbert I. *Mass Communications and American Empire.* New York: Augustus M. Kelley, 1969.
13. *Statistics on Radio and Television (1950–1960).* Paris: UNESCO, 1963.
14. *A Survey of Europe Today.* London: Reader's Digest, 1970.
15. *Variety,* 14 November, 1973.
16. Varis, Tapio. "Global Traffic in Television," *Journal of Communication* (Winter 1974), 102–109.
17. Wadsworth, A. P. *Newspaper Circulations 1800–1954.* Manchester: Manchester Statistical Society, 1955.
18. Wells, Alan. *Picture-Tube Imperialism? The Impact of U.S. Television on Latin-America.* Maryknoll, N.Y.: Orbis Books, 1972.
19. Wolfenstein, Martha, and Nathan Leites. "An Analysis of Themes and Plots in Motion Pictures," in Wilbur Schramm (ed.), *Mass Communications.* Urbana: University of Illinois Press, 1960, pp. 380–391.

CHAPTER 2

The Global News Wholesalers

OLIVER BOYD-BARRETT

The worldwide news agency or wire service is the most important source of foreign news for media throughout the world. The International Press Institute's 1953 survey (2) found that almost three quarters of all foreign news in 105 U.S. newspapers examined was supplied by three North American wire services: Associated Press (AP), United Press (UP), and International News Service (INS). In 1958 UP assimilated INS to form United Press International (UPI). American newspapers tend to subscribe to only one major news service (9)—for international, national, and state news. One informed observer has estimated that more than half the newspapers published in state capitals take state-house news from agencies rather than maintain their own journalists for such coverage (13).

A similar dependency on wire services has been demonstrated for European media. The 1953 IPI study drew estimates from editors of a number of European newspapers of the percentage of agency copy to foreign news published; these ranged from an average of 40 percent in some countries to 70 percent in others. This sample did not include provincial or regional newspapers of the European press, which often depend heavily for their supply of foreign news on the selection of items from international agency wires made by national news agencies. Studies by Starck and Thoren in the late 1960s indicate heavy dependence on the four major western-based global agencies by the national press of Sweden and Finland. The analysis by Galtung and Ruge (3) of the coverage by four Norwegian papers of three international crises showed that 87 percent of the examined news items came from these four agencies.

In this analysis I try to demonstrate the importance of the global news agencies as suppliers of foreign news throughout the world. Acceptance by media of the agency definitions of foreign news raised questions concerning the extent to which the agencies expressed or created a journalistic consensus. Such a consensus appeared more demonstrable in the developed regions of North America and Western Europe than elsewhere. This is shown to follow from a history of the agencies in which sectional, national, and commercial pressures had together produced a structural imbalance that favored Western-based interests which is still in evidence.

This situation reflects the continuing inequality of media resources between nations. Foreign news-gathering resources can also be regarded as a form of commodity, which a few nations have and most do not. Hachten has argued that the flow of news from less developed nations to more developed nations seems to be more closely related to the use of a world news agency than to geographical proximity or language similarity and that the reverse flow from more to less developed nations is greatly influenced by the particular world news agency that the less developed nations use (11).

An IPI study of news flow in Asia found that the world agencies were "by far the most important sources of Asian news for the press of Asian countries, and this also applies even to those few papers that have correspondents in Asian centres" (2). Markham (8) found that seven metropolitan dailies in Latin America relied almost entirely on AP, UPI, and AFP for their foreign news, even though they carried about twice as much foreign news as comparable U.S. newspapers. Foreign news in Africa was found by Hachten (5) to originate mostly from the European and American agencies and to be distributed through government-controlled national news agencies in most cases, many of which had been established with advice and technical aid from Reuters or AFP.

Nearly all attempts to establish world agencies to compete with those already mentioned have floundered and none have succeeded. An alternative source of regional news has sometimes been established where national news agencies enter into exchange agreements with one another. Such arrangements are limited in value where the agencies in question are government controlled, as they often are, and have very restricted resources even for coverage of their own domestic news. They are generally less well equipped to meet the requirements of media in neighboring countries than the established global agencies.

JOURNALISTIC CONSENSUS AND THE AGENCIES

The wire services help their clients establish news priorities in a number of ways: They make the initial news selection, apportioning more space to stories considered highly newsworthy than to others, and use a coding system that indicates whether a story is considered "urgent." In his study of 16 telegraph editors of a newspaper sample Gieber (4) found "the press association has become the recommender of news to the wire editor and thus the real selector of telegraph news. The wire editor evaluated the news according to what the AP sent him." Studies of one such editor, "Mr. Gates," in two periods, 1949 and 1966, largely support this view. The attention Mr. Gates gave to the various categories of news closely reflected the space allocated to the categories on the wire services he received. The consonance was not so great in the second study when he received only one news service, in contrast to the earlier period when he had received three services (10, 12). The selection of wire service news at any given moment of time may be influenced by "budget" statements announcing the news that is due to be sent in the near future. In a study of telegraph editor selection of wire service content, Liebes (7) reported that 25 percent of his respondents admitted that wire service budgets of what they considered the outstanding stories to come were decisive factors in their decision-making.

With continuous deadlines and an emphasis upon spot news developments, the wire services are frequently first with the news, even when the subscribing media have extensive alternative sources. In many parts of the world agency representatives may be the only journalists available when a major development "breaks," and in any case they generally have more men on the ground than alternative media. For this reason alone they might be expected to have a considerable impact on journalistic consensus of the importance of available foreign news items.

FACTIONAL AND NATIONAL INTERESTS

The origins of the European agencies are closely linked with the demand for financial intelligence. Charles Havas was a financier before he started his agency, and for the first eight years he catered only to private clients. Wolff, who founded the German agency of that name, was the son of a banker. For the first seven years of Reuter's operations in London the only clients were financiers, and news was mostly economic. The first exchange arrangement among these three agencies was to exchange news of the Bourse and trading information. By the mid-1860s Wolff's agency became dependent on government patronage and the support of the banking houses. The importance of speed, so essential in the canons of western journalism, was promoted by banks and governments in their concern for news of trade and war quite some time before it bothered newspaper editors.

Expansion of the European agencies followed the territorial and economic designs of their home governments. The interests of their clients and the paths of the new submarine cables lay in this direction. This was reflected in the cartel system consolidated in the treaties of 1870, which divided the world into exclusive distribution territories. After some further additions, Reuters emerged with the British Empire; Holland; and its dependencies, Australia, the East Indies, and the Far East. Wolff, or Continental as it came to be called, took Germany, Scandinavia, St. Petersburg, and Moscow and also enjoyed a special relationship with Corrbureau, the agency of the Austro-

Hungarian empire based in Vienna. Havas had France, Italy, Spain, Portugal, the Levant, Indochina, and Latin America. Some territories were operated jointly, such as the Ottoman Empire and Egypt; others, including the United States, were considered "neutral."

These divisions were based not only on the political interests of the respective clientele groupings, but the likelihood that an agency would have better access and communication facilities when covering territories controlled by its home government. The arrangements did not prevent the agencies from gathering news from the territories of their allies, only from distributing in those territories. In practice, however, the volume of newsgathering in each other's territories was far less than it might have been had the treaties not existed. But the purpose of the cartel was to avoid the heavy expenditure that truly global representation would necessitate for one agency. Such a responsibility might have brought an end to the formal independence of Reuters and Havas.

As it was, the business of general newsgathering for media markets was not immensely profitable. Havas became involved in advertising as early as 1857, a side of its business that fluctuated but was always important until World War II. Reuters exploited its strategic position at the hub of British and world communications by establishing a private telegram business which operated on the basis of secret codes. This was an important source of revenue until the development of good, less expensive public telegraph systems in the early 1900s.

To the extent that their news was not tailored to fit the convenience of political party factions, or indeed of any expressed ideology, and was released as quickly as technology allowed to all subscribers equally, Reuters and Havas were "objective" in their service. But naturally, their news reflected the interests of the governing and commercial elites.

The American agencies were conceived in a market already advanced in the popular field. Press freedom in the United States had a much earlier history than in Europe and was positively supported by federal government. By the mid-nineteenth century the United States had become the world center of the cheap daily press, which reached deep into the urban working classes even before the daily press of Europe had reached most of the middle class. By 1900 the U.S. press had moved decisively towards a commercial market orientation. At this time the revenue obtained by American papers was probably greater than that of all the papers of the rest of the world.

The struggle to secure domestic markets in the United States led to tactics and shifting alliances similar to those of the European agencies in their struggle for *both* national and international markets. When in the 1890s AP (of Illinois) established itself temporarily as a monopoly in the wire service field, it almost at once prepared the conditions for future domestic competition in a series of fundamentally restrictive measures that were intended to secure the loyalty of members. These included membership of the European cartel system through an exchange arrangement with Reuters, a continued bias in favor of morning newspapers, prohibition of alternative subscriptions by members, and the right of members to veto distribution to competing newspapers.

In reaction to these restrictions United Press Associations was formed in 1907 and International News Service in 1910. UPA's rapid expansion and the advantages of independent operation pushed AP gradually but surely to break away from the cartel, which came to be identified with European territorial imperialism. The American agencies promoted their expansion with the rhetoric of objectivity and free enterprise. These concepts seemed closely related, because the penetration of Europe's colonial markets signified a loosening in the monopolistic control over the supply of information. The terms were economically suitable as well, for in a free market the American agencies stood a very good chance of winning.

After World War I the advertising operations of Havas became increasingly important, and newsgathering deteriorated as a source of revenue. International news coverage was maintained only by virtue of large injections of government aid. Meanwhile the involvement in advertising brought the agency into considerable disrepute domestically. Pierre Lazareff wrote, "through its grip on the distribution of news and advertising, the Havas Agency was able to exert control over the biggest newspapers in France." Lazareff's condemnation is slightly misplaced. The essential point, as Al Laney wrote, was that the news supplied by Havas "was often, if not always, bent to fit its enormous volume of advertising. It enjoyed a practical monopoly and it could and did control news anywhere in France" (6, pp. 159, 295).

The extent and character of expansion into international newsgathering by the U.S. agencies tended to reflect their concern with domestic markets and subscribers or members. Between the wars "An America in isolation basically wanted foreign news that was compounded out of crisis or curiosity, sometimes both, and that is what was generally in the wire service foreign file in that era" (p. 282). The volume of international news was not great, and most of it that did not originate from the cartel came from UP, which concentrated on the entertainment-oriented afternoon press and was more populist in tone than AP.

UP was a privately owned enterprise belonging to Scripps newspapers. AP's cooperative structure, however, did not necessarily make it any more representative of national interests as a whole. It had a more high-brow image than UP, and until World War II it maintained a system of franchise rights to protect members' monopolies which made it something of an exclusive club.

World War II produced fundamental changes in the structure of the European agencies. Reuters became a cooperatively owned company representing national and provincial newspapers of Britain, and the press associations of Australia, New Zealand, and for a time, India. In this way she was protected from the kind of government-agency "understanding" that existed prior to the war. Moreover, the political atmosphere had changed: The government was not eager to be involved. A Post Office memorandum in 1946 read:

> AP and UPI have been agitating for some months for extension of their multi-destination Press wireless services. Although plant is available, we cannot give them the additional services they want—which would bring their facilities more nearly into line with those already afforded to Reuters . . . The agencies point out that the problem would be resolved if they were allowed to use their own operators. To concede this would be to provoke opposition from the U.P.W. (Union of Post Office Workers). It is difficult to continue to refuse facilities to the agencies, especially since a statement was recently made by the U.S. State Department that facilities given to the American News Agencies were less than those afforded to Reuters.

The memorandum recommended a relaxation of the rules, which indeed occurred.

Reuters had lost important markets as a result of the war. In response it elevated the importance of commercialism in agency operations. Economic news services especially were developed, and today Reuters depends on non-media organizations subscribing to financial and economic news services for over 50 percent of overall revenue. The marketing orientation was reflected again in a 1974 reorganization, dividing the company into a cost center and three profit centers. The profit centers are Reuters media service, Reuters Economic Services, and Reuters North America.

During the war Havas became the property of the Vichy government, and its advertising business was divorced from news agency operations. Ex-Havas journalists in London helped establish L'Agence Française Independent, which in 1944 became Agence France Presse but was not formally constituted until as late as 1957 when it assumed a cooperative character under the joint control of leading publisher and government clients and employees. Unlike Reuters, AFP was not able to maintain its independence from the government, and it became heavily dependent upon the payments of government agencies.

AFP chose to stress its character as a cooperative, perhaps to distinguish itself from the commercial and allegedly corrupt practices of its predecessor, Havas. Unlike Reuters, it had to start virtually from scratch after the war and needed government capital to retrieve lost markets. More closely controlled by interests outside the agency than its three western counterparts—interests that are not consistently served by its international newsgathering operations—it has experienced greater difficulty in finding the means to establish an independent capital base, and its success in this direction now seems highly improbable.

There have been no radical changes in structure in the American agencies. However, there have been fluctuations between emphasis on domestic and foreign markets and a substantial investment in both, in terms of computer technology and rationalization of news service. In UPI this has taken the form of a decentralized, computer-guided, multiaddress system that reduced editorial control in the world services. AP began to computerize its overseas operations in 1975. Content analysis of its overseas wires in 1974 indicated that AP regionalized its news services in foreign markets to a lesser extent than UPI; interviews suggested that the introduction of computer operations would not alter this situation (1). This might be interpreted in its effects as a form of rationalization that concentrates on the wealthier markets at the expense of the less affluent. AP's 1972 investment in a new domestic system of regional computer centers designed to eliminate manual operations and to concentrate editing was accompanied by remarks concerning the increasing importance of domestic news and the decline of American interest in foreign news. Nevertheless, there is no doubt that World War II promoted a considerable expansion of the U.S. agencies, which capitalized to some extent on the difficulties of the European agencies and on the international demand for American news that grew in response to the heightened American political and economic involvement in the world generally. Today there appears to be near saturation of media markets in the field of general news, which has given added revenue importance to the "subsidiary" activities of the American agencies. The spread of agency resources throughout the world suggests a tendency to concentrate on high revenue-producing areas. These are, inevitably, North America, Western Europe, and a few wealthy metropolitan areas in the rest of the world. Africa is particularly underrepresented. These same high revenue-producing areas receive most prominence in agency news services, although the absolute volume, and possibly the relative proportion, of news concerning the less-developed and nonwestern regions of the world is higher in the 1970s than in the 1950s. The foreign news content of the agencies appears to be heavily dominated by government-political, economic, and sports news. There is also a tendency to concentrate on international rather than domestic issues, which may follow from the added sales potential of stories that concern more than one country and the fact that such stories are often less controversial than stories of domestic politics.

REFERENCES

1. Boyd-Barrett, J. O. *Les Agences de presses mondiales.* Paris: Alain Moreau, 1976. News International research report available in Open University Library, Milton Keynes, U.K.

2. *The Flow of News.* Zurich: International Press Institute, 1953.

3. Galtung, Johan, and Mari Ruge. "The Structure of Foreign News," *Journal of Peace Research, 1* (1965), 64–90.

4. Gieber, Walter. "Across the Desk: A Study of 16 Telegraph Editors," *Journalism Quarterly, 33* (Autumn 1956), 423–432.

5. Hachten, William. *Muffled Drums: The News Media in Africa.* Ames: Iowa State University Press, 1971.

6. Homenberg, John. *Foreign Correspondence.* New York: Columbia University Press, 1964.

7. Liebes, B. H. "Decision-Making by Telegraph Editors—AP or UPI?" *Journalism Quarterly 43,* 3 (1966), 434–442.

8. Markham, John. "Foreign News in the United States and South American Press," *Public Opinion Quarterly 25* (1961), 249–262.

9. Schwarzlose, Richard A. "Trends in Newspapers: Wire Service Resources, 1934–66," *Journalism Quarterly 43* (Winter 1966), 627–638.

10. Snider, Paul. "Mr. Gates' Revisited: A 1966 Version of the 1949 Case Study," *Journalism Quarterly 43,* 3 (1966), 419–427.

11. Sunwoo Nam. "The Flow of International News into Korea," *Gazette XVI, 1* (1970), 15–26.

12. White, David M. "The Gate-Keeper: A Case Study in the Selection of News," *Journalism Quarterly 27,* 3 (1950), 383–390.

13. Williams, Francis. *The Right to Know.* London: Longmans, 1969.

CHAPTER 3

The International Film Industry

THOMAS H. GUBACK

In the early 1970s the nations of the world were annually producing about 3500 feature motion pictures. Although only about 5 percent were of American origin, American films occupied about 50 percent of theatrical screen time in what is called the Free World.

Pictures made in the United States dominate their own home market, and are shown in more than 100 other countries. About half of the theatrical revenues of U.S. film companies come from abroad. Probably no other large American industry relies so heavily upon overseas earnings as does film. In this respect, if one can talk about an *international* film industry, it must be American.

Although television usually is considered as competing with motion pictures, at least in the United States most programming is film, usually produced by the major film companies, some of which own television stations.* Like theatrical films, these series are rented overseas by Hollywood companies and are permanent fixtures on many of the 200,000,000 TV sets abroad (40). In this way telefilm is following the model provided by theatrical film. This is not surprising; the same companies are active in both fields.

EXPORTING AMERICA'S FILMS

Allied Artists, Avco Embassy, Columbia, Metro-Goldwyn-Mayer, Paramount, Twentieth Century-Fox, United Artists, Universal, and Warner Bros. are members of the Motion Picture Association of America (MPAA) and its

---

*The networks produce very little material except for news and public affairs. For example, 90 percent of all entertainment programming on CBS was supplied by outside sources, according to a network announcement in December 1973. In the previous year members of the Motion Picture Association of America provided seven of every 10 hours of prime time programming on the three national commercial networks. Motion pictures produced for theatrical release or television debut comprised about 40 percent; series made especially for TV made up the remainder.

foreign trade affiliate, the Motion Picture Export Association (MPEA). As vendors of TV programming overseas, they accounted for 80 percent of the $84 million reportedly remitted by U.S. companies in 1972. As sellers of films for theatrical presentation, the same firms earned 90 percent of the $258 million of revenue estimated to have been remitted by American distributors abroad.

An MPEA document pointed out as long ago as 1960:

From their long experience in distributing feature films overseas, the major motion picture companies were among the first to recognize the potential of the international market for television film. Just as foreign distribution now accounts for more than 50% of their gross revenues from features, they foresaw the day when the rapidly growing need for TV film programs abroad would bring about a similar situation in the electronic medium. The basic economic factors are identical. With the tremendous and steadily rising costs of production for both media, the domestic market alone cannot support a profitable operation. . . . The plush days of assured profit from the U.S. market in motion picture production ended many years ago, and the same thing is already true of television film. A producer is fortunate today if he can repay his negative costs from a network sale. His overhead and possible profit must come from the "residuals"—rerun sales after the network run and distribution in the international market (23, p. 2).

The overseas distribution of products from America's film companies is facilitated by the MPEA, which in the 1950s already was studying the small but quickly growing foreign television market. In early-1959 its Television Film Export Committee was established to "enable the member companies to move into new areas as soon as they become profitable sales outlets" and to "discover unfavorable developments in their early stages and to combat them before they have hardened into unilateral decrees or [foreign] Government regulations" (23, p. 4).

The MPEA itself is one of several MPAA affiliate organizations that the film industry has used to operate in foreign markets. The Export Association was established in 1945 and registered under the Webb-Pomerene Export Trade Act of 1918. This legislation provides certain exemptions from the Sherman and Clayton antitrust acts for associations organized by American companies, provided the groups operate only overseas. In effect the Webb Act allows firms supposedly competitive in the American market to combine to fix prices and allocate customers abroad—practices that are illegal domestically. Coming at a time when few companies were greatly concerned with foreign operations, the Act was an early effort on the part of the government to stimulate international expansion of American business.

The MPEA, created as it was in the wake of World War II, was the film industry's attempt to order and enlarge its foreign markets that were to become immensely important in terms of revenue. In many instances the war had disrupted existing patterns of film trade and had overturned systems of legislation abroad that had been aimed at protecting foreign film production from being smothered by Hollywood. This was especially the case in Western Europe, the principal foreign market for American films, which the American companies could not afford to lose and hardly wanted to share. Film distribution offices not only had to be reestablished, but more important was the development of a vigorous united front on the part of American companies to force higher rental prices from exhibitors, thwart foreign legislation that might hinder the circulation of American pictures, and develop means to export earned dollars from countries extremely short of hard currency (14, pp. 91–141).

The MPEA seemed to be the organization that could accomplish this because it brought together the most important American film distributors. It could exert leverage both by withholding films from a market that had come to depend upon them and by working through the American government whose own postwar policy called for extensive foreign propaganda programs in which films were included as "ambassadors of goodwill"—President Truman's term (16). In an early display of the powers of what are known now as multinational corporations the association also was capable of bringing pressure directly upon foreign states. The president of the MPEA, Jack Valenti, once declared: "To my knowledge, the motion picture is the only U.S. enterprise that negotiates on its own with foreign governments" (37). The MPEA concludes treaties as if it were an autonomous nation, reaffirming the political and economic nature of America's overseas film trade whose cultural consequences cannot be overlooked.

Although the determined effort to control foreign markets was made in the post-World War II era, the American domination of them often reaches back to the years after World War I. The difference, however, is that in the 1920s and 1930s for most American film companies revenue from foreign markets was simply an additional increment of profit upon which corporate lives did not depend. But due to the impact of television, coupled with antitrust action which divested Hollywood production-distribution companies of their theatres, market conditions changed radically in the 1950s, and the majority of theatrical revenue for the companies began to come from abroad. The domestic market no longer could entirely support an industry as it had been structured in the 1930s and 1940s—an industry producing 400 or so films annually with substantial investments in physical properties in Hollywood and large staffs and large overhead.

AMERICANIZATION OF EUROPEAN FILM INDUSTRIES

American films dominated European screens long before the coming of sound. By 1923 in the United Kingdom competition from U.S. pictures was so strong that only about 10 percent of films exhibited were British-made. Estimates indicate that by 1926 British pictures accounted for less than 5 percent of screen time. This was chiefly due to the facts that exhibition of American films was assisted by American distributors' block booking practices, and rental prices could be low because films' investments had been amortized in the American market (4).

The situation hardly was different on the Continent. For example, during the years 1924 through 1927 three-quarters of the 2543 features approved for exhibition in France came from the United States (13, pp. 469–471). American films not only outnumbered French films seven to one, but obviously blanketed pictures from other countries, likewise swamped by American exports. Therefore, the producer in any foreign country faced a twin peril: competition from American films in his own domestic market and competition from American films in other markets to which he might export in an attempt to redeem his investment.

During this period many European countries decided to protect the fate of film, a cultural medium, from being determined solely by forces of the international marketplace and narrow commercial imperatives. Measures were instituted to preserve what remained of domestic filmmaking. Import quotas and screen quotas were tried to reduce the imbalance by restricting the circulation of American films, thereby offering local productions a better chance to be exhibited. To these protective measures later were added state production loans or guarantees on loans and various subsidization programs. For example, British, Italian, or French films were allocated an increment of revenue over and above normal box office receipts to stimulate production by closing the gap between costs and earnings.

These programs were successful to the extent that filmmaking in the larger countries was able to survive against great odds. In the smaller countries, particularly Belgium, the present existence of film production can be attributed almost entirely to such measures and to the establishment of state-supported cinema schools that create a local cadre.

The programs had unusual consequences in another respect. While providing occasional flashes of temporary solvency for certain film industries, they also have provided the foundation for a slow but consistent erosion of a national film production with an identifiable cultural basis. This grew, strangely enough, from measures that restricted the exportation of earnings made by American films in the postwar years. With rapidly increasing accounts of blocked revenues, U.S. film distributors abroad searched for ways to transfer their funds to America. Because this could not be done in dollars, the companies usually were able to make arrangements permitting them to shoot films overseas to deplete their reserves and thereby export their earnings in the form of goods.

The process was well underway by the early-1950s and came to be known as runaway production—the desertion of Hollywood lots for the studios and countrysides of England, Italy, France, and later Spain, Yugoslavia, and elsewhere. Initially this resulted in American films shot on location for authenticity and local color. The depletion of accounts of blocked revenue by the early-1960s did not end the phenomenon, although its character by that time had changed. Realizing that subsidies were available for production in such major markets as the United Kingdom, Italy and France, the U.S. film companies turned from making "American" pictures overseas to making "British," "Italian," or "French" films. This was accomplished simply by subscribing to the legal definition of what constituted, say, a "British" film. Typically, this meant that the production company had to be incorporated under British law, that a certain amount of wages had to be paid to British workers, and that a specified share of the crew and cast had to be British. Such conditions could be fulfilled, and they were by foreign subsidiaries of Hollywood companies that employed foreign labor often at lower rates than those in the United States. In this regard the film companies more than two decades ago foreshadowed the movement of the American production facilities abroad by industry in general.*

Film subsidization plans abroad had not been initiated to attract American production from Hollywood. That they often facilitated it was viewed with considerable concern by some European businessmen who felt American penetration even in that facet of the industry as well as in its usual manifestation on foreign screens and the revenue flowing from box offices to American coffers. Evidence of this alarm is the mid-1950s statement from British Film Producers Association President John Davis (of J. Arthur Rank Productions Ltd.), who remarked concerning his country's subsidy scheme:

> The British Film Production Fund was established . . . on the initiative of the Government for the purpose of providing British producers with a supplementary revenue. . . . [I]t is obvious that the scheme would not have been put forward by the Government or accepted by the industry on the ground that the levy recoverable from box office takings was required to support films made in this country by American subsidiaries.†

An effort to restrict payments to wholly owned, as opposed to nominally British companies, was defeated with the help of American subsidiaries and certain British filmmakers who often produced for them.

The extent of the American presence was such that in the decade ending in

---

*This is also the case with phonograph records. Two, and sometimes three, symphonic recordings can be made in London for the cost of one in the United States, and costs in some European countries are even less than in England. This has not been overlooked by American producers and explains why there is so much recording activity overseas (43).

†Mr. Davis also complained that "American subsidiaries in this country not only have the benefit of Exhibitors' Quota but . . . claim British export licenses for foreign countries and even put forward their films to be presented at International Festivals as being British" (5).

1971 U.S. subsidiaries in the United Kingdom partially or entirely financed more than 60 percent of the "British" features released on the country's main theatrical circuits (24, p. 4). In terms of total film financing, the American share undoubtedly even was greater. U.S. companies were able to spend on a scale that their British counterparts could not match, which included bidding high salaries in a limited talent market.* "As in Italy so in the United Kingdom, production costs have under the influence of U.S. financing methods rocketed almost out of sight" (27).

By the mid-1960s American subsidiaries in the United Kingdom were so well entrenched that they were estimated to be collecting about 80 percent of the British production subsidy (39), although the share probably dropped somewhat around 1970 when American investment contracted. The tightening of finance created an unemployment crisis of sorts, thereby affirming that an authentic autonomous British film production had ceased to exist. In reality the industry was hardly more than a Hollywood annex.

American companies were able to achieve this position of dominance in Britain and other countries because, in part, they had larger sums to invest in production and were able to offer foreign producers an integrated global distribution system for their films. American companies have a virtual monopoly on the worldwide distribution of pictures; through their financing they are in a position to determine what kinds of films are made and circulated internationally. American products not only numerically dominate the universal flow of pictures but become the models of the international commercial culture. Moreover, the foreign films available for broad theatrical release in America generally are those in which American companies have investments. Because such financing tends to gravitate to a handful of western European countries, films and filmmakers from Latin America, Africa, Asia, and Eastern Europe often are unknown to most Americans. American distribution plays another role within continents, as Peruvian filmmaker Armando Godoy has pointed out:

> There are no procedures to follow in South America except to go to all 22 countries and talk to theater owners individually. This, of course, is impossible. So we have to go through the big North American companies such as Columbia to get our films distributed. Even so, it's not easy (36).

As for Columbia Pictures, its president, David Begelman, has declared:

> Basically I believe that the Majors, and Columbia in particular, must assume a closer control in all stages of production over all elements of the films which they

---

*"Last year (1973) four million and seven thousand pounds were invested in film production (in Britain). Of this, probably not much over seven hundred thousand pounds were British money. In 1972, the figure was twelve million pounds. I imagine that an even higher percentage of that sum was invested by Americans" (25, p. 69).

decide to produce and distribute. For several years, and even very recently, the Majors allowed their producers a greater and greater liberty and authority in the making of films. To my eyes, this is a grave error . . . [author's translation] (18).

The specifics of this new policy, obviously a response to the $50 million loss recorded by Columbia in fiscal 1973 as well as earlier deficits, entailed a $3 million ceiling on the company's investment in any given film, an intention "to deal more directly" with producers, directors, and writers, and finally a more thorough assessment of picture content before investment. Projects were to be measured in terms of their likely attraction to domestic and foreign audiences, acceptance by an American television network, and appeal to the 16-to-29-year-old age group that constitutes almost three-quarters of the American movie audience (8).

THE CHANGING FACE OF HOLLYWOOD

The movement abroad of American firms and production capacity is not unique to film. In 1972 the reported book value of American direct private foreign investment (branches and subsidiaries of U.S. companies) was over $94 billion, a figure that represents a doubling of the value every seven years since 1950 (30, pp. 24–27). Labor, for one, has insisted that this foreign manufacturing has meant a loss of jobs for American workers. The issue was explored officially as early as 1961 in hearings by the House of Representatives (31). Evidence in similar hearings a decade later indicated that the problem still was unresolved and was not likely to go away. Congressman John H. Dent emphasized the widespread nature of unemployment when he told Hollywood workers:

It's all coming together at one time. You fellows are feeling it now because you have gone through a protracted period now, of, let's say, 9, maybe 12, 13 years and it's beginning to hit home very seriously. But, it isn't new and it isn't only peculiar to you. It's every mill town in America. . . .

The primary interest of the corporate entities is to satisfy their stockholders. I mean, when we face that, we start to understand the problem (33).

Unemployment in many craft and technical unions in Hollywood has been running at 50 percent and more, while in 1972 half the membership of the Screen Actors Guild earned less than $1000 each. By 1970 over 40 percent of the earnings of SAG members came from television commercials, and only 20 percent from theatrical features (p. 84). This flows from production patterns that in 1969 saw American companies investing close to $235 million in 183 features made abroad, while $228 million was invested in 142 films made in America (p. 10).

The Domestic Film Production Incentive Act of 1971 was a stillborn effort to remedy the situation. It was an attempt to offset the lure of foreign subsidies, the alleged villain responsible for runaway production and unemployment in Hollywood. The bill sought to exclude from Federal income tax 20 percent of a producer's or distributor's gross income derived from the distribution or exploitation of an American production, which was defined in the bill in language reminiscent of British film legislation. The measure was referred to the Ways and Means Committee which apparently never received essential reports requested from the departments of the treasury, labor, and commerce. The bill died at the end of the Ninety-second Congress but was introduced again early in 1973. This climaxed a decade of effort to create an American subsidy that had even included a meeting at the San Clemente White House between industry leaders and President Richard Nixon who was cool to direct financial aid.

Although the Incentive Act was not approved, the motion picture industry did receive some assistance under the Revenue Act of 1971 which restored the 7 percent investment tax credit and created the Domestic International Sales Corporation (DISC) program. The MPAA apparently considered this legislation sufficiently important to hire a Washington lobbyist to represent its position.

The utility of subsidization, nonetheless, remains clouded. If the subsidy is to aid workers, by being allocated to producers, it would seem to be directed to the wrong quarters, for that will yield only indirect benefits to labor. This is especially true if the scheme is geared to gross income, for that allows companies to reap larger rewards on popular films without having to pass any of these rewards to the workers who made the films. If the subsidy is to aid production companies, it would seem to be pointless unless production is put on an entirely new structural basis. American subsidiaries already receive some subsidization abroad, which has not ensured that each will be financially sound and profitable from one year to the next. If the subsidy is to lure filmmaking back to Hollywood, is it not myopic to believe that the entire trend of industry in general, of which film is but a part, is going to be modified by one piece of legislation? The 1971 House hearings made clear and studies of multinational corporations have repeated that in business terms film is not exceptional. The problem of production in America is not going to be solved by piecemeal or narrow programs to assuage effects without reaching to the root of the matter.

There is another compelling reason to hesitate. Initiation of a subsidy, on whatever terms, without a prior detailed economic and social study of the industry would be folly, for it would commit the nation to aiding companies about whose internal and external operations very little is known publicly. A serious study must determine whether the deficiencies of the industry can be remedied by the kind of subsidy proposed—and indeed, if the deficiencies can be corrected by any form of subsidy. Material developed by Congressional hearings falls short of the kind that could be revealed by subpoena.

Unlike European countries, the United States has almost no reliable data about the operations of its film industry. Federal Trade Commission data, in some instances, is made available neither to other agencies of the government nor to the public. The Department of Commerce, which also collects and disseminates some industry data, lacks a definition of *American film* and therefore is unable to determine how well or poorly these pictures do in their own home market. Thus the Department also is incapable of determining the profits of "American" films abroad. In addition, without monitoring of the various above-the-line and below-the-line production costs, the Department (and therefore the public) cannot identify precisely what renders pictures costly and perhaps unprofitable. Fundamental economic information about the industry's operation, therefore, is absent or available only in fragmentary form. In its place one has access to data responding to questions often devised by the Department of Commerce in consultation with the MPAA. Furthermore, one sometimes must rely upon industry-provided figures that are unverifiable and whose derivation is obscure. Usually these pertain more to companies' operations than to American films, although the careful distinction between the two sometimes is overlooked. The former includes revenues from films made abroad and distributed abroad by U.S. companies, which is said by the industry to be a credit to our balance of payments. If this is true, the $342 million allegedly remitted from abroad in 1972 to the United States by American film companies represents a significant loss of revenue for foreign film industries.

One can turn, of course, to foreign data for a glimpse of how American companies and American films do in various countries. However, U.S. investment is masked in dozens of films that appear to be "British," "French," "Italian," or another nationality; revenue accruing to these pictures would not be reflected in earnings for "American" films. Between 1956 and 1967 in Italy the "American" film share of the box office slipped from about 63 to 34 percent, while the share for "Italian" films climbed from 28 to 52 percent (2, p. 70). Hidden behind these data, yet probably explaining them, is the fact that during the decade to 1967, U.S. companies were spending an average of $35 million annually to acquire and finance Italian films and to make their own pictures in Italy (22). The camouflage becomes more elaborate when it involves official coproduction, a form of filmmaking that joins technical, artistic, and financial resources from at least two countries. The resulting picture carries two nationalities, such as Italian-French, even though production money may have been supplied by an American subsidiary.*

---

*During 1972 at least one quarter of the Italian-French coproductions involved an American subsidiary as producer (6).

MULTINATIONALS AND CONGLOMERATES

Film companies, as multinationals, have the ability to shift revenues and expenses from country to country to suit their own interests. In the early 1970s a British study of the film market highlighted the obstacles facing the researcher:

Because of the multi-national nature of the American film companies operating in Britain, it is impossible to arrive at any accurate calculation about the real foreign earnings of films made in Britain but distributed by the American companies here and abroad. Accountancy methods used by these companies in charging distribution fees and expenses make it impossible to determine what the actual revenue from film exhibition is, and how much would be recouped to recover the production cost of a film once distribution charges, and inflated distribution expenses have been eliminated. The same argument applies to film budgeting, once inflated overheads and interest charges are also eliminated (1).

The multinational character of American film business has been overlooked in studies of industry generally and film particularly. In 1973 both the United Nations report *Multinational Corporations in World Development* and the U.S. Senate Finance Committee studies and hearings on multinational corporations ignored the cinema. The U.S. Chamber of Commerce 1970 survey of 160 American-based internationals did not include a motion picture company in its sample. Studies by Europeans from a broad political spectrum have not considered film, even though they dealt with other aspects of American control and Americanization.*

American film companies, as multinationals, have the ability to shift men, material, and money from one country to another to suit their own corporate interests, without regard to the economic stability of foreign film industries or the cultural needs of the countries those industries are supposed to serve. Even in America this was perfectly clear 25 years ago when companies began transferring some of their production to Europe, leaving behind the great studio labor forces that had been built up over decades when Hollywood was a picture factory. There was no more concern for American workers than has been shown more recently for their British counterparts when U.S. film investment was reduced in that country and partially shifted to other European nations offering more attractive conditions. For example, as part of a huge reorganization beginning in 1969, MGM began firing thousands of workers around the world. The following year it sold Boreham Wood, its British studio facilities that included 115 acres of land and decided to concentrate on low-budget films and those that would not cost over $3 million. These changes obviously had impacts in countries in which MGM was doing busi-

---

*For example, see Claude Julien (17), Ernest Mandel (19), Jean-Jacques Servan-Schreiber (26), and Pierre Vellas (41).

ness, yet these decisions were made solely on the basis of corporate needs. However, that was only Act I of a drama whose climax came in late 1973 when MGM's chief executive officer, Kirk Kerkorian, decided to take the company virtually out of the film business altogether, fulfilling a principle he described in these terms: "I'm an MGM stockholder and if it was decided that MGM had to go out of pictures entirely, and if it went into ball bearings and made money . . . I'd cheer" (42). The company sold its interests in foreign theatres and then signed contracts giving theatrical and TV distribution rights at home and abroad for all MGM films to United Artists and Cinema International Corporation, a Netherlands company formed in 1970 by Universal (MCA) and Paramount (Gulf & Western).

The intersection of the multinational character of American film business with the rise of conglomerates since the mid-1960s has added another dimension to the matter. Typically this has meant that theatrical film production and distribution become only a segment, usually a small one, of a parent company engaged in a diversity of fields. Strangely the impact of conglomerates on the film industry, which a quarter century ago was the object of antitrust action, was not thoroughly examined in the 1970 House Judiciary Committee hearings on conglomerate corporations.

The usual pattern involves a film production-distribution company being absorbed by or merged with a larger corporation. In 1967 Transamerica Corporation acquired United Artists, whose film, broadcasting, and recording activities subsequently became subsidiaries along with car rentals, data processing, insurance, and air travel. In 1972 motion picture rentals accounted for only ten percent of Transamerica's total revenue (28). Similarly, Universal's theatrical film releases represented only eighteen percent of the 1972 gross revenue of its corporate parent MCA (21).

Probably one of the better-known conglomerates, not only for its acquisitions but its rapid growth, is Gulf & Western Industries. It acquired Paramount Pictures in 1966, selecting the company not for where it was ("the bottom of the barrel") (32, 37), but for what it could be made to yield. Apparently Paramount's attractiveness lay in its large film library whose real value G&W officials believed to be underestimated and a hidden source of future wealth. The extensive merger and acquisition program of G&W, according to a House Judiciary Committee report, was made possible by a small number of key banks, among them Manufacturers Hanover, Bank of America, Chase Manhattan, and First National City.* Once in control of Paramount, G&W outlined a production program. This obviously had ramifications overseas in view of the company's extensive foreign activities (32, pp.

*These banks themselves are multinationals with 25 to almost 50 percent of their deposits at foreign offices (34). The same banks also are among the principal entries in *Disclosure of Corporate Ownership* (35).

475–478, 486–492, 510–515). Paramount's operations also became subject to approval by its parent, whose management principles were spelled out by its president:

. . . Gulf & Western operates with detailed annual business plans to provide each of our companies with a blueprint for the year ahead. A business plan is prepared by each operating unit, analyzed with Gulf & Western's top management and, upon approval, is carried out by the subsidiary. The plan is jointly reviewed each month and up-dated each quarter. This system not only provides detailed information to top management at Gulf & Western headquarters, but it enables each company to take a continuing look at itself (32, p. 10).

Although *The Godfather,* a Paramount picture, is probably one of the biggest money-earners in cinema history, the film company's theatrical revenue contribution to G&W stands small in relation to the parent's other enterprises such as auto replacement parts, cattle ranching, minerals, insurance, tobacco, and vegetables. Theatrical film revenue in fiscal 1973 represented 43 percent (49 percent in 1972) of the total for the Leisure Time Group, of which Paramount is but a part, and only 5 percent (7 percent in 1972) of G&W's total revenue (15).

As part of conglomerates, the film industry must be made to fit into the parents' total international manufacturing and marketing strategies. Foreign film industries, which rely upon American companies for financing and distribution, not only remain subject to the imperatives of film headquarters in New York or California but now as subsidiaries obviously are affected by how real estate, computers, sugar, cigars, and insurance are doing on the market—as well as by parents' needs for cash and their financial ties to America's largest banking houses.* Therefore, the amount of money allocated and available for film financing in, say, the United Kingdom is far beyond the decision-making power in that country. The European producer seeking U.S. investment for a project or a Latin American director looking for an international distributor for his film can hardly be immune to these forces over which they have no control. In the same way European film industries that have courted American financial penetration during a quarter of a century find themselves living in a balloon of synthetic prosperity that can be burst at any moment by the acts of a few large American companies. These can decide summarily to halt their film activities and to put their money into other ventures, leaving to wither the overseas facilities and cadre that once had served them. The artistic medium of film and its potential to tell the stories and aspirations indigenous to a people becomes a pawn that can be

---

*As an example, Charles Bluhdorn, chairman and chief executive officer of Gulf and Western, proposed to the MPAA that rental prices be increased on American films distributed in certain oil-supplying nations: "He said he wanted the film industry to set an example for the rest of the country in learning how to deal with the oil-rich and other rich countries" (3, p. 18).

sacrificed in the global gambits that are part of international industrial warfare.

FILM IN THE EUROPEAN ECONOMIC COMMUNITY

Some persons abroad believe that only a new unified Europe can answer effectively the American technological, industrial, and financial challenge and that this new unity must be achieved within the European Economic Community (EEC). The Common Market, which came into existence in 1958, aims to reduce barriers among member states to promote an easier and greater circulation of goods, capital, and manpower. Its application to the cinema has been slow, because film ranks low in priority for discussion compared to agricultural and monetary policy, heavy industry, chemicals, and so on and because film is an art as well as a business. The Common Market is primarily an economic association, and therefore its authorities in Brussels have approached film from that perspective, considering it a commodity to be made, distributed, and consumed.

Since 1963 EEC authorities issued several film directives aimed at abolishing quotas on the internal flow of pictures made by community members and liberalizing the movement of producers from one country to another. Other directives would harmonize and probably merge production subsidy schemes of member states, liberalize the establishment of distribution companies in the community, create a uniform public film registry system to facilitate finance, and standardize cinema technical training in member states.* The objective, some declare, is to create a *European* film industry by replacing present competition with cooperation, thus effectively answering the American challenge.

There are numerous difficulties with this argument. It is based on the assumption that Europe must compete on the same terms and scale with the United States, which means little more than the construction of a European model of American industrial prowess—in short, Americanization. The second assumption is that European film industries actually exist now as economically and culturally autonomous units. This position is hard to support in view of the significant penetration by American companies into the economic, political, and artistic fibre of filmmaking in the major producing countries in Europe, all of which are EEC members. EEC authorities have neither touched nor recognized this problem. Perhaps the issue has not been thoroughly examined on the national level for fear of offending U.S. interests and frightening away their investment. If American production, financing,

---

*The Common Market's relation to the film industries of member states is examined by Claude Degand (9, 10).

and distribution were to disappear from Europe today, film industries there would be ill-equipped to deal with the disaster. Cultural autonomy and economic independence can be achieved only by a thorough reorganization of filmmaking in Europe—something the Common Market seems incapable of doing. Its present trend is toward creating a unified European industry, not only on the American model, but realized or not, on the foundation of American companies. In reality these efforts are directed less to protecting film and more to perpetuating and safeguarding the economic-industrial structure that makes it.

Film trade unions in Europe naturally are split over this problem. Since its founding in 1953 the European Union of Film and Television Workers (affiliated with the International Confederation of Free Trade Unions) has supported European unity, more specifically the EEC. It sees integration as the way to resolve economic problems facing European film industries and believes that some, but not total, independence from American interests is desirable. This could be achieved by the establishment of a European film distribution consortium and revitalized systems of local finance, both offering alternatives to U.S. distribution and investment. Such a plan was introduced at an international symposium in 1968 in Brussels. Subsequent periodic meetings, climaxed by another symposium in 1974 in London, revealed that little progress had been made toward realization.

As might be expected, a somewhat different position is held by the left-wing Confederazione Generale Italiana Lavoratori and the Confédération Générale du Travail (and its entertainment industry subsidiary Fédération Nationale du Spectacle), both affiliated with the World Federation of Trade Unions in Prague. Although eager for international cooperation, they have denounced the form it has taken in the EEC, as they earlier protested the Marshall Plan for being an instrument of American imperialism. The unions charge that the EEC approach is narrow because its purpose is to build a cinema through concentration of enterprises, which will leave no room for a film d'auteur or an experimental short. The distribution of these types of film is already obstructed by commercialism. Also charged as accomplices are the French and Italian governments which, the unions claim, have renounced their responsibility in the area of film culture while acknowledging it in art, music, and broadcasting. Popular cultures must be respected and cultivated, the unions urge, and this cannot be done when artistic creation is the pawn of business interests. They argue that whatever will be accomplished will be at the expense of workers because EEC authorities demonstrate no concern for labor. Meanwhile, the position of labor becomes even more precarious as circulation of capital and opportunities for establishment in the community are liberalized. The unions declare that the EEC is perpetuating film capitalism rather than eliminating it.

A similar view is espoused in the United Kingdom by the 18,000 members of the Association of Cinematograph, Television, and Allied Technicians. Yet in one respect ACTT has been more emphatic. In May 1973 it released a report that called for nationalizing the British film industry (including U.S. subsidiaries) on a confiscation-without-compensation basis and placing it under worker rather than state control. Early in 1974 ACTT hosted a meeting of trade union representatives largely from European countries. That resulted in the founding of the International Federation of Audio-Visual Trade Unions, probably the first such group in film and broadcasting to bring together artistic, technical, and laboratory workers. It will create stronger bonds among entertainment and technical unions in the community and will establish more formal links with those in non-EEC states, Eastern Europe, and elsewhere.

AFRICAN NATIONS: MARKETS OR CULTURES?

The achievement of formal political independence by many African states did not guarantee autonomy. In many cases African independence meant a restructuring of film-marketing patterns and offered American companies the opportunity for a foothold on the continent. American firms seem to be banking on Africa as a long-term investment because present economic dividends, although increasing, are not great. As markets, the United States and Western Europe are saturated and stagnating, if not exhausted. Significant growth in earnings, however, could be expected to come from developing countries where consumption of all kinds is bound to rise. With few exceptions, these nations have sparse film-production capabilities. Because of the easily exportable nature of film, the rising demand will be met with films manufactured either in America or in Europe with American investment. In this way many African nations are faced with films produced by an alliance of European colonialism and American imperialism—films whose values will probably submerge, if not pulverize, distinct African cultures and heritages or menace them with extermination by a global commercial culture flowing from a few centers in the industrialized world.

As long ago as 1962 a meeting at Unesco headquarters considered media in Africa and urged that national film units be supported "to promote rapid development of the production and distribution of films that are truly African in style and content" and, moreover, that these "films should reflect African realities as exactly as possible" (29, p. 31).

In contrast to that program were the militant economic policies of the American industry which had decided, according to *Variety*, that the "time is ripe to strike in emergent Africa. Planned is a united invasion of the Dark

Continent . . ." (38). The spearhead was the American Motion Picture Export Company (Africa), founded in 1961 and, like the MPEA, registered under the Webb-Pomerene Export Trade Act. Its establishment culminated several years of planning and study. Member companies licensed AMPEC (Africa) to distribute their films and to act as the sole bargaining agent and representative, thereby eliminating competitive price-cutting among U.S. distributors. The cartel had the power to monopolize the supply of films handled by its distributor-members and to turn the supply on or off depending upon the rental terms it could arrange with exhibitors. It was licensed to operate in the English-speaking countries of Ghana, Gambia, Sierra Leone, Nigeria, and Liberia—all but Liberia newly independent—and thus in a potential market, where theatre-going was still in its infancy, of close to 60 million population (about that of the United Kingdom). The company's initial successes involved raising rental prices, doubling or tripling American film earnings in the market, and heading off restrictions on the circulation of U.S. films.

With that technique a proven success, the interests of the American Industry turned elsewhere on the continent, specifically to the French-speaking republics south of the Sahara. To handle that region and to develop it commercially, U.S. companies organized in 1969 the West Africa Film Export Co., Inc., changing its name later the same year to Afram Films, Inc. Its purposes, policies, and tactics are essentially those of its sister organizations, AMPEC (Africa) and the MPEA. Its 15-country market has a population of about 60 million. But here, as in the Arab nations of North Africa, American interests often must compete with those of the French, who have long-standing positions they wish to protect and enlarge, even though what filmmaking there is on the continent is largely centered in North Africa.

After almost two decades of independence, few African states have been able to develop a national policy for their cinemas. Consequently, film relations *among* these countries have hardly been established. Yet a *de facto* policy has been imposed by American and European interests, and its essence is decidedly commercial, with little concern for cultural identity. Unless drastic changes occur, African states will be cinematically isolated from one another. They will not be exchanging films with each other (for that presupposes production) but will be receiving them from American and European distributors who obviously have no interest in encouraging filmmaking on the continent, although they do wish to augment exhibition facilities. The problem in Africa remains essentially that outlined by Tom Mboya in the early 1960s:

> It appears to me that although Africa is getting rid of Western colonialism and is still fighting against its hangover, known as neo-colonialism, there is yet another fight to be waged—the fight against intellectual imperialism. This fight must be waged now, side by side with the fight for economic independence (20, p. 251).

INDUSTRY AND GOVERNMENT

A sketch of the international film industry would be incomplete without attention to the relations between government and film companies. Space here permits only the briefest consideration—and that in the American context. Our traditional conception of freedom of the press creates the impression of a jealously guarded separation between American government and American media, with the latter strongly resisting the kinds of contact that might influence their operations. This is not entirely accurate, for relations between the two are cultivated and in some ways are beneficial to each. Government does not necessarily meddle in the content of specific films, a possibility that seems abhorrent, but relations between government and industry are more pervasive and less obvious. In fact, they can involve industry influencing government—the reverse of what our mythology would have us believe.

As an industrial enterprise, filmmaking is not exceptional in attempting to manipulate or persuade government to certain points of view. As an *international* industrial enterprise, filmmaking also becomes involved in foreign policy and enters into a symbiotic relationship with the U.S. government. I have mentioned earlier that the postwar exportation of American pictures was encouraged by the government for their propaganda value and that film was just one medium whose dissemination was assisted by the government's Informational Media Guaranty Program. Moreover, equity investment abroad was viewed as a way of rebuilding and stabilizing war-torn Europe while simultaneously binding it to American interests at a time when the world was becoming polarized politically. Henry Fowler, former Secretary of the Treasury, has pointed out:

Transcending the private commercial importance of the foreign operations of domestic multinational corporations is their significance and role in a United States foreign policy. . . . Since World War II, every President [and] practically every Congress . . . have emphasized the importance to national interests of the role of these private companies. . . . For example, the various foreign aid enactments beginning with the Marshall Plan in 1948 have all stressed the importance of promotion of American private investment abroad, in their provision for investment guaranties and other means of encouraging foreign investment by American business (12, pp. 123–124).

These kinds of considerations provided the grounds for a close alliance between government and film interests. American pictures disseminated Hollywood's version of the good life, while American investment supposedly offered the means to achieve it. More recently the MPEA claims that the activities of American film companies around the globe favorably contribute to our balance of payments; $342 million was reportedly remitted from abroad by the industry in 1972, according to Jack Valenti. Coming to a period when the United States has suffered trade deficits, the unrestricted circulation of American films abroad is enthusiastically encouraged by government.

Relations between industry and government have been direct and intimate. The three heads of the motion picture trade association (the MPAA and its predecessor, the Motion Picture Producers and Distributors Association of America) have been closely tied to government. Other officers of the MPAA-MPEA have shifted back and forth between government and industry, making it difficult to determine at times who was on loan to whom.

The dynamic and many-faceted development of America's international film industry over the past 30 years has helped to change the face of the globe. The industry's trends and achievements—indeed the very problems it has posed and the impact it has had—are summarized well in two statements made more than a quarter century apart. In Hollywood in 1945 French filmmaker René Clair observed: "Even before the end of the war in Europe, there was talk of the coming struggle for the conquest of film markets. Certain industrialists are already making plans for an invasion of the most vulnerable of them" (7, p. 132).

Introducing the Domestic Film Production Incentive Act of 1971, Representative James C. Corman (D., Cal.) declared:

We must make it our national policy to save this vital American industry without further delay. The motion picture is, after all, the industry which has "sold America" to the world by a graphic display of the American system, and of the productivity of free, competitive enterprise (33).*

REFERENCES

1. Association of Cinematograph, Television, and Allied Technicians. *Report of the A.C.T.T. Nationalisation Forum* (May 6, 1973).

2. Associazione Nazionale Industrie Cinematografiche ed Affini. *L'ANCIA per l'industria cinematografica,* relazione all'assemblea generale dell'ANICA. (December 16, 1971), Rome.

3. Bluhdorn, Charles. *The New York Times* (January 25, 1974).

4. *British Film Industry. Political and Economic Planning.* London, May 1952, pp. 40–41.

5. British Film Producers Association. *Fourteenth Annual Report, 1955–1956.*

6. Centre National de la Cinématographie. *Bulletin d'information, 108* (December 1967).

7. Clair, René. *Reflections on the Cinema.* London: William Kimber, 1953.

8. Columbia Picture Industries. *Annual Report Fiscal 1973.*

9. Degand, Claude. *Le Cinema . . . cette industrie.* Paris: Editions Techniques et Economiques, 1972.

10. ———. "1972/3: A Turning Point for European Cinema?" *Sight and Sound, 42,* 2, (Spring 1973), 107–109.

*There was one dilemma that was not confronted satisfactorily: If the film industry truly is the paradigm of the glories of the free enterprise system, how did it manage to slip so low that government should be urged to bail it out?

11. ———. "Europe's Film Industry." *European Review, 23,* 4 (Autumn 1973), 16–20.

12. Fowler, Henry H. "National Interests and Multinational Business," in George A. Steiner and Warren M. Cannon (eds.), *Multinational Corporate Planning.* New York: Macmillan, 1966.

13. "French Motion-Picture Policy." *European Economic and Political Survey, 3,* 14 (March 31, 1928).

14. Guback, Thomas H. *The International Film Industry.* Bloomington: Indiana University Press, 1969.

15. Gulf and Western Industries. *Annual Report 1973.*

16. Johnston, Eric. "Messengers From a Free Country," *The Saturday Review of Literature, 33,* 9 (March 4, 1950), 9–12.

17. Julien, Claude. *America's Empire.* New York: Pantheon, 1971.

18. *Le Film Français* (October 19, 1973).

19. Mandel, Ernest. *Europe Versus America?* London: NLB, 1970.

20. Mboya, Tom. "African Socialism," in William H. Friedland and Carl G. Rosenberg Jr. (eds.), *African Socialism.* Stanford: Stanford University Press, 1964.

21. MCA, Inc. *Annual Report 1972.*

22. Monaco, Eitel. President of ANICA. Quoted in "Centre National de la Cinématographic," *Bulletin d'Information 108* (December 1967).

23. Motion Picture Export Association of America. *Interim Report on Television* (October 21, 1960).

24. National Film Finance Corporation. *Annual Report and Statement of Accounts for the Year Ended 31 March 1972.*

25. Raphael, Fredric. "What Hope for British Films?" *The Listener 91* (January 17, 1974).

26. Servan-Schreiber, Jean-Jacques. *Le Défi Américain.* Paris: Editions Denöel, 1967.

27. Terry, John. "Film Financing in the United Kingdom," *The Journal of the Producers Guild of America, 12,* 3 (September 1970), 32–34.

28. Transamerica Corporation. *Annual Report 1972.*

29. UNESCO. *Developing Information Media in Africa.* Reports and Papers on Mass Communication 37. Paris: UNESCO, 1962.

30. United States Department of Commerce. *Survey of Current Business, 53,* 9 (September 1973).

31. United States House of Representatives. *Impact of Imports and Exports on Employment.* Hearings before the Subcommittee on the Impact of Imports and Exports on American Employment of the Committee on Education and Labor. Washington: Government Printing Office, 1962.

32. ———. *Investigation of Conglomerate Corporations.* Hearings before the Antitrust Subcommittee (No. 5) of the Committee on the Judiciary, on Gulf and Western Industries, Inc., July and August 1969. Washington: Government Printing Office, 1970.

33. ———. *Unemployment Problems in American Film Industry.* Hearing before the General Subcommittee on Labor of the Committee on Education and Labor, October 1971. Washington: Government Printing Office, 1972.

34. United States Senate. "U.S. Multinationals—The Dimming of America," in *Multinational Corporations.* Hearings before the Subcommittee on International Trade of the Committee on Finance, February and March 1973. Washington: Government Printing Office, 1973.

35. ———. *Disclosure of Corporate Ownership.* Hearings before the Subcommittees on Intergovernmental Relations and Budgeting, Management, and Expenditures, of the Committee on

Government Operations, 27 December 1973. Washington: Government Printing Office, 1973.

36. United Press International, news story, Champaign, Illinois *News Gazette* (October 30, 1972).

37. Valenti, Jack. "The 'Foreign Service' of the Motion Picture Association of America," *The Journal of the Producers Guild of America, 10,* 1 (March 1968).

38. *Variety,* 17 May 1961.

39. *Variety,* 26 January 1966.

40. Varis, Tapio. *International Inventory of Television Programme Structure and the Flow of Television Programme Between Nations.* Tampere: University of Tampere, 1973.

41. Vellas, Pierre. *L'Europe face à la révolution technologique Américaine.* Paris: Dunod, 1969.

42. *Washington Post,* 9 December 1973.

43. Whyte, Bert. "The $$ Crunch in Classical Recording," *Audio, 53,* 5 (1969).

CHAPTER 4

Television International

ROBERT LEWIS SHAYON

The most comprehensive inventory of the cross-national flow of television and film programs available was compiled by Tapio Varis of Finland's University of Tampere. He found: "The United States is still the biggest TV programme exporter in the world and in most countries of the world American TV programmes compose a major part of all the imported programmes" (24).

However, a recent study of the flow of exports and imports in the American film and television industry, prepared in the office of telecommunications, United States Department of Commerce, suggested that the world market for American film/videotape production might be decreasing. The author, concerned about the "national character" of the industry, suggested the initiation of "programs (such as subsidy, quota or levy) that would insure employment and remittances to the American balance of trade in the film/videotape industry" (26).

The very idea of protectionism, arising out of a Department of Commerce survey, represented a significant turning point in the history of international television. The key words *national character,* when applied to United States film/videotape production, strike one with novel force. Students of international television are accustomed to cries of "sovereignty, integrity, defence" emanating from nations intent on protecting their vulnerable indigenous cultures from the "imperialist" thrusts of American exporters who "gobble up the international TV market" and dump programs at low prices in nations too weak to resist the cultural invasion. As early as 1959 in his study of Mexican family life, Oscar Lewis noted the high visibility of American TV commercials in that country, observing that certain beauty products were touted in their American linquistic forms or *pochismos*—"Touch and Glow," "Bright and Clear" (15).

In 1963 Gordon, Falk, and Hoddap noted "reprisals against American TV" as "the result of this Americanization of television over so much of the world. . . . In Canada 55 percent of all TV fare must be homegrown; only 14 percent of the programs on Britain's ITA network may be foreign-originated;

Japan has a relatively low ceiling on prices that may be paid for United States shows; shows for Argentina must be dubbed in Argentine dialect—not Mexican, not Castilian, and not Peruvian" (6). In 1971 Peru witnessed a takeover of the radio and television industry in that country by the non-Marxist, revolutionary military government. In explaining its action the government noted that "only 36 percent of the mass media shows" were of Peruvian origin. The rest of the programs are mostly dubbed U.S. and European shows or come from Mexico and Argentina." The foreign content of broadcasting time, the military promised, would be reduced to 40 percent, and henceforth the Peruvian airwaves would be used for "cultural, educational and social purposes, as well as for state security" (10). In November 1973 *Variety*, the American weekly, front-paged its annual Canadian Films and Entertainment Review with the headline "Show Biz & Canadian 'Nationalism.' " The issue's lead story noted:

English-speaking Canada's entertainment for several decades, willingly or not, has been a branch plant, a mere adjunct of the wider, better financed U.S. show biz. Only in the last five years have there been strong voices raised in opposition. . . . It is more a plea for an assertion of nationalism that doesn't force its talents to emigrate because of unconcern towards poor work opportunities at home (1).

In the early 1970s there were evidences of some success by other national television systems in their efforts to strike a more equitable balance with the American giant. The decades since the end of World War II had given them opportunities to build or rebuild their national economies, to foster their own national television systems, and to produce in many cases a surplus of product that could compete for a share of the international television exchange market. Of course the United States would itself have to adjust to the new conditions by various measures—"runaway production" overseas; coproductions with other nations; efforts, in international trade agreements, to have tariff barriers lowered against American products; partnerships in foreign-producing firms and development abroad of "spin-offs," subsidiary products of film/videotape programs. But that the United States should even consider joining the international chorus of voices singing the necessities of protection of the "national character" of their cultures—not to speak of "subsidy, quota or levy"—was a development few observers of the international television scene would have predicted.

A BACKWARD GLANCE

Let us go back in time to another Department of Commerce publication *Radio Markets of the World, 1930*. The patterns that characterize television around the world today in programming, advertising, scheduling, and marketing were permanently in place in the United States as early as 1926 when the first network was established; and the American model, with due regard for structural and ideological differences in capitalist and socialist nations, is the model that has come to be most widely imitated.

The 1930 Department of Commerce publication was designed "to present accurate information as to the development of radio broadcasting in foreign countries, for the guidance of American exporters of radio apparatus in entering and maintaining sales in such countries." With psychic insight appropriate to the rhetoric of Futurism, the author of *Radio Markets of the World, 1930* remarked in his Introduction that after 10 years of remarkable progress around the world, radio was not only developing "a catholicity of tastes in the phonic arts," but was also "giving the people a great moral foundation for international peace and goodwill" (3).

Having genuflected ceremoniously to the shrine, the 1930 Department of Commerce survey and three other related publications that followed in 1931 and 1932 addressed themselves in more careful detailed fashion to the more significant objectives of trade. In their survey of radio advertising in Europe; in Latin America; and in Asia, Africa, Australia and Oceania, they pointed to the promising demand potential for consumer goods waiting to be cultivated. Radio had powerful appeal everywhere. It was used primarily for amusement. Certain universal program types had been demonstrated. True, in scattered areas, there were resistances. Europe was wary of commercial advertising, but the author of the first Department of Commerce publication expected that local prejudices would subside as soon as European listeners became familiar with "actual conditions" in the United States. In South China broadcasting was viewed by the government "as a dangerous instrumentality for the dissemination of propaganda inimical to the welfare of the country," and radio, therefore, was under strict supervision. Nevertheless, on all continents there were "opportunities for exploitation of American products and services over the air, despite a variety of government restrictions and natural economic limitations." American firms were already sponsoring broadcasting records ("electrical transcriptions") on foreign radio stations (7, 16, 23).

Latin American markets seemed especially receptive to the United States model of consumer goods cultivation via radio.

In the growth of radio advertising Mexican big business has borne the brunt of the burden. . . . Now, however, even small retail shops are buying programs or short announcements, and the returns have been gratifying. . . . The radio audience in Mexico now learns of the qualities of an American radio; that an American insecticide will free their kitchen of roaches; that the Centro Mercantil has the best bargains in ladies' hats; that a talking-machine hour is sponsored by the Mexico Music Co.; that Aguila or Buen Tono cigarettes are as good as any imported brand; that a well-known light six is the car of their dreams; and many other statements which by repetition cannot fail to build up a preference in the minds of consumers (23).

The editors of the Broadcast Advertising Trade Information Bulletins caution again and again that radio is a luxury item for upper classes who can afford to buy luxury goods. Thus, an American Consul reported from Syria: "Radios rank distinctly in the luxury class and are available to a limited wealthy group, as only the barest necessities of life are obtained by the general population" (p. 7). And in the Introduction to the Latin American bulletin, the editor writes: "Only the well-to-do people have sets, yet these are the ones most likely to purchase goods advertised over the air, since many of the poorer classes lack the necessary buying power" (p. 1). In Washington, D.C. the Department of Commerce experts saw the world through neocolonial glasses—a globe efficiently divided into haves and have-nots.

Angola (population 2,481,856) has not seen any great development in radio. The class to be interested are the Portugese . . . (p. 102). The development of radio in Algeria (population 5,992,770, Language, French and Arabic) has been restricted mainly to the French residents. . . . Radio provides contact with France which otherwise is impossible. The native population is not interested (p. 101).

Later in the 1930s sponsors themselves became active in promoting their products in Latin America. The Gillette Safety Razor Company purchased scripts in the United States of *The Shadow*, a popular radio series, and had them mailed to Argentina and Brazil where they (along with safety razor commercials) were translated into the local languages (12).

The early commercial emphasis in international broadcasting was not exclusively an American phenomenon. Australian and British radio entrepreneurs, among others, looked to the United States for start-up supplies of radio programs. Since the inception of networking in 1926, the presence in the United States of the world's largest domestic market had already generated a stockpile of programs that could be sold abroad for marginal profits. The same giant domestic market for cultural finished goods had been responsible for America's dominance of the world film market and would in due time provide the basis for the leadership of American industry in world television.

In Europe sometime during 1939–1940 the noncommercial BBC was about to be challenged by a new powerful 50,000 watt transmitter atop the Normandy Cliffs across the English Channel. The International Broadcasting Company, an English consortium, was setting up shop to penetrate the British Isles with commercially sponsored radio. The manager cabled an American agent for samples of 50 to 100 radio series. Within two weeks electrical transcriptions of 40 series were crated and shipped, including *Omar, The Wizard of Persia, The Count of Monte Cristo,* and *The Weird Circle.*

In the late 1930s when NBC and CBS, among other communications corporations, began operating shortwave broadcasting transmitters to Latin America, they maintained that their commercial overseas operations would be an aid to hemispheric unity. NBC asserted that its overseas programming would show "the dividends that democracy pays." Commissioner George H.

Payne, a member of the Federal Communications Commission, in 1937 asserted that the real motive of the "misguided captains of industry," as he called them, was "a desire to devote the channels to nostrum peddling." Commissioner Payne wished to promote shortwave radio as an instrument of United States government abroad, because the political elites of totalitarian countries in Europe and Asia had begun during the 1930s to use shortwave broadcasting as an instrument to be played upon for their own preconceived ends. A move to establish America's own shortwave stations for counterpropaganda purposes was supported by President Roosevelt, but the broadcasters resisted it. The 38 active shortwave "experimental" stations in the hands of the broadcasters had been allowed to rebroadcast domestic programs including commercials, and the operators pressed hard for permission to sell time. The broadcasters blocked the proposal for non-commercial government operated shortwave stations, and, in 1939, they succeeded in having the FCC authorize the sale of shortwave broadcast time. Sponsors paid $25,000 a year for 15-minute programs daily. NBC and CBS executives traveled through Latin America lining up affiliates and arranging for local rebroadcasts for commercial sponsorship (2, pp. 30–34).

The export of American programs for the purposes of product salesmanship abroad was one of the earliest casualties of World War II. The armed forces and the government took over shortwave broadcasting for military and propaganda objectives. American broadcasters did not renew their interests in international commercial broadcasting after the war. The military and the government retained their possession of the shortwave transmitters. The overseas nations, their economies shattered by the war's devastation, were too preoccupied with the satisfaction of basic needs to be receptive to the lure of advertised luxuries.

In 1953 UNESCO, in its first survey of world television, declared: "International cooperation is beginning to open up new fields for television and it is increasingly recognized how effective it can be to bring about greater awareness about each other among nations differing in language and character." The survey recognized that undesirable consequences could flow from programming's necessity to "take account of . . . mass appeal and meet it. . . . The broadcaster finds himself in a position of sometimes conflicting responsibilties," being at the same time the three-fold servant of audiences, advertisers, and the community at large, "even if he conducts a station for private profit." Nevertheless, "the educator, the writer and the artist must learn how to present their contribution in a manner which can be accepted and enjoyed by a wide public, while the spectator learns to share in treasures of man's civilization which hitherto had been remote and inaccessible" (21, pp. 30–31).

In a 1955 supplement to its first world television survey (20), UNESCO reported how some of these "treasures of man's civilization" were already becoming near and accessible: "Television is bursting its national seams; international programme cooperation is becoming a regular feature of the industry." Western Europe, under the auspices of the European Broadcasting Union (EBU) had grown into "a reciprocal network covering eight countries." Plans were under way to link the Soviet Union and the Warsaw Pact nations with an East European network. North and South America had their own links by stratovision or on film or kinescope, and the first North American programs had been released in Europe and Japan. Foreign countries had already become places for shooting of television films for the United States.

There has also been progress in the international contact made between the broadcasters themselves. UNESCO, in cooperation with the BBC, organized the first study course for producers and directors of educational and cultural television programmes, which brought together professionals from 12 countries and nonself-governing territories.

The fruit of all this international cooperation designed to unify peoples and bring about a deeper comprehension had been a coronation in the United Kingdom, a World Football Association Cup Championship in Switzerland, and a number of other unidentified "significant events." "Theoretically, it might be possible," UNESCO pulsated, "to relay directly the 1956 Olympic Games from Australia to Europe" (pp. 7–8).

One can distinguish between the rhetoric of the equipment manufacturers, broadcasters, and advertisers and the rhetoric of the UNESCO experts. The object of the first group was profit; UNESCO wanted to use this great new instrument to further world peace and understanding. The UNESCO surveys, for all their affirmative thinking, of necessity ignored the fact that the decade following the end of World War II had been marked by the bipolar confrontation of the world's two great nuclear powers: the Cold War between the United States and the Soviet Union. UNESCO, as an instrument of the United Nations—the larger organization dominated by the rivalry of these two giant powers—could not, for political reasons, call attention to the realities of the international situation which cast its shadow astride the unfolding path of worldwide electronic communications.

THE HUTCHINS COMMISSION REPORT

Some of those realities had been constructively set forth in the *Report on International Communications from the Commission on Freedom of the Press* published in 1964. Television was not considered in the Hutchins Report (Robert M. Hutchins, Chancellor of the University of Chicago, was chairman). The report, as it surveyed the state of international communications immediately after World War II, confronted for the first time a number of issues that would become increasingly crucial in debates about television's role in the year ahead. The new instruments for "direct communications across national boundaries to the masses of the people of the world" could be used responsibly to enlarge mutual comprehension; yet, their use could be "incomplete, undirected, and irresponsible . . . with the risk of an increase in international hatred and suspicion as a consequence" (25).

The Hutchins Commission was remarkably prescient on the question of the "free flow of information." It conceded that barriers to communication should be eliminated progressively wherever possible, but it stressed the world's great need for "objectively realistic information—*true* information, not merely *more* information; *true* information, not merely, as those who would have us simply write the First Amendment into international law seem to suggest, the *unhindered flow* of information" (p. 2). There were special circumstances, the authors maintained, that affected "the free market place of ideas" in foreign lands. In large areas a major concern was that of "personal security and authority among peoples deprived for years . . . of free exchange of information. Freedom of the press is peculiarly the child of confidence, security, and stability. It almost never lives undiminished in times of war, disorder, and revolution" (p. 8). "In mass communication, information is circulated in three forms: as raw material, as semifinished goods, and as finished product. . . . We may hesitate to insist that any people have a right to flood other people with finished products . . ." (p. 57).

The authors exhibited some ambivalence in discussing the international role of mass-media operators. "The directors of mass-communications media must recognize frankly that the need to know runs almost in reverse ratio to the ability to pay, and they must devise means of reaching those who can pay little or nothing" (p. 14). In the end, the authors assumed "that the present advertising-commercial control of programming in the domestic field is quite unsuitable in the international field" (p. 94).

The Hutchins Commission report, although ahead of its time, made a permanent valuable contribution. It was an admirable attempt to treat the then-known dilemmas of freedom and responsibility in international communications in an evenhanded scholarly manner. It had directed attention to the fact that the "free flow of information" is a two-way street and that the *receiver* of messages as well as the sender had a stake in the freedom-responsibility debate. In 1951 upon his retirement, Raymond Rubicam, cofounder of Young and Rubicam, one of the largest advertising agencies in the United States, had sent a letter to Senator William Benton in which he declared his opposition to "what amounts practically to a monopoly of radio and television by advertisers to the point where the public's freedom to choose any programme is more of a theory than a fact and to the point where the public service of the two media is only a shadow of what it could be."

A "MARSHALL PLAN OF IDEAS"

The question of choice was at the core of the rhetorical fireworks that exploded when people realized that Stalin had dropped his iron curtain around the Soviet Union and Eastern Europe. The argument in the United States ran that Stalin had not only thrown up barriers to prevent the free flow of ideas from reaching his captive millions, but that he was also from behind those barriers spreading "big lies" about the true motives and objectives of the democratic nations. This had to be countered by a worldwide communications offensive to penetrate the screens of censorship and suppression that were blocking people abroad from knowing "the truth" about the United States. Oddly enough, two of the more prominent leaders in propagating the notion of the information offensive were William Benton, Senator from Connecticut who had founded the advertising agency of Benton and Bowles, and Brigadier General David Sarnoff, chairman of the Board, Radio Corporation of America, which owned and operated the National Broadcasting Company. Benton had introduced Senate Resolution 243: An expanded International and Education Program, which he had dubbed, "a Marshall Plan in the field of ideas," and he campaigned vigorously on its behalf on radio, in print, and in public speeches.

General Sarnoff appeared with Senator Benton on a "University of Chicago Round Table" radio program, broadcast over the NBC network, in which he supported the Senator's proposal "that the international propagation of the democratic creed be made an instrument of supreme national policy," and in Senate hearings on Resolution 243 he urged that "our immediate objective should be to ring the iron-curtain countries with radio broadcasting. To do this, strategic sites must be obtained on American and other free territory upon which both shortwave and medium-wave broadcasting stations can be installed and operated" (14).

American trade objectives were incompatible with closed doors and blocked spheres of influence. The United States, its production quadrupled during the war, looked forward to leadership in the exploitation of international markets. Furthermore, there was a strong connection between foreign and domestic policy. One week after Japan's surrender, Secretary of State James F. Byrnes noted: "Our international policies inevitably affect employment in the United States. Prosperity and depression in the United States just as inevitably affect our relations with the other nations of the world." Byrnes believed "that a durable peace cannot be built on an economic foundation of exclusive blocs . . . and economic warfare . . ." (9). The Soviet Union, unable to compete on equal terms economically, was attempting to create exclusive spheres of influence and markets: Stalin would surely attempt to extend them in Asia and Africa. From the viewpoints of advertisers and program exporters, here was another domino theory—one of mass communications.

While the advocates of "a Marshall Plan in the field of ideas" were calling for "steady and steadily increasing pressure in behalf of worldwide freedom of information" (14), the equipment manufacturers, broadcasters, and advertising agencies in the United States were steadily building up their capacity to penetrate the international television market. The domestic market had already reached and passed its takeoff point. Production costs were rising, and the mass appeal programs were spectacularly outdistancing more thoughtful programs. In short, the television industry had already perfected the model it would shortly begin to mass distribute abroad. While Canadian television did not make its formal debut until 1952, when stations in Toronto and Montreal went on the air regularly for three hours a day, 100,000 sets had been sold to Canadian homes along the United States border, and the Canadians had already "acquired a pattern of viewing similar to that of the public in the United States." The Chairman of the Canadian Broadcasting Corporation's Board of Governors recognized that Canadian station-operators could avail themselves of a source of American programs at a far cheaper cost than they could produce their own, but he expressed the hope that Canada would be able to resist becoming "a country of recipients and not developing anything worthwhile of our own. I believe if this situation developed that in 30 or 40 years we would become pretty well mentally a part of the United States" (21).

In Italy Radio Audizioni Italia (RAI) had imported from the United States a complete television plant, including transmitter and studio equipment and was planning to start regular broadcasting in 1954. RAI had also purchased about 300 television programs from the United States. Mexico had six stations on the air by the spring of 1953, and the primary concern of program directors was "to create a series of broadcasts which will be commercially successful at low cost. . . . Types of programs successful in the United States are reproduced in Mexico, while Mexican stations broadcast kinescopes of United States productions." One paragraph in the UNESCO report on television in Mexico may have recalled, for some readers, the concern of the 1946 Commission on Freedom of the Press for the inequalities to be found among the world's potential television audiences. "Press reports say that television sets are to be found only among higher income groups, perhaps 10 percent of the total population. Collective reception has been organized by commercial establishments who charge an entrance fee to poorer people" (21, pp. 52–56).

THE INTERNATIONAL MARKET

International television had become big business and it was getting bigger and bigger. While the United States was the unquestioned leader in the export of films and tapes, England, West Germany, and Japan had become aggressive competitors. Even the smaller African nations were going on the air with American programs and commercials. John Tebbel may have been the first to introduce the maxim that would become a staple of the conversation among international film and television program salesmen: When a new nation is formed, the first things it wants are an airline and a television system—for status (19). The major Hollywood film studios, after a holdout action, had joined the television parade and released their "vaulties" (old films) for television sale abroad. These, along with old television serials, were the backbone of foreign television systems. Wilson Dizard in 1964 wrote: "Today overseas sales account for 60 percent of all U.S. telefilm syndication activities and represent the difference between profit and loss for the industry" (4). Just as American films had followed the flag around the world during World War II, so now American advertisers were following the television programs.

American firms have begun to make substantial investments in television advertising abroad, particularly in the European and Japanese markets. General Foods and Lever Brothers are, for example, heavy advertisers on West German television. The expansion of U.S. advertising agencies into the international market has served to spur this development. Within the past two years, the American networks have moved into this market. The leader in this case has been ABC. "You can," ABC promises American advertisers, "sell to a $136 million foreign market with ABC Worldvision." ABC does not restrict itself to American products. It has not only placed advertising for American cigarettes in Teheran, but also for British soap and Japanese transistor radios in Latin America" (pp. 67–68).

Dizard recognized that criticism of America's low-grade foreign television exports had been growing. Asserting that there "will always be a strong export market for lightweight television features, primarily because television overseas, as in this country, is primarily an entertainment medium," he nevertheless found "a definite trend—towards the merchandising of quality programs to meet the new demands of overseas buyers" (pp. 72–73).

Such a demand was not to materialize. According to the top foreign sales executive of the largest British telefilm exporter, what most overseas buyers wanted then, and still want, particularly in the developing nations, is "something to keep the natives quiet. Keep 'em watching TV and they won't talk against the government." The executive recalled his first major deals with the Prime Minister of Egypt, and remembered watching a television set on a pedestal in a village square, surrounded by viewers astride camels. "People all over the world are the same," he declared. "They all want the chase, cowboys and Indians—a little bit of escapism" (8). The view from some sectors of the underdeveloped world is different. In 1961 Frantz Fanon published his angry defense of violence for effecting social change, and writing of the disintegrating influences on the youth of the Third World spread by the cultural products of industrialized nations, said:

It is to the youth of an underdeveloped country that the industrialized countries most often offer their pastimes. . . . But in underdeveloped countries, young people have at their disposition leisure occupations designed for the youth of capitalist countries: detective novels, penny-in-the-slot machines, sexy photographs, pornographic litera- ture, films banned to those under sixteen, and above all alcohol. . . . The news which interests the Third World does not deal with King Baudouin's marriage nor the scandals of the Italian ruling class. What we want to hear about are the experiments carried out by the Argentinians or the Burmese in their efforts to overcome illiteracy or the dictatorial tendencies of their leaders (5, pp. 195–203).

The realities of television in the Third World can overwhelm high hopes even when the latter are not mere rhetoric. Timothy Green cites the case of Ghana, which originally planned to operate its television system with more than 80 percent of its own programs, mostly educational. The planners were determined not to develop the appetite for cowboy pictures.

The only trouble was that the money simply was not there to sustain them. With less than 15,000 sets in the country, the annual license fee of $12 could not provide enough revenue. After a while, Ghanian television began to accept advertising and as a corollary, the advertisers demanded popular shows. So the floodgates to the western opened after all, and today Ghana's television service provides only 40 percent of its output (7, p. 251).

The fact that international television as a big business was not inescapably a corporate contribution to unifying peoples and effecting world peace was clear to students of the medium by the mid-1960s. What was not yet clear was the pattern of America's fundamental policy and practice in the field. It may be expressed as follows: The United States wanted no barriers against trade, for both technical facilities and the content of programs ("hardware and software") in international exchange. It was opposed to "narrow nation- alism" everywhere. This policy has enabled it to take the initiative in film/ videotape program exchange across borders and to expand its world leader- ship. American television products were everywhere shown on national televi- sion systems—almost no products of other nations were shown on America's television stations.

SATELLITE COMMUNICATION

We must distinguish between the use of satellites by common carriers whose managers are indifferent to the nature of the messages they relay from point- to-point around the globe and their use by television systems, where content is important to the operators who compete for mass audiences. Television systems are the customers of common carriers. They pay the latter for sending and receiving news and television programs, via satellites and ground-stations, in real-time, live relays, or in delayed transmission of film or videotape. Common carriers and broadcasters do not have equal stakes in satellites. Without satellites common carriers could not carry on their business at all; users would have to go the alternative route of undersea cables. Television systems can live without satellites, for most of television's programming is not in real-time, but on film or tape, which can be transported fairly quickly across frontiers and oceans. For television systems, the advent of satellites meant essentially a heightened image in the public mind of television's glamour and importance. One could speak with awe of the new age of instant interchange among peoples.

Actually, the broadcasters knew from the start that satellite transmission, except for daily news exchanges—a small part of television schedules—would be used only sparingly for big-time sports or ceremonials. Advertising time on real-time satellite broadcasts is almost exclusively sold on a one-shot basis. Delayed repeats are rare and cannot be regularly syndicated or sold in series. The "meat and potatoes" of television, the staple products, are the feature films, old and new, and the television series, first, third, or fiftieth run. Satellite transmissions for networks and stations, particularly in the United States, offer fluctuating competitive advantages in the fierce struggle for leadership and prestige.

Although the Commission on Freedom of the Press had warned in 1946 that private agencies could not or would not undertake the necessary tasks of postwar international communications "on the basis of normal commercial incentives," President Eisenhower declared it to be government policy to "aggressively encourage private enterprise in the establishment of satellite relays for revenue-producing purposes." President Kennedy reaffirmed his predecessor's policy, but added a convenient rhetorical grace note with his invitation to "all nations to participate in a communications satellite system in the interest of world peace and closer brotherhood among people throughout the world" (15, pp. 128–129). In the short space of three years Congress passed the Communications Satellite Act; the Communications Satellite Corporation (Comsat) was organized as a private corporation for the profit of its shareholders; the United States pressed for and won an international agreement for immediate allocation of the radio spectrum for space communication, although other nations argued for delay to give them time to prepare for the new game; and the United States led in the organization of Intelsat, the international satellite system of a consortium of nations. Comsat managed the system and had originally more than 50 percent of the voting power, and United States contractors and manufacturers supplied 98 percent of the system's hardware procurement. Most of the other nations who joined the consortium did not relish the lesser role to which they were assigned by the United States but they joined up on unfavorable terms lest they be left out of the game. Voting power among 11 members was distributed according to the power to pay, and what could be done for the poorer countries of the world was left to be worked out (15, p. 141; 13, p. 26).

In subsequent years the United States dominance in Intelsat was considerably cut back in voting power and monopoly control. If the United States had not agreed to substantive amendments in the original Intelsat agreements, other nations might have defected from the consortium; and although the United States still holds fast to the concept of a single unitary satellite system serving all nations of the world, it faces escalating efforts by other nations to organize supplementary and competitive systems. Thus, while the United States was pursuing a highly nationalistic policy in space communications, American industry spokesmen inveighed publicly against the virus of narrow nationalism—a disease more easily spotted in foreign nations than at home.

"FREE FLOW" VS. SOVEREIGNTY

In the early 1970s freedom of information became a rhetorical issue in international television. In a newspaper article Dr. Frank Stanton, who had become the vice chairman of CBS as well as chairman of the U.S. Advisory Commission on Information, noted that the Soviet Union had introduced a proposal in the United Nations General Assembly that, along with a similar report by UNESCO, would "negate the principle of international freedom of communication" (17).

The draft proposals had been generated by the technological probability of direct-satellite-to-home television broadcasting. The Intelsat system had not been designed for such purposes, and consequently a new system or systems would have to be organized and developed. Many nations had begun to plan for domestic and regional satellites that would beam educational, informational, and cultural broadcasts to world areas, and they had to coordinate their use of the radio spectrum and geostationary orbits.

Studies had been initiated both by the United Nations General Assembly and UNESCO and by other international agencies. They agreed that direct broadcasting by satellites should respect the sovereignty of States, nonintervention, and equality and should promote the free flow of information. This meant that no nation could beam a satellite broadcast to another nation without the latter's prior consent and agreement; this undertaking included not only scheduling but also content (22).

The American strategy was to delay any agreement that would freeze regulatory principles on direct satellite broadcasting. But in 1972 the United Nations General Assembly voted not to delay but to press ahead for an international convention establishing principles for regulating direct satellite broadcasting. The vote was 102 to 1. The lone vote in opposition was cast by the United States.

World Bank President Robert S. McNamara, in his 1973 report to the bank's 122 members, noted the "absolute poverty" that he said affects 800 million people in 100 or so developing nations. He defined absolute poverty as a "condition of life so degraded by disease, illiteracy, malnutrition, and squalor as to deny its victims basic human necessities." Among the developing nations, Mr. McNamara reports that 55 percent of the national income goes to the upper 20 percent of the population and only 5 percent to the lowest 20 percent (11).

How can television be primarily an instrument for the sale of goods at home, but when it crosses a national border, even by permission, become teacher, philosopher, and health and welfare guide to peoples in countries falling even farther behind in the race for the exploitation of the world's resources? No one knows how the television systems of the world can be deflected from their present course of cultivating obedient citizens and plea-sure-seeking customers; but until things change on the world's domestic scenes they will hardly change on the international stage.

REFERENCES

1. Adilman, Sid. "Show Biz and Canadian 'Nationalism,'" *Variety,* November 1973, p. 1.
2. Barnouw, Erik. *The Golden Web, A History of Broadcasting in the United States,* Vol. II, 1933–1953. New York: Oxford University Press.
3. Batson, Lawrence D. *Radio Markets of the World.* 1930 Trade Promotion Series 109, United States Department of Commerce, Bureau of Foreign and Domestic Commerce. Reprinted in *World Broadcast Advertising, Four Reports.* New York: Arno Press and *The New York Times,* 1971.
4. Dizard, Wilson P. "American Television's Foreign Markets," *Television Quarterly, The Journal of the National Academy of Television Arts and Sciences 3,* 2 (Summer 1964), 57–73.
5. Fanon, Frantz. *The Wretched of the Earth.* New York: Grove Press, 1963.
6. Gordon, George N., Irving Falk, and William Hodapp. *The Idea Invaders.* New York: Hastings House, Communications Arts Books, 1963.
7. Green, Timothy. *The Universal Eye.* New York: Stein & Day, 1972.
8. Kaufman, Elkan. Associated Television Corporation Limited. Personal Interview. London, 1973.
9. LaFeber, Walter. *America, Russia and the Cold War, 1945–1966.* New York: Wiley, 1967.
10. Maidenberg, H. J. "Why Peru Seized TV," *The New York Times,* Financial Section (November 1971), p. 11.
11. McNamara, Robert S. Quoted in Phil Newsom, "Starvation, Disease Rising, World Bank Study Shows," *The Philadelphia Bulletin,* 28 September 1973.
12. Michelson, Charles. Pioneer exporter of American radio and television programs. Conversation with author. New York, 1973.

13. Riegel, O. W. "Communications by Satellite; The Political Barriers," *The Quarterly Review Economics and Business.* Bureau of Economic and Business Research, University of Illinois, 2, 4 (Winter 1971), 26.

14. Sarnoff, David. In "Can We Defeat the Propaganda of International Communism?" An NBC Radio Discussion. "The University of Chicago Round Table," *647,* 20 August, 1950.

15. Schiller, Herbert I. *Mass Communications and American Empire.* Boston: Beacon, 1971.

16. Schutrumpf, E. D. (ed.). *Broadcast Advertising in Latin America,* 1931.

17. Shayon, Robert Lewis. "TV Etiquette Across the Borders," *Saturday Review,* 6 October 1962.

18. Skornia, Harry J., and Jack William Kitson. *Problems and Controversies in Television and Radio.* Palo Alto, Calif.: Pacific Books, 1968.

19. Tebbel, John. "U.S. Television Abroad; Big Business," *Saturday Review,* 14 July 1962.

20. *Television, A World Survey.* Supplement 1955. Paris: UNESCO, 1955.

21. *Television, A World Survey. Reports of the Facilities of Mass Communications.* Paris: UNESCO, 1953.

22. United Nations. *Direct Broadcasting Satellites.* Working paper presented by Canada and Sweden. United Nations General Assembly, Committee on the Peaceful Uses of Outer Space, 2 May 1973.

23. United States Department of Commerce. *Trade Information Bulletin 771.*

24. Varis, Tapio. *International Inventory of Television Program Structure and the Flow of TV Programs Between Nations.* Finland: Institute of Journalism and Mass Communications, University of Tampere, 1973.

25. White, Llewellyn, and Robert D. Leigh. *Peoples Speaking to Peoples, a Report on International Mass Communication from the Commission on Freedom of the Press.* Chicago: University of Chicago Press, 1946.

26. Will, Tom. *Initial Study of Import and Export Film and Videotape.* Working draft. United States Department of Commerce, Office of Telecommunications, 1973.

CHAPTER 5

American Television in Latin America

ELIZABETH DE CARDONA

The three major networks (ABC, NBC, and CBS), together with Time Inc., represented the primary U.S. interests in the promotional stage of television in Latin America. During this period crucial decisions on technical specifications (such as line span) were made that would later influence the source of hardware equipment and consequent television programming.

The American Broadcasting Company (ABC) made its first contact in 1950 with *Telesistemas Mexicanas* (an affiliation they continue with channel 4 in Mexico City). The United States was then leading the world in the development of television equipment, so the assistance given by the networks and specifically by ABC was in the form of technical aid. They advised the stations on types of hardware needed and sent equipment and technicians. Concurrently the networks began to experiment with production and programming sales for the new markets. ABC had an early trial run in Latin American programming sales with the production of *Meet the Professor*—in Spanish—but ran into conflicts with its customers concerning the nationality of the professor. Each country wanted the professor to be of its own nationality. The program was soon abandoned. ABC also entered into an association with private interests in Mexico for the production of soap operas that could be produced in Mexico at one-fourth the cost of their production in Hollywood. These programs had the advantage of being closer to the Latin American humor and lifestyles.

The cost in these early days of television was about $5000 or $6000 for the production of a half hour of Mexican soap opera. A similar production in Hollywood would have cost three times as much.

In 1939 the National Broadcasting Company (NBC) began the first international transmission of daily news in Latin America, sponsored by the United Fruit Company. Two years later, when the Federal Communications Commission authorized the commercial development of television, NBC created the Pan American Network, made up of 92 radio stations, to transmit programs to South America. NBC operations were coordinated by its mother company, RCA, which assumed leadership in the manufacturing of radios, record players, and television sets in Argentina, Brazil, Chile, Mexico, and Venezuela. NBC continues to have interests in a radio and television station in Caracas (20 percent of the stock of Channel 2, Radio Caracas Television) and a television channel in Mexico. It has headed consulting projects in technical and administrative assistance in various Latin American countries, for example, Mexico and Peru. Through RCA, it manages numerous recording houses in countries "south of the border."

In 1942 the Columbia Broadcasting System (CBS) founded the Latin American Network, composed of 64 radio stations in 18 countries. In addition, it founded and still operates various recording houses on the continent. It also has investments in at least three TV production companies: Proartel of Argentina, Pantel of Peru, and Proventel of Venezuela (1).

Companies producing television programming, independent from the networks, also entered the Latin American market at its inception. Producers like Warner Brothers, United Artists, Twentieth Century Fox, MGM, Screen Gems, Paramount, Universal Pictures, Allied Artists, and MCA (Music Corporation of America) went into the Latin American TV market in the 1950s. They did this to meet the demand of the private broadcasters who would come north to shop for American programming. To increase their sales the U.S. companies began to send sales representatives to South America. These representatives played an important part in the introduction of U.S. films into the Latin American market. They traveled extensively throughout South America showing pilots of new programming offered in the United States and selling a combination of used-programming and syndicated programming from their home studios. These packages included old Hollywood movies.

By direct investment Time Inc. began its penetration of Latin American television in the 1960s. Its two primary contacts were Emilio Azcarraga in Mexico *(Telesistemas Mexicanas)* and Goar Mestre in Argentina. Time Inc. started operations with Mestre in Argentina because he had been Director of Television in Cuba before the revolution, and it wanted to begin with people of experience. In Brazil it began with Roberto Marinho of *El Globo*, the country's most important newspaper. Although Time Inc. initially planned to furnish only technical assistance in both these ventures, it eventually supplied 50 percent of the capital.

The Argentine station was licensed in the name of Mrs. Mestre, an Argentine.* *Proartel,* the production company, a partnership of Mestre, Time Inc.,

---

*This arrangement of ownership was due to the limitation in the Argentine laws of foreign ownership of television channels.

and CBS, sold programs to Channel 13 in Buenos Aires and to other stations in Argentina and other Latin American countries as far north as Colombia. Time Inc.'s subsequent operation was a similar production company in Venezuela in which Mestre supplied the expertise and connections, while Time Inc. and CBS supplied the capital. This company also included investments by the Vollmer family, important industrialists of Venezuela.

The Venezuelan operations were not as successful as the Argentine. At this time, about 1964, Caracas already had two other commercial television stations. Though Channel 8, Caracas had the best equipment money could buy, with capital provided by Time Inc. and CBS, it suffered from a shortage of trained local TV personnel. There were constant administrative problems. Its two competitor stations were also affiliated with U.S. companies. The strongest one, Channel 2, owned by the Cisneros family, was affiliated with ABC. The other, Channel 4, owned by the Phelps family, was affiliated with NBC. The investment of CBS and Time Inc. in the Caracas station was greater than they would have made in a comparable U.S. station. Problems with the Venezuelan business included the fact that the Vollmers were more interested in the political role than the economic role of television.

ROLE OF THE NETWORKS

The initial role of the U.S. networks was one of technical assistance and capital. Most of the investments were preceded by technical assistance to get the station on the air. ABC was the most active in this initial type of setup; CBS, the least. Time Inc. would probably have been more successful in its Latin American ventures if it had been able to set up an effective fourth network in its U.S. homeland; however, the only country where Time Inc. suffered an actual loss was Venezuela.

Some prominent members of the U.S. television industry* feel that the networks took a beating in their Latin American investments and that the initial decision of the networks to enter the Latin American market was unwise. The decision was made during an expansionist phase of the U.S. economy when many thought the expansion could be extended limitlessly outside the nation's borders. The networks believed the lack of technical ability of the Latin American countries would make them an easy market for U.S. entry, but the political factors were not fully taken into account.

ABC had hoped to control programming through minority interests in Latin American stations, but the trend toward local control thwarted this

*Ralph Franklin, Head of Overseas Sales for MCA; William Fineshriber, V.P. MPEAA; Charles Michelson, Independent Agent, C. Michelson, Inc.

plan. ABC had originally hoped to sell programming and commercial time to a single company such as Coca-Cola or Gillette. When this proved to be impossible, ABC withdrew from many of its stations but continued to earn fees as a buyer for them.

Time Inc. has sold or closed down all of its telecommunication facilities in Latin America.

CHANGING U.S. INVESTMENT

As U.S. investments have declined, U.S. advertising in Latin American television has increased. The initial investment plan of Time Inc. and the networks had been to attract the advertising dollar, in one package, for their affiliated stations. Today advertisers are no longer willing to commit themselves to the whole Latin American market as a bloc. They prefer to plan their advertising on a country-by-country basis.

Approximately 10 to 15 percent of TV programming in Latin America is sold directly to multinational advertising agencies. These companies buy a program and time on a television station and then sell slices to their clients. Most of the current sales in Latin America are made directly to the station by the program producer or syndicator. In the past a multinational company like Singer, Coca-Cola, or Gillette would contract a show in the United States and then send it to their subsidiaries or associates in other countries as a "carrier" for their advertising. The trend today is toward more local autonomy. In reaction, the multinational corporations have established separate operations in each country and try to decentralize the control of the company to placate the nationalistic tendencies of the host. The parent firm no longer directs its branches in writing advertising copy, nor does it send them translated copies of programs. Resident managers are now more independent in their advertising budgets. ABC occasionally works with the international branches of U.S. advertising agencies to sell time on the program of its associated stations—for example, its Sales Representative Department works to place advertising on programs in the Latin American market—but this activity is an exception.

The advertising dollar has also shifted its center because of the FCC ruling separating the networks from their domestic syndication and from some of their foreign distribution activities. Most of the rights for overseas sales now remain with the production company. Because the networks in many cases are buying series at prices below the production costs, the production companies must take advantage of overseas distribution revenue to make a profit.

Although there are still television stations in Latin America in which U.S. companies have investments, the primary influence of U.S. culture and commerce is now through the sales of TV programs.

The major U.S. exporter of television programming is the Motion Picture Export Association of America (MPEAA). Members of this association are Allied Artists Television Corporation, Avco-Embassy, MCA Television, Metro-Goldwyn-Mayer TV, Paramount TV Enterprises Inc., Screen Gems International, Twentieth Century Fox, United Artists Television, and Warner Brothers Television. A smaller share is exported by Viacom, a company established in 1970 to operate the foreign and domestic program distribution business and the cable systems of CBS. Viacom was founded by National Telefilm Associates Inc., which recently purchased the stock of NBC films and certain assets of NBC International, and by Independent Television, which is a British corporation and therefore cannot be a member of MPEAA.

MPEAA is said to favor a gradual growth by national stations and national television producers. One of the problems of the less developed countries, however, is that no television industry can exist solely on the local market. When these countries enter the international market, they must compete with the United States, England, and other developed nations for the sale of their domestically produced—and usually inferior—programs.

One counterbalance that has been proposed by the countries that buy American television is the formation of a bloc among the national stations to bargain as a cartel. Of course the MPEAA is against this proposal and has said it will not sell to the cartel, except when there is no other alternative, as in the case of Italy and France where the television industry is already a national monopoly.

At the same time as MPEAA is fighting the formation of monopolies among its buyer countries, the Webb-Pomerine Act, a protectionist measure that exempts U.S. industry from some antitrust limitations in its international operations, is permitting the American producers of television programs to act as a cartel themselves in their dealings with the world market. Under this act associations can be formed that have the power to deal as a unit and represent all their members in price decisions.

Each foreign country pays a different price for American programming. The price is determined by the number of television sets, the population, and the general income level of the host country. The MPEAA supplies its members with confidential information concerning the market in each country, the going price for programming, market potential, limitations, and prospects for the future.

Coproductions have been done in almost every country of Latin America. They have had exciting beginnings, but unfortunately many have failed through lack of commitments. The Coca-Cola special *Raquel* was filmed mainly in Mexico with the assistance of national artists and technicians, but they neglected to advise Coca-Cola that the use of Aztec pyramids in a dance scene would be offensive to their fellow countrymen.

One problem with coproduction is that the nationalism of each country limits the acceptance of different cultures and accents. A coproduction with Mexico will have limited acceptance in Peru. The absence of a unified market is one of the main obstacles to foreign investment in Latin American coproduction. Nevertheless, there are those who regard coproduction as the trend of the future because of its lower costs and fewer labor problems.

REFERENCE

1. Mattelart, Armand. *Agresion desde el espacio: Cultura y napalm en la era de los satelites,* Vol. XXI. Buenos Aires, 1973.

CHAPTER 6

Satellite Communication and National Power

O. W. RIEGEL

The politics of space is an extension of the politics of earth. The objective of governments in communications is not to promote "world-mindedness" or education in the sense of increased understanding and appreciation of the ideas and cultures of other nations and peoples in a world community, but rather to preserve and strengthen the sense of nationality and the national status quo. "Bringing emerging nations into the twentieth century" in communications usually translates into providing governments with tools to combat indifference and tribal and other fragmenting loyalties for the purpose of promoting national unity and discipline. Bluntly stated, this means turning nomadic Africans into soldiers.

Another basic fact of life in communications politics is that in the first decade of satellite development two nations, the United States and the Soviet Union, have dominated space through launching capacity, with a duopoly in the launching of heavy satellites (over 250 pounds) and a monopoly by the United States in the launching of geostationary satellites. This means that the two superpowers have largely determined how many satellites should be launched and for what purpose. This dominance will be increasingly challenged. France, Japan, China, and the United Kingdom have launched satellites. Other countries are in various stages of planning and experimentation. The Soviet Union may be expected to end the American geostationary satellite monopoly by 1977, and the European Space Agency (ESA) hopes to have a similar capacity by the end of this decade. As more nations acquire larger and more sophisticated satellites and launching facilities, the problems of competition and accommodation will become acute.

The four operational satellites of the INTELSAT system and their three spares, the Canadian TELESAT, and the Russian Molnyas are a minute fraction of the thousands of satellites now in space or of those planned for

63

self-serving national and military purposes.* In addition to American Defense Satellite Communications Systems (DSCS) already launched, the Army, Air Force, and Navy are all embarked on a variety of new systems to be operative within the next few years (15). Military communications satellites have been provided by the United States to NATO and the United Kingdom. Governments, including their military branches, are also users of the INTELSAT system.† Moreover, *communications* is a word of broad definition, and it is difficult to see why satellites with surveillance, detection, camera and sensor devices, which communicate all kinds of information from weather conditions to warship and nuclear silo locations do not qualify as communications satellites as well as those that transmit command, supply, and navigation messages. The National Reconnaissance Office, a top-secret agency, spends an estimated $1.5 billion a year on surveillance that includes sophisticated satellites (7, 15).

The American Earth Resources Technology Satellite (ERTS), with its revealing sensors, is understandably regarded as a spy satellite by many of the nations over which it passes. Even though the raw data, the United States insists, are available to all, nations ask why satellites are used when less-expensive authorized aircraft equipped with sensors would do as well and why an enterprise that invades sovereignty should not be internationalized. Even more difficult to understand is why surveillance and military satellites are not considered in violation of both the spirit and the letter of the United Nations Treaty on the Peaceful Uses of Outer Space. The Soviet Union has similar surveillance satellites (Cosmos satellites monitored the 1973 Arab-Israeli war), and other nations will have them as they acquire launching capacity. Seen in perspective, then, space is dominated by communications satellites serving narrow national purposes. The four satellites of the global public communications network in world service are like four lonely sunfish in a sea of eels.

No nation has ever surrendered sovereignty over telecommunications entering the country across national frontiers or from space. Binational and multinational agreements affirm the devotion of nations to the principle of free flow of information, but no nation has ever renounced the right to interrupt that flow. The escape hatch in all international agreements is a clause permitting interference with any messages that might damage national security or disturb domestic tranquillity.

---

*The monthly *Satellite Situation Report* of the Goddard Space Flight Center (NASA) lists 3313 objects in orbit as of April 30, 1975, of which 2168 were American and 1145 Russian. The same report shows 4468 decayed objects, 1314 American and 3154 Russian.
†One example: The Hot Line via satellite between the White House and the Kremlin. The Defense Communications Agency has awarded a contract to IT&T WORLDCOM for teleprinter service over the INTELSAT system. Payment to IT&T is about $5500 monthly (2).

As technologies develop and the political situation changes, the focal points of national policy and action also change. At this time the problems of national interest cluster around two issues that appear to be crucial to the future development of satellite communication: one is the problem of ownership, control, and operation of the satellites; the other is the problem of direct television broadcasting from space to home and neighborhood receivers.

When the communications satellite became a reality, questions of who was to use the satellite and for what purposes became paramount. The nationalist view was that because the United States had developed the satellite at great cost, the United States was entitled to exploit the satellite for American benefit. A government agency was proposed that would launch, own, and operate a satellite communications system and enter into bilateral agreements with other countries for the use of the system.

A practical objection was that an international communication circuit is impossible without a willing partner at the other end. According to the proposed plan, the United States would be asking our governments, who for the most part own and operate their telecommunications systems, to cooperate as partners in a venture in which they would in fact be only commercial clients. Moreover, the American government was sensitive to the charges of monopoly and arrogance that such a course would suggest, even to its allies. The question was complicated by the clamor of American private, competing, commercial international carriers for a share in the new satellite business, as well as by a strong American prejudice against government ownership.

The result of the debate was the COMSAT Act of 1962, which created the Communications Satellite Corporation, a private commercial stock company designated as the chosen instrument of the United States for the development of an international space communications system. The nations of the world were invited to join in an international consortium in which, by mutual but temporary agreement, each nation would have investment ownership in the system roughly in proportion to the amount of traffic it generated. Although there was to be an international governing committee, the United States would have the dominant role by virtue of ownership of more than half of the investment and control of operations through management of the system by COMSAT.

The irony in the story of the interim INTELSAT, as the consortium was called, is the contrast between the dissatisfactions of its non-American members and the success of INTELSAT under COMSAT management. The record is impressive: an increase in membership from the original 14 in 1964 to 89 in 1975; an increase in ground station antennas from five in five countries in 1964 to 103 antennas at 81 ground stations in 50 countries in 1975; increase in traffic (e.g., 150 leased half-circuits in 1965 to 9814 in 1973 and increasing by 1975 at the rate of 20 percent a year); decrease in cost (e.g.,

$10,000 for a voice-grade half-circuit to Europe per month in 1965 to $4625 in 1974); and improvements in satellites, service, and profitability (5).

The reason for dissatisfaction was not the efficiency of COMSAT. The reasons, both material and psychological, stemmed from national interest. At base was dissatisfaction with the dominating role of the United States in INTELSAT affairs, the feeling of other nations that they were minor or insignificant partners in an enterprise in which they were nominally equals but in which they had little authority or power.

The underlying psychological dissatisfaction found expression in a number of specific and practical complaints. One was that COMSAT was a mongrel among purebloods—a three-headed creature that was at the same time the official United States government representative in INTELSAT; a private corporation; and a business with a primary interest in being profitable, not as a part of a national telecommunications system, as in the case of most other INTELSAT members, but for the benefit of private, mainly American, stockholders. Another complaint was that COMSAT was too autonomous and secretive; it did not share expertise with or hire personnel who were citizens of member nations eager to develop their own capabilities in space. Still another complaint, related to the one above, was that COMSAT, whether justifiably or not, favored American subcontractors in the procurement of hard and software for the INTELSAT system to the detriment of the engineering and space industries of member nations.

When negotiations for a permanent INTELSAT organization began in 1969, the United States took a hard line in defense of its priority position but subsequently yielded to the inevitable. The permanent agreement that became effective February 12, 1973, represented a substantial retreat from the American position under the interim agreement and a substantial increase in the internationalization of INTELSAT. The permanent agreement set up the machinery for the take-over of the management of INTELSAT over a five-year period by a new Director General (interim title, Secretary General) who is responsible to a greatly strengthened international Board of Governors which is broadened in membership to include representatives of regional blocs of small or underdeveloped nations (an African bloc was among those added). COMSAT was given a transitional management services contract for a period of six years; at the end of the period INTELSAT will decide whether to continue with COMSAT or award the service contract to another manager, which could conceivably be itself. In the latter case it might simply take over a COMSAT technical and managerial staff. The investment interest of the United States in INTELSAT was reduced from its majority interest to about 40 percent as of 1973, which was in line with the percentage of INTELSAT traffic generated by the United States, a percentage that has been shrinking as traffic increases among other member countries (1, 4, 12).

How international is INTELSAT? In spite of setbacks, the position of the United States remains strong. With its launchers, technology, large investment share, and allies within INTELSAT, U.S. primacy is not really in jeopardy at this time. Conspicuously absent from INTELSAT, however, are countries representing about a third of the world's geographic area and half of its population—the Soviet Union, China, and the smaller nations of the Communist blocs. The first Soviet reaction to INTELSAT was to denounce it as a tool of American imperialism. It called upon the United Nations to establish a satellite system in which all nations would have an equal voice (17). It also created its own INTERSPUTNIK system using Molnya eccentric orbiting satellites (INTELSAT uses geostationary satellites), but INTERSPUTNIK until recently has served only Soviet domestic telecommunications and ground stations in the Soviet bloc of Eastern Europe.

The conventional view in the West is that the Soviet Union has refused to join INTELSAT because it develops so relatively little international traffic that it would consider its minor position in INTELSAT under the voting system as incompatible with its role as a great power. However, in spite of the rhetoric, Soviet behavior toward INTELSAT has been correct, and it sent an observer to the permanent INTELSAT negotiations. It cooperates through INTERVISION in television exchanges and it is, of course, a member of international telecommunications entities. In fact, it is a client of INTELSAT through terrestrial connections with the Swedish ground station and is building a ground station for "Hot Line" Kremlin-White House satellite communication; the station will interconnect with INTELSAT. China now has four ground stations that interconnect with INTELSAT in a client non-member relationship and appears eager to move ahead with a comprehensive combined satellite-terrestrial telecommunications system. It could be a large user of INTELSAT. There is a feeling in INTELSAT that with the internationalizing reforms of the permanent INTELSAT, the diminution of the American role, and the new detentes with the United States (if they last), the Soviet Union may change its policy, and both the Soviets and Chinese may apply for INTELSAT membership. A development not compatible with this view was the completion in Cuba in 1974 of an earth station providing linkage with INTERSPUTNIK. This is the first intrusion of INTERSPUTNIK into the Western Hemisphere and, in fact, the first INTERSPUTNIK link outside the Soviet bloc.*

While INTELSAT membership is open to any nation and its services are

---

*It has been reported (5) that in 1970 some Canadians were proposing that Canada negotiate with the Soviet Union for rental of channels on the Soviet Molnyas orbiting in northern latitudes, thereby saving the $7 million launching fee paid to the United States. The idea is said to have produced a strong negative reaction from the United States.

available to any user who can pay the tariffs, because of its weighted voting system and the nonmembership of many nations, it falls short of answering the call of the United Nations resolution for a global satellite communications system available to all on an equal basis.

How feasible is a global satellite system under the ownership and control of a truly supranational and politically neutral governing body? One proposal would create such a body under the auspices of the International Telecommunications Union (ITU). Another proposal would have the United Nations create such a body within its own organization. The difficulties of these proposals are obvious. As successful as the ITU has been (up to a point) in bringing order to international communications through spectrum allocations, it is becoming increasingly politicized and is without police power to enforce its rules. There is no reason why this one-nation-one-vote organization should be any more successful than INTELSAT in resolving differences between have and have-not nations. Nor is there any way that the ITU can force sovereign nations into providing launching pads and satellite technology. These objections can be raised with even greater force against operation of a global telecommunications system by the United Nations, a highly politicized body that is ineffectual against the claims of national sovereignty.

Meanwhile many nations are pursuing their own launching and satellite communication plans and projects, creating new problems of national interest. What, for example, should be the response to the challenge to the American-Soviet duopoly of the launching pad? Should an effort be made to blunt the proliferation of launching capacities by making existing pads available to other nations? If so, to whom and under what conditions? As the usuable spectrum for satellite communication becomes more congested, how will channels be allocated among rival national claimants? How will domestic and regional satellite systems affect the viability of a global system like INTELSAT? How can a proliferation of communication satellites avoid violations, intentional or unintentional, of national sovereignty from space?

DIRECT TELEVISION BROADCASTING

The prospect of direct television broadcasting from satellite to the home receiver has created another paradox of satellite communication: the contrast between the worldwide potential of this technological advance and the alarm and controversy the prospect has provoked among nations.

We may begin by assuming that the age of direct television broadcasting has arrived in respect to technical feasibility, although actual reception on standard home sets may be five or 10 years away. In simplest terms, the technical problem has been either to increase the transmitting power of satellites, or the sensitivity of receiving antennas, or both, so that television signals can be received by small inexpensive antennas on standard receiving sets. A transitional stage toward direct broadcasting has been achieved. There is broadcasting to community or neighborhood antennas that are small compared to the great saucers of the ground stations of the INTELSAT system but are too large and expensive for the home. There is no good reason to doubt that advancing technology will soon achieve a capability for practical home reception.

The obstacles are political and economic, and they are formidable. Basically the political obstacle is the fear of violations of national sovereignty. The beauty of the ground station from the point of view of governments is that it simplifies control of incoming communications at the gateway; communications may be edited, revised, or totally embargoed before domestic distribution. Control of the multiple stations of a community system might be a little more difficult, at least in theory. The real fear, however, is of home reception, which governments seem to assume may elude effective control.

The reasons nations most commonly offer for their apprehensions cluster in three main areas:

1.   Fear of propaganda and provocation, especially material that will increase tensions domestically or with other nations, rouse passions, cause disunity, or disturb domestic or international tranquillity

2.   Fear of commercial aggression—for example, in material that will rouse desires for different products or a different standard of life, creating unrest, disturbing the economic order and putting nations at a disadvantage in domestic and world markets

3.   Fear of corruption of culture—for example, in material that offends traditions, damages values, and seduces the population with alien culture and standards, which are naturally considered inferior to the native ones

An irony of the agitation over direct broadcasting is that electronic intrusion on national sovereignty is no novelty. Shortwave and medium-wave radio broadcasting have violated national frontiers for half a century. The propaganda content of such broadcasts has been bitterly denounced and at various times combatted with jamming and penalties for listening, but proving that such broadcasting has seriously affected target nations or changed the course of history would be difficult.

Frontiers have been violated by "pirate" radio stations, which nations have suppressed by individual and collective action, but the reasons for suppression are not political or cultural subversion but violation of frequency allocations, luring listeners away from authorized stations and eluding the tax collector. Television spillover across national frontiers is substantial—for example, between Canada and the United States, East and West Germany, Austria and Czechoslovakia, Hong Kong and China, and many other frontiers in Europe and the Middle East. Spillovers may not be liked, but nations learn to live with them.

Other problems are time zones and language. The economic advantage of satellite broadcasting is its ability to transmit simultaneously to as much as one-third of the earth. This advantage is substantially diminished if a considerable part of the audience is asleep or can't understand the language. Nor are nations defenseless against unwanted television signals. They can jam, enforce laws against illegal viewing; provide sets with attachments to limit reception; confine television transmission to cable systems; or, in extremity, blast noxious satellites out of space.

Costs considered, if terrestrial propaganda broadcasting is economically marginal, it would be even more questionable with the much higher costs of satellite transmission, especially when it would jeopardize the cooperation upon which a nation's international communications depend. What advertiser or government commercial agency is prepared to spend huge amounts on satellite transmissions to promote products, from automobiles to body deodorants, in foreign markets where a nationalist backlash, import quotas, embargoes, and other reprisals might be expected? Most television receivers are situated in a few industrialized countries where customers can be reached more economically in other ways.

Direct broadcasting has been a subject of study and debate at high levels of international discourse for a decade. By the mid-1960s the subject was being discussed at private conferences, at meetings of experts summoned by UNESCO, at the UN's Committee on the Peaceful Uses of Outer Space, and at meetings of official and private broadcasting organizations (3, 8, 9, 11).

The controversy became an agenda item of international diplomacy in 1972, when Andrei Gromyko presented to the General Assembly of the United Nations a draft convention on "principles governing the use by States of artificial earth satellites for direct television broadcasting." The salient features of this draft included (1) the stipulation that nothing could be broadcast to any country without the express consent of the country and with notice to the Secretary General of the United Nations and UNESCO; (2) the exclusion of "any material publicizing ideas of war, militarism, naziism, national and racial hatred and enmity between peoples, as well as material which is immoral or instigating in nature or is otherwise aimed at interfering in the domestic affairs of foreign policy of other states."

In the debate American Ambassador George Bush called the proposal premature and in probable conflict with the freedom of expression guaranteed by the Universal Declaration of Human Rights. Soviet Ambassador Yako Malik said the Soviets opposed "freedom of information such as the one to which the Voice of America resorts in its broadcasts from West Germany" and called the Soviet proposal a fight against anarchy and against the imposition of unilateral information by one power.

The General Assembly's Political Committee in a close vote rejected consideration of the Soviet draft and then referred the matter to the Committee on the Peaceful Uses of Outer Space, which it charged with devising a set of principles to govern the control of satellite broadcasting. The vote to refer to committee for recommendations was 102 to 1, the United States casting the sole negative vote.

Meanwhile the experts of UNESCO had formulated guiding principles scarcely less restrictive than the proposed Soviet convention (3). The key passage in the guidelines says that States must reach or promote prior agreements concerning direct satellites broadcasting to other states. The United States, the United Kingdom, Canada, and West Germany voted against the Guiding Principles; 55 members voted for them; there were 22 abstentions.

Sweden and Canada have presented a compromise proposal to the Working Group of the UN Committee on Outer Space that is preparing a recommendation on guidelines. The proposal accepts the principle of controls but would require that complaints of violations be settled by consultation, conciliation, arbitration, and courts, rather than through unilateral action (such as destroying satellites) by the offended nation (13).

In the United States Commissioner Robert E. Lee of the FCC has suggested that the time has come for the United States to reevaluate its position "in accord with international political realities," by which he appears to mean that some kind of convention for broadcast control is inevitable and that the United States should stop acting intractably and stop delaying accommodation (10).

On the other side, Frank Stanton of the Columbia Broadcasting System, who plays the role of elder statesman of the broadcasting industry, belabors the State Department and especially its UNESCO representatives for being soft on freedom of information.

The argument over American advocacy of an unrestricted flow of information everywhere is an old one. The sentiments of the United States, say its critics, are based upon the circumstance that the United States happens to have a glut of domestic communications and is the leading exporter of communications products. Its advocacy of freedom of information is therefore good business. The situation is quite different, the argument runs, on the savannahs of the Mato Grosso and along the banks of the Congo and the Indus, where peoples are relatively deprived of television and other forms of communication and vulnerable to communications imperialism. Would the United States continue to champion laissez-faire international communications if a foreign satellite were saturating the country with pornographic programs? Or if a satellite beamed into the country incited racial minorities or radical groups to overthrow the government?

The indicators of popular convictions—attitude polls, elections, the reflexes of populations in times of stress and war—show that most people approve policies that promote national self-interest. Most people are xenophobic when the national order or national culture appears to be threatened from land, sea, air—or space.

REFERENCES

1. Aelard, Charles D. "The INTELSAT Definitive Agreements: A Recapitulation," *EBU Review 128 B* (July 1971).

2. *Aviation Week*, 19 November 1973.

3. *Broadcasting from Space: Reports and Papers on Mass Communications.* Paris: UNESCO, 1970.

4. Colino, Richard R. *The INSTELSAT Definitive Arrangements; Ushering in a New Era in Satellite Telecommunications.* Geneva: European Broadcasting Union, 1973.

5. *COMSAT, The First Ten Years: COMSAT Annual Report to the President and The Congress.* Washington D.C.: Communications Satellite Corporation, 1973.

6. Dowd, Erik. In *Washington Post*, 23 January 1973.

7. Klass, Phillip J. *Secret Sentries in Space.* New York: Random House, 1971.

8. Koslosov, Yuri. Article summarized in *IPI Report*, Zurich, 22, 4 (April 1973).

9. Kozluk, Tadeusz. "Problems of Television Satellite Broadcasting," *The Democratic Journalist*, IOJ, Prague, 7–8 (1973).

10. Lee, Robert E. West Virginia Broadcasters Fall Meeting, White Sulphur Springs, W.V., August 24, 1973.

11. Ploman, Edward W. "Satellite Broadcasting for Europe." Prepared for Council of Europe, Strasbourg. Document No. CCC/EES, 72, 7.

12. Riegel, O. W. "Communications by Satellite: The Political Barriers," *The Quarterly Review of Economics and Business, 2*, 4 (Winter 1971).

13. Smith, Delbret D. *International Telecommunication Control.* Leyden: A. W. Sijthoff, 1969.

14. United Nations Working Group of Direct Broadcast Satellites. *Working Paper on Direct Broadcasting by Satellites.* Presented by Canada and Sweden, Fourth Session, June 11–12, 1973.

15. United States House of Representatives. *Review of Department of Defense Worldwide Communications, Phase II. Report of the Special Subcommittee on Defense Communications of the Committee on Armed Services.* House of Representatives, Ninety-second Congress, Second Session, October 1972.

16. *Washington Post*, 9 December 1973.

17. Zhukov, G. P. and E. G. Vasilevskaya. *Legal Aspects of the Utilization of Artificial Satellites for Meteorological and Radio Transmission Purposes.* Moscow: Nauda Press, 1970.

CHAPTER 7

Trends in Middle Eastern Societies

HAMID MOWLANA

For more than a century mass media in the Middle East have been considered phenomena imported from the West—products, so to speak, of the impact of the West upon the Middle East. To a large degree this image persists in the minds of Middle Easterners: Mass media never have been "export" commodities. Importation of mass media usually has occurred on two levels: via communication technology—through introduction of the printing press, telegraph, telephone, radio, and television—and via their content—various forms of nationalism, "modernization," ideology, news, and most recently entertainment. Each level has stimulated growth of the other, and although communication content has come to reflect indigenous cultures, the influx of Western technology has remained unabated.

The dawn of the mass media era in the Middle East is a comparatively recent event. For example, introduction of newspapers in Turkey, Iran, and Egypt dates only to the first half of the nineteenth century. Before that time social life provided abundant intercourse (e.g., the mosque, with its extra Friday meetings; the coffee houses; and the market place), and dissemination of news and opinion was also the concern of religious leaders.

In borrowing Western military, transportation, commercial, and communication technology, the Middle East allowed and at times welcomed penetration first by Europe and later the United States. To the invading corps of political ambassadors and military experts were added missionaries and others who established printing presses, newspapers, educational institutions, and marketing organizations.

With a few exceptions, the mass media—especially the press—of the Middle East have followed the style and format of French and British newspapers and periodicals; lately they have also been influenced by American journalism. At times wholesale imitation has resulted. Only for short periods such as the 1905–1911 Constitutional Revolution in Iran, was the indigenous press able to develop its distinct cultural and regional characteristics. Nevertheless, the asumption that the mass media are tools of nationalism and politics is strong in Middle Eastern societies.

Introduction of mass media into the Middle East during the nineteenth and early-twentieth centuries accelerated development of political consciousness and brought autocratic/aristocratic systems, such as those of the Ottomans in Turkey (6) and the Qajars in Iran (2), into collision with nationalism. Popularization of the print medium and its use for political purposes marks the dawn of modern history and birth of independence for many Middle Eastern countries. As a number of related developments, such as introduction of telegraph and telephone and adoption of modern postal systems, fostered growth of the media, they too became tools of political and nationalistic drives.

MASS MEDIA AS A TOOL OF SOCIOECONOMIC AND CULTURAL POLICIES

Middle Eastern leaders and planners—and to a large extent the public as well—assume that the media must serve the people and the country and must promote national development. This is the expectation whether in the Arab countries, Israel, or the non-Arab countries of Iran and Turkey.

Thus, a recent campaign by the Iranian government to promote national development objectives outlined their policy objectives for mass media:

In view of the appreciable effect of the mass media on public opinion, especially among children and young adults, all the media will be utilized in accordance with a comprehensive and balanced program to achieve the following objectives: (a) to strengthen religious foundations and national cultural unity and promote greater interchange of ideas between officials and the public concerning important social, economic and cultural policies; (b) to motivate the public to accept new ideas; (c) to create a sense of discipline, perseverance and vocational conscience, prepare the public to fulfill their social responsibilties, and encourage active public participation, especially on the part of young people, in development affairs, while at the same time utilizing all democratic and progressive organizations, such as the village, municipal, urban district and provincial councils, the Universal Welfare Legion and the Revolutionary Corps, to attract public participation and mobilize the younger generation to prepare and implement development programs (3).

In Egypt utilization of mass media has been the backbone of programs by both Nasser and Sadat for social reform and national development. Nasser (10) used a two-prong approach: He discredited media by telling the masses that the enemy would use it to spread rumors and false reports; at the same time, however, he expressed his pleasure at the media for promoting programs of the Egyptian Revolution.

In accordance with his ideas about the media while he was a student and a military officer, Nasser's revolution began with the occupation of Marconi House, headquarters of the Marconi Radio Telegraph Company and the Egyptian Broadcasting Company. Later he also nationalized and centralized print media. Sadat (11)—then a journalist and information minister—asserted that the proper role of the media was to help "to get Egypt out of the Middle Ages, to turn it from a semi-feudal country into a modern, ordered, viable state, while at the same time respecting the customs of the people."

Other countries of the region have followed this example. For the past decade mass media in Iraq have been orchestrated to play a significant role in promoting political and economic education of the citizenry. Important allocation was made for broadcasting in the Iraqi budget as ". . . the importance of radio and television became evident in their being the chief media for general education and popular entertainment through which to acquaint the citizens with events occurring inside the country and to educate them by scientific and social talks" (4).

Encouraged by the growth of its educated class and by domestic and external support, Saudi Arabia issued a reform program that included strengthening Islamic communication/propaganda and developing Saudi mass communications. Despite the firm opposition of religious leaders, the government established a state-owned television station and substantially increased the number of newspapers.

The relationship of mass media to social reform in the Middle East today represents only the latest phase of a long process of transformation and change which began in the late-nineteenth century and extended through at least three generations. Whereas reformers of the early years, inspired by the ideas of the French Revolution and the libertarian ideas of Europe, emphasized individual freedom and the traditional concept of the democratic media, reformers of today uphold a more collective and socialist concept of democracy and freedom.

The religious heritage of the Middle East has retarded the growth of film more than it has any other media. In assimilating the print arts into their cultures, for example, the peoples of the region skillfully used them as tools of reform and even of revolution. The assimilation process of film, however, has not been so smooth. Rather, there has been a hostile confrontation between the cinema and traditional Islamic culture; the religion of Islam has never favored the use of the human figure in art forms because it is thought to be the equivalent of "making a god" opposed to Allah. The prohibition of images comes from the traditional Moslem literature rather than from the Koran itself. The Koran criticizes the pagan worship of images but contains no specific commandments against the creation or use of artistic representations.

Despite this sociocultural factor, filmmaking and film viewing vary widely from country to country in the Middle East. This fact permits comparison of

Saudi Arabi and Yemen (both produce no motion pictures and discourage the showing of entertainment films) to Lebanon and Israel (both have active film industries catering to an avid moviegoing public). The average movie-goers in these latter two countries sees three times as many films as the average American.

STRUCTURE AND CONTROL OF MASS MEDIA CHANNELS

The Development of Film and Cinema

Only three countries in the Middle East—Lebanon, Israel, and Egypt—have been active in the production of long films. This does not mean, however, that the other countries have been idle. Iran is gaining an increased share of the Middle East market with its locally produced films. Other countries, such as Syria and Iraq, have made efforts at developing their film industries (5, 12).

Egypt is the birthplace of Arab cinema and the most important film pro-ducer in the Middle East. Among the factors responsible for the devleopment of film industry in Egypt have been the government's interest in its use as a source of hard currency and as a tool of propaganda. In 1957 the National Organization for the Consolidation of the Cinema was formed under the Ministry of National Culture and Guidance to improve and control the cine-ma by initiating legislation and planning for development. More recent at-tempts to improve the quality of Egyptian films were taken in the estab-lishment of the High Cinema Institute, a four-year school for the training of prospective film artists. The Institute's 200 students are drawn from countries throughout the Middle East. Since the Revolution of 1952 and as a partial result of the cinema's close ties with the government, the number of patriotic films produced in the country has increased.

In the wake of the 1973 October war the Egyptian government has em-barked upon a policy of trying to create a better economic and psychological climate in the country. The government's decision to return the country's movie theatres to private owners has been one result. This measure is the first denationalization of the public sector since Egypt began nationalizing private property in 1952.

Film in the Middle East has not had an impact upon the intellectuals alone. The cinema also serves as the only inexpensive vehicle of communica-tion (besides radio) that is amenable to the large illiterate sections of the population. For this reason film has become one of the most widespread means of the penetration of foreign customs and ideas. Likewise, an impor-tant factor in the development and growth of film in the Middle East has been the lack of entertainment available in urban areas. Because it is primarily educational and propagandistic, broadcasting has proven unsuccessful in competition with the cinema for audiences.

Although Lebanon has many well-attended cinemas, Israel leads the Middle East in this area. Every Israeli community is within reach of either fixed or mobile cinemas. In both seating capacity and film attendance Israel leads the Middle East and is well ahead of the United States. The subject matter of Israeli films is diverse, ranging from patriotic dramas and documentaries (*Five Days in Sinai*, a war film, and *Forty-Two Six*, the life of David Ben Gurion) to comedies, to romantic love stories and intellectual dramas.

Until recently the film industry in Iran has been hampered by stiff competition from India and Egypt where film industries began at least three decades earlier. This situation, however, has improved considerably, with Iranian films doing well in regional markets. Iran has several advantages over its competitors. Unlike Egypt and Turkey, Iran's foreign exchange reserves and the film industry's financial resources allow the studios to secure advanced technical equipment from abroad. In addition, the scenarios of Iranian films are generally more sophisticated than Egyptian scripts. These technical and formal qualities of Iranian films have increased their appeal to Middle Eastern audiences.

Despite the growing production and popularity of the native films, the Middle Eastern cinema is dominated by Hollywood productions with Italian, French, and British films as close competitors.

The Politics and Economics of Broadcasting

In the Middle East radio and televion broadcasting is a state monopoly, financed through fees or government subsidies. Only Lebanon maintains private television stations supported by advertising, while its radio broadcasting is exclusively government-owned and operated. In the past two decades radio has made dramatic advances in the Middle East as evidenced by the number of receivers in countries such as Bahrain, Kuwait, Yemen, and Syria. Both sociopolitical and technological causes have accounted for these advances. A succession of political crises, the need to use broadcasting as an instrument of foreign policy and propaganda, and the accelerated pace of economic growth and social change have led to a continuous expansion of the radio networks in Egypt, Iran, Israel, and Lebanon. In short, social revolutionary forces, technological advancement, and socioeconomic factors have combined to make radio the principal medium of mass communication in the Middle East.

On the basis of geographical factors alone the audiences in the Middle East are constantly exposed to international broadcasting. At the crossroads between Europe, Asia, and Africa, the Middle East receives a significant number of broadcast messages from stations in Europe, India, and the Soviet Union. The British Broadcasting Corporation (BBC), Voice of America,

Egypt's Voice of the Arabs, and to a degree Radio Moscow are the most listened to and discussed international broadcasting channels in the area.

Radio is a many-faceted instrument of mass communication in the Middle East. In the absence of strong and diversified telecommunication systems and press in many countries, the medium of radio is used to mobilize and integrate the nation, disseminate propaganda and information, provide cultural and educational programs, present entertainment and music, and extend religious services and sermons beyond local and traditional settings.

Radio has had a formidable effect upon popular culture in the Middle East. At the same time that it has helped to spread and diffuse each country's traditional music, literature, and poetry, it also has accelerated westernization, especially promoting the contemporary American and European popular music and lifestyle.

Visitors to the Arab states of the Persian Gulf area, such as Bahrain and Kuwait, are surprised to see television sets in almost every house. Despite the large number of sets currently registered for the Arab emirates of the Gulf area, at one time there was no television broadcasting there. The sets were sold to the natives by importers who described the "magic box" as the surest way to the heart of the modern world. Today everyone in that region can put the television set to good use and choose one of the several channels offered by the country's broadcasting systems or by stations in neighboring Iran. Kuwait already has its own television stations while Qatar's are fast joining them. Entities such as Abu Dhabi and others with rapidly rising oil income will undoubtedly enter the television contest soon.

In fact, for the first time television is becoming a channel of interstate communication and politics as the Persian Gulf enters a new era of military, economic, and political competition. Iran, not a newcomer to the region's competitive market of ideas and power, has recently succeeded in making its voice heard by expanding its television network to cover the entire Persian Gulf and the Gulf of Oman.

The potential of television both as a medium of popular culture and as an instrument of national policies has been recognized in the Middle East as each government has tried to have control over its operation and programming. For example, television was introduced into Iran in 1958 as a privately owned and commercially operated monopoly by the Sabet Pasal group, the company that earlier had introduced Pepsi Cola. Upon termination of the monopoly concession in 1963, however, the government incorporated the company into a newly established state-owned public broadcasting system, the National Television. It has now become the second channel in the Iranian television network. Iran also possesses closed-circuit educational television and an American Armed Forces television station in Teheran.

Lebanon and Egypt are the major producers and distributors of programs in the Arab countries. In Egypt the television service, a state-owned and operated network, is divided into three programs: The first two cover most of the country's populated areas and broadcast the same type of material; the third program is geared to a limited audience in Cairo and its suburbs, with content prepared for viewers interested in sophisticated artistic material. Egypt considers providing low-cost receivers for both radio and television necessary. Therefore, in addition to exempting television sets and parts from customs duties and other import restrictions, Egypt has embarked on a program of manufacturing her own sets. In the interest of spreading television to the countryside and rural areas, she has encouraged buying through long-term credit. Profits for the sale of sets are applied to the financing of television broadcasting.

Television programs in the Middle East are a combination of both locally produced shows and popular American and European television series dubbed in the local language (13). However, in recent years audiences are becoming more discriminating and thus more imaginative cultural programs and documentaries are being offered.

Lebanon has one of the most developed television systems in the Middle East and is the only country with two privately owned national services. Next to Kuwait, Lebanon has the highest number of television receivers per 1000 inhabitants. Both of the Lebanese services are largely foreign-owned. The Compagnie Libanaise de Television is owned by French interests and draws heavily on French sources, while the Compagnie de Television du Liban et du Proche-Orient (Tele-Orient) broadcasts British and American material and has as its largest shareholders the British Thomson Organization.

The Press and the New Alignment of Social Forces

Unlike radio and television, the press in the Middle East continues to be a medium through which the intelligentsia and the ruling political and economic elites articulate their goals; it reflects their perception of domestic and foreign policies.

The Middle East moved into the age of modern mass media before its people were literate and its economy developed. Writers and journalists, therefore, used their power not to defend an existing order and economy but to create new ones. Thus political, bureaucratic, and intellectual elites play the major role in shaping the structure and function of the press (8). This new intelligentsia is radically different from the great families, landholders, and politicians of the past. Its social origin and psychological outlook are rooted in modern nationalism, social revolution, and technological advancement. It finds its expression in the modern regional press.

The press of the Middle East is neither a traditional Western "libertarian press" nor a constricted and arbitrary "authoritarian" one. Even in such traditionally democratic countries as Lebanon (1) and Israel (7), certain degrees of social and political control are exercised. The Middle Eastern press has the following structure:

1. A mixed system of both privately owned newspapers (Iran, Turkey, Lebanon, Israel) and a party-controlled public press (Egypt, Iraq, Syria)
2. A licensing system through which political and economic controls are exercised
3. Laws and constitutional provisions by which security matters, educational qualifications, and press codes are checked
4. National and centralized publication in the capital cities and a few large metropolitan areas
5. A national news agency, often controlled by government, in charge of distributing local and national news (Israel, Lebanon, Turkey, Egypt, and Iran are the only countries with correspondents abroad, including in the United States)

With more than 50 daily newspapers and a large readership drawn from a population of less than three million, the Lebanese press is the most competitive in the Middle East and is the only one in the Arab world that is still exclusively in private hands. Although a majority of newspapers and magazines continue to receive support from various political and economic groups, the government has promoted a financially independent press and has proposed giving grants for the amalgamation of newspapers. The Arabic press dominates the print media, but there are a number of well-edited journals in French, Armenian, and English. The most important and influential papers are *Al Nahar, Al Hayat, The Daily Star,* and *L'Orient* which are also distributed in neighboring countries.

With a broad range of multilingual news coverage, the Israeli press continues to be one of the most vigorous in the Middle East. Party-subsidized newspapers have dominated the Israeli press since its foundation in 1948, and today only three of the regular Hebrew dailies and a few of the foreign language dailies are independent. Reflecting the fact that a majority of Israel's three million population is nonnative, the foreign language dailies produce about 20 percent of the country's total circulation.

The second category of the national press system in the Middle East is what may be termed the Arab socialist system and includes countries such as Egypt, Syria, and Iraq. Here the press has been restructured and centralized in support of socialist programs and national development objectives. Individual privately owned newspapers have been closed in favor of those owned by political parties, religious organizations, and labor organizations.

Egypt, with the most influential and quoted press in the Arab world, has four main publishing houses which operate separately and compete with one another, but the publications and their foreign affairs content reflect the views of the government.

The structure of the press in Syria and Iraq is more or less similar to that of Egypt, with the ruling parties exerting control and influence over its content.

The third category of the print media in the Middle East characterizes the press of the two non-Arab countries of the Middle East, Turkey, and Iran. Privately owned with a strong family tradition, it has shown a remarkable ability for survival and a unique capacity for adaptation.

Striving to imitate the West European press system, journalists and press associations in Turkey have been rather successful in forming the government's liberal attitude toward the press. This has been accomplished in part through adoption of a system of self-control based on a code of ethics, or Basin Yasasi, signed by all major newspapers and periodicals. A course of honor, similar to the press commissions in Britain and Sweden, has been established to censure those violating the voluntary code.

Iran provides an excellent laboratory for the study of the intricate intermingling of the press and political and economic elites (9). The country has a privately owned and commercially operated press, which is national and urban in character and content, providing the major media link between the governing elite and the nation's intelligentsia. Although the role of the press as a major channel of information and news has decreased in recent years, its role as a supplier and reflector of official and national developmental policies has been enhanced considerably.

What course will the mass media take in the future development of the Middle East? Iran is perhaps the most fully described society in which the question can be addressed.

In an attempt to integrate the social, economic, and political problems, the Iranian government has launched a major campaign for national development in which telecommunication plays a considerable role. At the heart of Iran's new system is the Integrated National Telecommunication System (INTS), which will eventually link every part of the country, including more than 90 cities. The new microwave system is being followed by the creation of a telephone, telegraph, and automatic Telex network among the country's towns; installation of a domestic satellite system; and creation of a communication research center and a communication training center.

Given the region's strategic military and economic importance, such national telecommunication policies may eventually be followed in other Middle Eastern countries. This kind of development, no doubt, will transfer the structure and institutional bases of mass media and will map the course of mass communication in the Middle East.

REFERENCES

1. Abu-Laban, Baha. "Factors in Social Control of the Press in Lebanon," *Journalism Quarterly, 43* (1966), 510–518.

2. Browne, Edward G. *The Persian Revolution.* Cambridge: Cambridge University Press, 1910.

3. Iranian Government. *Iran.* Teheran: Ministry of Information, 1974.

4. Iraqi Ministry of Culture and Guidance. *Law No. 87 of 1965, The Five Year Economic Plan: 1965–1968.* Bagdad: Iraq Government Press, 1965.

5. Landau, Jacob M. *Studies in the Arab Theater and Cinema.* Philadelphia: University of Pennsylvania Press, 1958.

6. Lewis, Bernard. *The Emergence of Modern Turkey.* London: Oxford University Press, 1961.

7. Lowenstein, Ralph. "The Daily Press in Israel: An Appraisal After Twenty Years," *Journalism Quarterly, 46* (1969), 325–331.

8. Mowlana, Hamid. "Mass Media Systems and Communication Behavior," in Michael Adams (ed.), *The Middle East: A Handbook.* London: Anthony Blond, 1971, pp. 584–598.

9. ———. *Mass Media and Public Communication in Iran* [in Persian]. Teheran: College of Mass Communication Press, 1974.

10. Nasser, Gamal Abdel. *Egypt's Liberation: The Philosophy of Revolution.* Washington, D.C.: Public Affairs Press, 1955.

11. Sadat, Anwar el. *Revolt on the Nile.* Cairo: Government Printing Daprtment, 1957.

12. Sadoul, Georges. *The Cinema in the Arab Countries.* Bierut: Inter-Arab Center of Cinema and Television, 1966.

13. Varis, Tapio. "Global Traffic in Television," *Journal of Communication, 24,* 1 (Winter 1974), 102–109.

CHAPTER 8

Trends in Tropical African Societies

SYDNEY W. HEAD

Patterns of mass communication do not, of course, emerge from a neutral background: "The development of a mass-media system embeds traditional channels of contact within a new system of intercourse" (23, p. 201). To summarize how patterns from the past blend into present patterns in African communication we might picture first a relief map of the continent as a *tabula rasa,* then imagine a series of overlay transparencies representing successive motifs that contribute to the final composite pattern.

The first overlay might show the language distribution pattern prior to major incursions from the outside. It would depict a linguistic crazy quilt of astonishing variety, for even the greatest of the ancient African empires (within each of which, one supposes, some universal *lingua franca* of government and trade must have existed) seems to have encompassed no more than about 5 percent of the continental land area. Today we are talking about a total of 58 states and dependent territories, if we include the offshore islands. In most of this chapter I refer primarily to 42 political entities, excluding the North African states, South Africa, and the smaller islands. In only four countries does a single indigenous language serve the entire population—Lesotho, Malagasy Republic, Rwanda, and Somalia. Linguistic fragmentation has major significance for the mass media—not simply because of the practical problems of polylingual production, but also because media language policies have important political implications.

A second continental overlay might depict the linguistic effects of foreign incursions. Nonindigenous foreign languages have been adopted as the official media in nearly all African states and territories. In North Africa the invaders' tongue has, of course, long since become the majority as well as the official language, and indeed Arabic is the most widely spoken language on the continent. Nevertheless, Berber dialects still survive and are used in broadcasting in the Maghreb. Most countries, however, continue to adopt a colonial language for official purposes, even though it still may be understood by only a minority of speakers: English, French, Portuguese, or Spanish have been adopted, either singly or paired with an indigenous language. Tanzania is exceptional in having adopted a nonuniversal (though widely understood) indigenous language, Swahili, as its official tongue.

Publication tends to be restricted to the European languages and a very few widely spoken vernaculars, such as Swahili. Radio, however, adapts itself more readily to polylingualism. Nearly every country uses a number of vernaculars in broadcasting as well as the official language. The average is about four per country, but as an extreme example, Nigeria uses 30.

Another colonially inspired overlay might depict the radical cleavage between urban and rural cultures. Intense concentration of economic and social development in cities on or near the coast contracts abruptly with underdevelopment in the rural interior. In urban centers such as Abidjan or Lagos, one finds all the modern amenities of European cities, including newspapers, radio and television services, telephone, cable, telex, and even satellite ground stations capable of sending and receiving television. But a short drive into the country can produce a startling change—the artifacts of industrialism quickly disappear and we find ourselves back on the land pretty much as it always was.

The region of interior underdevelopment assumes the pattern of a broad curved figure 7, starting on the shores of the great western bulge at Mauritania and Spanish Sahara, sweeping 2000 miles eastward through Mali, Niger, Chad, and Western Sudan; then the down stroke, running another 2000 miles southward, down through the heart of the continent, as far south as the Kalahari desert. Much of this great landlocked interior consists of deserts, lakes, and savannahs little touched by modern development. Exceptions exist where climate and soil favored European inland settlement, producing such upland cities as Nairobi and Salisbury.

Yet another overlay, depicting the colonial network of telecommunication and mass-media facilities, reinforces this rural-urban cleavage. Colonial radiotelegraph and radiotelephone circuits tended to radiate outward from the urbanized fringe, linking colonial centers of administration with London, Paris, Brussels, Lisbon, and Madrid. In most cases there was no lateral interconnection from one African territory to the next; newly independent African states found themselves unable to communicate directly with each other. Messages had to be routed thousands of miles out of the way through Europe to reach an African capital only a few hundred miles up or down the coast. The 1965 chart of intra-African telecommunication routes graphically outlines as an empty space the figure 7 of the interior previously described: Even by 1975 only three links were expected to bridge the great central gap between east and west, two via Zaïre and one via the Sudan and Chad (14).

Newspapers and radio broadcasting were initiated in the colonies primarily to provide links between European expatriates and settlers and their homelands, secondarily to further the Europeanization of educated Africans. World War II, however, introduced a new and urgent note, the need to reach a wider African audience to ensure loyalty and cooperation in providing foodstuffs and "native" troops. The French as well as the British increased the use of broadcasting in Africa during the war.

The new African nations inherited a communication system profoundly unsuited to their needs as independent states—not because of any conspiracy to deprive them of their due, but simply as natural consequences of their economic dependency and of the nationalistic rivalries of the colonial powers.

The distorting influence of foreign interests continued even after independence. In the 1960s Africa became a Cold War arena, with the ex-colonial powers trying to maintain their preferred status, while staving off the efforts of the Communist Bloc to gain footholds on the continent. The media systems of the new nations made especially prized targets in this power struggle. France, for example, kept a tight rein on her former colonies, offering them independence under a form of Gallic hegemony called the "French Community." It was supposed to be an offer the colonies could not afford to refuse. Guinea alone opted to withdraw from the community, creating a vacuum which the Communists immediately filled, and for a time Guinea became their West Africa showcase (Browne, 1963). Mainland Tanzania has adapted socialist dogma to African conditions. Zanzibar, the other portion of the Tanzania union, however, became the Communists' East Africa showcase.

Western governments encouraged private media interests to fill the gap left by removal of colonial control. Lord Thomson of Fleet set up not only a commercial subsidiary to contract with developing countries for construction and management of television stations, but also a charitable foundation to train African personnel—admittedly maneuvers designed explicitly to counter Communist media influences (1, p. 181). African leaders, however, with their intensely practical experience in the political uses of communication, were exceedingly chary about entering into agreements that seriously compromised their control over their own media.

Historical influences continue to affect the media as a result of the differing colonial experiences arising from differing colonial policies. The French tended toward highly centralized control in the colonies. Mastery of French language and culture was the only road to improvement for Africans. The British, by contrast, tended broadly to rely on "native administrations" and decentralized control, encouraging rather than discouraging indigenous languages and cultures. The distinction between the two colonial policies is clearly traceable, not only in events and institutions, but even in the psychological impact of the colonial experience on indigenous populations.

In a variety of ways these differences in policy continue to echo in the mass media of today. British West Africa, for example, had a tradition of a lively and relatively free African press dating back to the nineteenth century, whereas in French territories the emphasis was heavily on importation of publications from Paris. Britain decentralized broadcasting and encouraged the use of vernaculars, while France placed more stress on regional broadcasting in the French language.

On a higher level of generalization, however, one might ask to what extent mass media technology and economic constraints dictate the direction of media growth in any country, quite irrespective of politics. Africa provides two cases in point, Ethiopia and Liberia, neither of which inherited an imposed colonial broadcasting system designed originally in imitation of a foreign model. True, both countries have necessarily depended on a variety of foreign sources for equipment, advice, and training, and perhaps this dependence is tantamount to colonial influence. Still, one might have expected, if we assume that freedom to improvise exists, that one or both of these countries would have developed some uniquely African version of broadcasting. One cannot find, however, anything markedly different in the systems of these countries from those in other countries of comparable economic status where the broadcasting system was imposed from without by a single colonial power. The one distinguishing feature that comes to notice is that both Ethiopia and Liberia have proved hospitable to major international missionary stations on their soil.

THE MEDIA IN THE STRUGGLE FOR INDEPENDENCE

The independence movements in the African colonies relied, of course, on mass communication for generating essential popular support. Often the leaders had to depend on traditional media when modern media were denied them. The mass political rally, a lineal descendent of traditional tribal gatherings, served the freedom movement well in East Africa in particular, where there was far less access to the press than in Anglophone West Africa. Such rallies became highly organized and effective. As the late Tom Mboya wrote:

> The rallies tackled the task, in the early days of a national movement, of creating among Africans a sense of self-confidence, a feeling that it is not only right to fight for his independence but that it is possible to win his independence . . . (18, pp. 62–63).

As early as 1928 Jomo Kenyatta edited a vernacular journal, the first one in the Kikuyu language (15, p. xix). In 1959, while Kenyatta was in confinement, Tom Mboya and others published a cyclostyled broadsheet called *Uhuru*. As Mboya describes it:

All African newspapers had been banned with the [Mau Mau] Emergency, and the English-language papers gave little African news. For instance, a speech, however trite, by a settler leader, to fifteen Europeans would be given a front-page column, while a speech by an African leader to 10,000 people might get an inch in an obscure corner (18, p. 80).

Uhuru was quickly suppressed and the party leaders arrested—"the Government's way of paying tribute to our effectiveness," Mboya adds.

In Anglophone West Africa the political press had a long and remarkable history, though primarily in English because of the larger number of Africans there with European-style education. The extraordinary educational development that took place in the two territories founded by freed slaves, Liberia and Sierra Leone, account to a large extent for this early development of an African-oriented journalism tradition. The most celebrated African leaders in the region were all newspaper editors of note, men such as Azikwe, who founded the *West African Pilot,* and Nkrumah of the *Accra Evening News.*

African political leaders during the independence movement had no comparable access to radio, which remained a tight government monopoly. In this respect Tropical Africa differed significantly from North Africa. There the universality of the Arabic language and of Islamic culture and religion made it possible to take full advantage of radio's unique ability to surmount political boundaries. Nasser used Cairo radio extensively and effectively in support of freedom movements in other Arabic-speaking countries. In more recent years, however, vernacular broadcasting has become an important factor in the remaining freedom movements of Tropical Africa, such as Rhodesia and South Africa.

PATTERNS OF OWNERSHIP AND CONTROL

During the colonial period newspapers were generally privately owned in Anglophone areas, although colonial administrations exercised much more control than would have been tolerated at home. The largest newspapers were financed from abroad by British, French, and South African press and mining interests. Since independence, the trend has been away from private ownership and toward government or political party ownership and control. The remaining independent organs must exercise stringent self-censorship to avoid giving offense.

Broadcasting facilities have always been either directly controlled and operated by government or kept on a very tight tether if owned by statutory corporations, private clubs, missionary organizations, or commercial concerns. Prior to granting independence the British set up public broadcasting corporations in its colonies on the model of the BBC. Most of these were soon dismantled after independence came. Corporations do persist in Ghana, Liberia, Malawi, Mauritius, Nigeria, and Rhodesia. Although corporate status does not necessarily protect these broadcasting organizations from direct manipulation by government when officials feel the need to intervene, in some cases at least they appear to benefit from it. Exceptions to government operations of broadcasting are Protestant missionary stations, notably those in Ethiopia and Liberia; some minor commercial stations licensed to foreign venturers, such as Radio Syd in the Gambia; and a few small stations run by mining interests for the benefit of their employees.

Several consequences for the broadcasting services flow from the prevailing pattern of government ownership and control. First, the systems are highly centralized and thus representative of whatever class or group is in control at the center. Services to other ethnic groups, whether minorities or majorities, may be inadequate. The absence of local and regional services in most countries precludes groups far from the main centers having effective input to the programming of the system. An exception to this, unique in Africa, is the system of Nigeria. It provides not only for a federal service, with regional as well as central outlets serving the entire country, but also for separate, independent, state-owned services representing the specific interests of the several regions. The federal service insists that its regional outlets carry certain national programs, such as the national news and important political statements; otherwise the individual regional station directors of the federal service are free either to take the national programs or to originate their own material locally, according to local circumstances. One result is that Nigeria broadcasts domestically in 30 languages, more than any other country in Africa.

A second consequence of the general pattern of government ownership and operation is the fact that the national civil service system usually controls personnel appointments, wage scales, and promotions. Rigid civil service criteria for clerks, accountants, and other bureaucrats take little account of the creative qualifications needed in broadcasting (24, p. 39). Usually talented personnel soon find themselves at the top of their civil service career ladders and so become administrators or shift to other employment to obtain advancement. One advantage of corporate status in some cases is freedom from civil service constraints.

Third, the monopoly position of government broadcasting means as absence of competing stations, either as a source of optional employment or as a source of standard-setting comparison of performance.

A fourth consequence of the centralized pattern of government control is the conversion of broadcasting into a public relations mouthpiece for the government, which in most cases narrows down to serving one, or a very few, leading personalities in the government. Broadcast news departments are often reduced to little more than translation offices for preedited news supplied by the government Information Department or by a national news agency. The latter usually serves as the gatekeeper for the international news services that may be received. This can amount to an *ad hoc* unregulated type of censorship which for unpredictability and petty interference can sometimes be much worse than a more formally constituted censorship office, because the bureaucrats in the gatekeeping roles tend to avoid trouble by following the maxim, "When in doubt, suppress."

Government control is rationalized on both economic and political grounds. As to economics, the national broadcasting systems of Africa all depend in varying measure on direct government subvention. Collecting radio receiver license fees is impracticable and has been abandoned in many countries. Only 10 of the 42 systems under discussion operated noncommercially in 1972. But commercial revenue potential is limited; moreover, government controlled commercial operations tend to be inefficient so that not all the possible revenue from commercial sources is realized. Legislators resist voting substantial subventions to undertakings over which they have no direct control. More important, however, political leaders take the view that a medium as important as broadcasting cannot properly be left in private hands. The government must have direct access to the people to further the job of nation building.

Ali Mazrui, who as an African social scientist has a keen appreciation of the sociopolitical role of the media, calls this function "cultural engineering." He defines it as "the deliberate manipulation of cultural factors for purposes of deflecting human habit in the direction of new and perhaps constructive endeavors" (17, p. xv). He goes on to characterize this process as "indigenizing what is foreign, idealizing what is indigenous, nationalizing what is sectional, and emphasizing what is African" (p. xvi)—as neat a description as one can devise for the way the role of the media is conceptualized in Africa.

The most systematic and philosophically integrated attempt to carry out this formula in practice was probably that of the late Kwame Nkrumah. When Ghana television was in the planning stage, he assured Parliament that the new medium "will not cater to cheap entertainment nor commercialism" (8, p. 1). A brochure announcing the advent of Ghanaian television declared:

Our television will be a weapon in the struggle for African unity. It will be a weapon in Africa's fight against imperialism, colonialism and neo-colonialism. It will resurrect forgotten glories of African history, of African culture. We shall attempt to organize a quick exchange of films with other African countries, and eventually have travelling news units all over Africa, disseminating news of Ghana and televising what is happening in our sister states (8, p. 5).

As to domestic news policy, Nkrumah flatly declared: "We do not believe there are necessarily two sides to every question: We see right and wrong, just and unjust, progressive and reactionary, positive and negative, friend and foe. *We are partisan"* [italics added] (9, p. 45).

Nkrumah's attitudes are still shared by most African leaders, though others tend to be purely pragmatic. Mazrui wrote:

The Kenya government felt that the mass media ought to play a part in promoting a climate that should reduce the mystique of violence as a method of personal fulfill-ment. . . . In Nairobi a systematic attempt was made to do away with television programs containing excessive violence. . . . A resort to censorship was regarded as unavoidable (17, p. 59).

The term *censorship* is, however, avoided. The key word heard again and again is *responsibility*—the media should be free of restraint, but only so long as they behave responsibly. Criticism is all right as long as it is "constructive." The government should not tell the media what to say, but it should give them "guidance."

MEDIA FACILITIES

The comparative status of the print and broadcast media in Africa is indi-cated in Table 1. Comparisons between numbers of newspapers and numbers of radio stations or between newspaper circulation and radio receivers in use have no simple one-for-one significance; still, the differences between the media are sufficiently marked to justify saying rather more about broadcast-ing than about newspapers in this chapter. There are, for example, over three times as many radio transmitters as daily newspapers.

Table 1 also reminds us that Africa is very thinly populated, relative to the world as a whole, indicating that the problem of media distribution is acute.

Table 1   Media Comparisons: Africa and the World

Comparison Base	Africa[a]	World	Africa's Share
Area (million square kilometers)	30	136	22.3%
Population (millions)	354	3,706	9.5%
Radio transmitters	650	19,110	3.4%
Radio receivers (per 1000 population)	45	232	
TV transmitters (principal)	82	3,925	2.0%
TV receivers (per 1000 population)	3.2	89	
Daily newspapers	210	7,680	2.7%
Daily newspaper circulation (per 1000 population)	19	130	

[a] Includes North Africa and South Africa.

Sources: Media data, for 1969, UNESCO (27); area and population data, UN (26).

Although broadcasting overcomes some of the barriers of distance and terrain that defeat newspaper circulation, even broadcasting has difficulty in coping with the vast spaces of the African continent and the unfavorable propagation conditions of the tropical zone. Other factors that put newspapers at a disadvantage are polylingualism and high levels of illiteracy, ranging from 97 percent to 40 percent, with the mean at 84 percent (20, p. 70); data refer to 32 independent countries in 1967 and earlier.

The quantitative limitations shown in Table 1 fail to reveal another important physical factor, the maldistribution of facilities. During the 1960s the International Telecommunication Union held a series of conferences aimed at closing the gaps in the telecommunication infrastructure and the frequency spectrum allotments in Africa (12–14). Restructuring the system had been going forward rapidly despite the economic problems involved. Improved facilities will make it feasible technically, for example, for a Pan-African news agency to emerge, relieving African media of total dependence on foreign newsgathering organizations. At the very least an improved telecommunication infrastructure will make it easier for national news agencies to do their job internally, for neighboring countries to exchange media materials, and for domestic broadcasting networks to obtain interconnection facilities.

A baker's dozen satellite ground stations scattered around the periphery of the continent tie Africa into the world network of Intelsat. At present these facilities serve telegraphic and telephonic traffic rather than broadcasting traffic. High costs of satellite use relative to small audience potentials make routine use of satellites for the relay of television programs impracticable. Of more promise, perhaps, is the syndication of educational materials by securing the cooperation of a number of countries in a joint program of direct relays from satellite to local receiving centers. The operation of such a system by the end of the century was envisioned at a UNESCO-sponsored meeting in 1974. The plan called for a 35-country cooperative that would join in financing and using special educational satellite relay stations. Ground receivers could be used at 1.6 million schools and other communal reception centers, reaching 130 million adult and school-aged pupils (5, pp. 42–43). The conference calculated that the system could provide a choice of languages, according to local needs, and that as few as eight languages (Amharic, English, Fulani, Hausa, Ibo, Lingala, Swahili, and Yoruba) could serve half the school-aged population, though 48 languages would be required to serve the adult population. Raising the $1 billion needed to finance such a scheme might be the smaller part of the problem; much more difficult might be the problem of getting 35 different countries to coordinate their teaching programs and to agree on mutually acceptable educational matter.

Few countries have the present terrestrial microwave-relay capacity to tie their radio and television stations together into true simultaneous intercon-

nected networks. Most depend on shortwave broadcasts to distribute programs to outlying transmitters for rebroadcasting.

The aggregate medium frequency (AM, or standard broadcast) transmission facilities for all of Tropical Africa averages only 98 kilowatts per country, less than the aggregate power of the stations in a single large city in the
United States (for sources of these and other facilities data in this section, see
Head, 11, pp. 401–405). Five countries in fact have no medium-frequency
service at all, which means that they rely entirely on high-frequency (shortwave) transmissions to reach both urban centers and distant parts of their
countries.

Because of limitations on frequency-spectrum space in the medium-frequency band, Africa as a whole cannot in any event expect to obtain complete coverage with medium-frequency stations alone. Frequency modulation
transmission in the very high or ultra-high frequency bands is the ultimate
answer to this problem, but only 15 countries of the group of 42 under consideration have FM stations, mainly on an experimental basis. South Africa,
however, has a comprehensive FM network that blankets the whole country.

The tendency to concentrate radio transmission facilities in the capital city
is understandable. There they can be maintained and programmed and kept
in government hands in case of emergency. Only Angola, Malawi, Niger,
Nigeria, and Zaïre have medium-frequency transmitters widely dispersed in
the country. If we measure dispersal by the number of geographically separate transmitter sites relative to the total area of a country, the average for
the entire continent is 95,000 square miles per site, and some countries run up
into the hundreds of thousands. Because of Africa's large deserts and other
sparsely inhabited areas probably 4000 to 5000 square miles would be a
realistic target. In short, the pattern of radio coverage in Africa is highly
uneven, with satisfactory signals available in capitals and other major cities,
but with smaller towns and rural areas covered by domestic services only
spottily, if at all.

The urban pattern of television distribution is more sharply defined than
radios, because radiations at the frequencies used for television are line-of-
sight waves whose reach is limited by the horizon. In no case does a country
have enough television transmitters to provide anything approaching universal coverage—unless one chooses to regard the Zanzibar-Pemba island system
an entity unto itself, apart from mainland Tanzania. Moreover, we are talking of a single television service in each country in Tropical Africa—that is,
only one program available, no tuning from one channel to another.

The television haves and have-nots are nearly equally divided (counting
the former Portuguese territories as separate entities). The division follows
per-capita income closely, with the nontelevision countries mostly at a level
below $125 a year. Some of the exceptions to this rule are worth noting.

Ethiopia, one of the poorest countries in GNP, has television primarily because it was needed as part of the furnishings provided by Emperor Haile Selassie to make Addis Ababa a suitable setting for the Organization of African Unity Headquarters. Another low-income country, Niger, has a UNESCO-sponsored station devoted entirely to educational experiments.

The strangest television situation in Africa is that of the United Republic of Tanzania. The loose union of the islands of Zanzibar-Pemba and the mainland territory formerly called Tanganyika does not extend to a common policy on broadcasting. Mainland Tanzania, under the moderate leadership of Julius Nyerere, has so far adhered to a policy of self-denial, on the grounds that its limited resources ought to go toward further development of radio, which can reach the country as a whole. Tiny Zanzibar, however, officially inaugurated the first color television system in Africa in January 1974. The system includes production studios both on Zanzibar and on Pemba, its nearby sister island; microwave interconnection between the two islands; and a well-equipped mobile unit for picking up broadcasts outside the studio (19). If, as seems inevitable, the Zanzibar transmitter's signals are picked up by receivers on the mainland only 20 miles away, Nyerere may not be able to maintain his Spartan resolve to keep the lid closed on Pandora's box.

Centralization of daily newspaper production is similar to that of television transmissions. Most countries had only one city of publication in 1973. The average number of publication locales per country for dailies was 1.5; even for newspapers published less than daily it was only 1.9 (based on data of Feuereisen and Schmacke, 6).

The rates of 45 radio and 3.2 television receivers per 1000 population (Table 1) are parlously low, even for the limited transmission facilities in use. Most African governments nevertheless erect artificial and regressive economic barriers to participation in mass media by imposing high import duties and taxes on receivers and spare parts. Few administrations have taken positive steps to encourage audience growth. Zanzibar seems to be a striking exception; the island government not only bought sets at wholesale for resale to the public at no markup, but also provided interest-free loans to purchasers (25, p. 83). This policy seems to have paid off handsomely, for 3500 sets were reported in use within a few months of the station's opening, a remarkable record considering the small size of the potential market and the poverty of the people.

SERVICES OF THE MEDIA

Newsmen who grew up in an era of intense party rivalries and dramatic struggles for independence found themselves at a loss as to how to continue to attract readers once freedom had been won and rival parties suppressed. They discovered that reports of routine official activities, rewrites of government handouts, news of arrivals and departures at the airport, and coverage of other standard reportorial beats did not sell papers the way the politics of independence movements had. Worse, most reporters discovered how ill prepared they were to deal seriously with the kinds of technical specialized information that makes up the bulk of significant news in a developing country. African officials constantly complain that newsmen fail to grasp the significance of what is going on and neglect to report adequately the great agricultural, hydroelectrical, industrial, and social schemes by which their countries are trying to achieve economic progress. Referring to a press conference given by the president of Tanzania on the East African Community, Kenya's Minister of Finance Mwai Kibaki noted: "You could not help being impressed by the fact that either the people who were interviewing had just not read anything about the Community or if they had they had not read enough . . ." (16, p. 3).

But the most intractable dilemma for the news media is how to deal with the rural-urban gap. Quoting Kibaki again: "Each morning you just take any of the Kenya papers and count how many news items have to do with rural communities in the country. . . . The press has begun to reflect and in fact to reinforce . . . urbanization and the question of urban men talking to each other" (p. 5). Some African journalists go so far as to say the gap cannot be bridged. A panelist from Zambia in the same seminar is quoted as saying:

Are we being realistic when we talk about newspapers assisting rural development? Is the idea to bring news to the rural areas or to bring the rural areas to the news? Newspapers are published in towns and if you produce a newspaper in town full of news about how the cattle are behaving in the rural areas or how the tsetse fly campaign is going, people in the towns are going to say, "What has this got to do with us?" And remember, it is the townspeople who buy your papers. If it could be done, I suppose what is needed is two editions—a rural edition and a city edition (3, p. 11).

The speaker's conclusion is sound: The gulf is probably too great to bridge with a single medium. First regionalization, then localization of media is essential for an adequately responsive system.

In their simplest form radio systems provide a single nationally oriented service from the capital city, usually over a medium frequency transmitter for the immediate environs and over a shortwave transmitter for the rest of the country. The latter is switched to different frequencies at different times of the day to adapt to varying propagation conditions. With only one set of transmission facilities available, such a system cannot provide a continuous service of vernacular programming. Sierra Leone, as an example, had two transmitters in 1973, one medium frequency, one high frequency, each of 10-kilowatt power. The two operated in tandem 16 hours a day, with a closedown period in midmorning. About 65 percent of the schedule was in English, the official language; the remaining 35 percent was allotted to four major vernaculars, plus short weekly news summaries in nine other local languages (7).

Also typical is the fact that in 1974 Sierra Leone was planning a quantum leap in power, a 250-kilowatt transmitter (5, p. 83).

Most countries want also to provide an external service. Even Sierra Leone's modest schedule, for example, included 15 minutes a week in French, designed for listeners in neighboring Francophone countries, but using the regular domestic transmission facilities. The richer countries mount complete independent external services, using high-power shortwave transmitters, feeding complex directional antenna arrays. Egypt and South Africa have the most powerful and sophisticated external in Africa and can be picked up virtually anywhere in the world. All the major international broadcasters, from both the West and the East, also direct external services to Africa. Research indicates that substantial numbers of the more highly educated Africans listen to foreign stations, among which the Overseas Service of the British Broadcasting Corporation is generally the leader (2, pp. 184–185).

The relative amounts of radio programming, considered by gross categories, appear not to differ markedly from one country to another throughout the world. UNESCO sent questionnaires to all broadcasting administrations on amounts of programming by category, classified also as to whether locally produced or imported, for its 1972 statistical yearbook (27). An analysis of replies from 108 radio systems and 76 television systems is shown in Table 2. A number of particularly large systems, such as those of the United States and the Soviet Union, are not included in the data. Insofar as the replies represent a fair sampling, they indicate that African programming is somewhat more serious than world programming as a whole, with more time, proportionate to total time, devoted to education and information.

The relative amounts of television programming by category follows closely the distribution of time to radio program categories. African systems again average slightly higher percentages of serious programs as against light entertainment. The relatively high percentages of educational programming reflect the fact that virtually every African system has a schools broadcasting unit. Some such as Nigeria, have had many years of experience and have become well integrated into the educational system. Television, with its shorter reach, affects fewer schools in most countries, but has proved effective as a teaching medium. The Ivory Coast provides the world's leading example of the restructuring of an entire national system of education deliberately to enable making the most of television's potential (25, pp. 102–104). There, of course, the television transmission system itself has been expanded to support the national program of fundamental teaching by television.

Table 2   Amount of Programming by Type

| | Average Percentage of All Program Hours | | | |
| | Radio | | Television | |
Category of Program	Africa (N = 27)	"World" (N = 108)	Africa (N = 11)	"World" (N = 76)
Light entertainment[a]	35	40	34	37
Information	25	21	27	27
Arts, letters, sciences	15	18	12	8
Education	10	6	11	13
For special audiences	10	10	12	11
Advertising	4	4	4	4
For ethnic minorities	2	2	1	1

[a] Read as follows: Among the 27 African countries reporting, the category "light entertainment" occupied on the average 35% of their total radio time, whereas among the world total of 108 countries reporting, "light entertainment" occupied on the average 40% of their total time, etc.

Source: Based on 1969 data reported in (27).

The preponderance of United States network serials and feature films in the international exchange of television programming is often a subject of comment (see Chapter 20 below). The UNESCO data previously mentioned enables a comparison of the relative amounts of programming imported by a number of systems, most of them in developing countries. The data in Table 3 indicate, as one would expect, that considerably more television than radio programming is imported by all countries. The average African station's imports are not strikingly greater than those of other countries and in some program categories are less. The overall impression is of surprising uniformity among countries.

The general compulsion to use imported materials is, of course, the inherent necessity for syndication in the mass media. When the home market is too restricted to support syndication, markets from different countries have to be combined until the critical mass (i.e., the capacity to pay enough to defray high production and intermediate distribution costs) is reached. This principle is illustrated in television by the high percentage (more than half on the average) of programming imported in the largest category—entertainment.

We get but a dim idea of the African media environment from such statistics. Even if we had more complete information on program content, we would still know little about the extent of actual listening and viewing. Consumption of radio seems to be relatively low generally, but quite high for urban educated Africans. The one survey that gives an in-depth analysis of media consumption in a population as a whole, rural as well as urban, was made in Zambia under the auspices of the Zambian Broadcasting Corporation and the Institute of African Studies at the University of Zambia (21). According to a national sample of 4505 respondents, only slightly more than half of the population (53 percent) ever listened to Zambian radio. Of those who did listen, nearly half (48 percent) listened also to foreign stations. The two leading attractions of foreign stations were music and news, but twice as many mentioned music as a reason for listening to foreign stations as mentioned news. As for other media, 77 percent reported never seeing a daily paper, and 53 percent never seeing motion pictures (the relatively high percentage of film viewers is due to an extensive program of mobile screenings of agricultural training films).

Of the five most popular radio programs among Zambians, the leader featured a traditional storyteller; the second in popularity was a panel discussion of personal and social problems, broadcast in each major language; the third, a folk comedy series featuring impromptu acting—a series that had been running for twenty years; the fourth, recorded music requests in English; and the fifth, recorded music requests in Bemba. These choices, which seem typical, are significant for what they tell us of the way in which broadcasting has been able to absorb traditional art forms. Radio and television have naturally been far more successful in this than have the print media.

Broadcasting can play a role in preserving traditional African arts and culture. The former Uganda president, Milton Obote, observed that "entertainment" should actually be called "development of culture"; he went on:

Since the Radio began broadcasting these various languages, there has been a new spirit in Uganda, simple composition of songs, dance teams and various competitions around the countryside. Every village is eager to surpass the other in its cultural activities with a view that one day Radio Uganda recording vans will pass around the village and record the songs and the poems of a particular group (22, p. 6).

Unfortunately, the cost of producing such unique materials in quantity is prohibitive. Syndication cannot work when the users, in terms of stations, amount to only one, and the audience, in terms of language groups, amounts to an insignificant number relative to the total audience requiring service. Small African broadcasting systems have hundreds of empolyees to provide a quantity of programming that could be assembled and broadcast over a station of equal power in a developed country, using syndicated material by a staff of half a dozen or even less. Unfortunately, there simply is no mass market for syndication of serial plays in Kupsbiny, documentaries in Amharic, and traditional songs in Tambouri. The hard facts of mass media econom-

Table 3   Extent of Program Importation

| | Average Percentage of Program Hours Imported | | | |
| | Radio | | Television | |
Category of Program	Africa (N = 13–23)[a]	"World" (N = 34–74)	Africa (N = 3–8)	"World" (N = 14–54)
Advertising	34	18	13	23
Arts, letters, sciences	33	25	40	36
Light entertainment	30	27	57	55
For ethnic minorities	27	20	67	62
Education	13	14	30	31
For special audiences	8	11	29	38
Information	7	12	26	25
All categories	18	19	43	43

[a] Ns vary because not all categories were reported by all countries.

Source: Based on 1969 data reported in UNESCO (27).

ics, rather than either neo-imperialist conspiracies or failures of local imagination, account for much of the program importation indicated in Table 3.

News represents another program category crucially dependent on syndication. African media have no choice but to subscribe to one or more of the major world news services. Egypt (in 1956) and South Africa were the first countries to develop a national news agency. The Ghana News Agency started in 1957. During the Algerian war of independence the Cairo agency "was able to challenge the French version of events" and during the Congo civil strife "Ghana could provide a voice for the 'Lumumbists' when they had been deprived of all others (1, p. 8). Nkrumah tried to develop the Ghana agency into a Pan-African and even worldwide service. The creation of a continental agency free of dependence on non-African sources was a major item on the agenda of the Organization of African Unity's first conference in 1963. Once again the economics of syndication intervened. With so much concentration of media in government hands, each country constitutes in effect virtually a single customer; the entire continent would provide perhaps under 100 newswire customers. In contrast, the major world agencies have subscribers in the thousands. A seeming short cut might be the welding of the rapidly developing individual national agencies into a supranational agency. However, its international editors probably would not be able to satisfy all customers when they received conflicting stories about the political disputes among African countries; each country could not be its own gatekeeper, denying news about internal events to the international wire.

The individual national agencies themselves in fact have great difficulty in obtaining prompt and complete coverage even within their own territories.

As government employees, the local bureau chiefs and stringers tend to spend their time in attendance on the local government officials, acting in effect as public relations men rather than newsmen. Feuereisen and Schmacke (6) describe in some detail the problems faced by Zambia's emergent news agency, ZANA, founded in 1969. Lack of skilled personnel, the civil service straitjacket, interference by politicians, delays, and overdependence on government handouts severely limited the usefulness of the young agency at the time of Eapen's analysis.

FUTURE DIRECTIONS

Recalling Mazrui's formula for building national identity—"indigenizing what is foreign, idealizing what is indigenous, nationalizing what is sectional, and emphasizing what is African" (17), let us conclude this survey by speculating about some of the future directions media development may take.

Indigenizing the Foreign

The choice in Africa must ultimately be, perhaps, among alternative ways of institutionalizing the media. Broadly speaking, two models are available— the communist and the western, differentiated for purposes of the present discussion in terms of the ways in which they achieve media consumption by the mass public. In the Communist model motivational qualities of media are low, but the government compensates for this by assuming major responsibility for facilitating consumption. For example, the communist countries have invested massively in wired radio systems, to the point where in a number of cases they represent by far the dominant mode of program distribution. These systems enable participation at minimum cost to the consumer. The West depends on the attractiveness of media content to motivate the public to make its own investment in consumption facilities.

The position of the African countries between these poles is ambivalent. The same Nkrumah who told newsmen to be partisan also declared that "once a journal gains a reputation for even occasional unreliability or distortion, its value is destroyed" (8, p. 28). African leaders would like their press to speak with the authority of the autonomous Western press, but not at the price of losing control of what the press says. Looked at from another viewpoint, this ambivalence reveals itself in the emphasis on production facilities without corresponding emphasis on distribution and consumption facilities. With no additional transmission or production cost whatever, every broadcast transmitter is physically capable of serving a far wider audience than it now reaches. Every newspaper press is capable of running off far more papers than can be sold. Yet investment in new and larger transmitters and presses continues at a high level. Governments have assumed major responsibility neither for removing economic barriers to media consumption by direct sub- vention, as in the Communist model, nor for removing barriers to improve- ment of the motivational qualities of media content to stimulate private initi- ative, as in the Western model. For a distinctively African alternative to emerge the tactic of both having one's cake and eating it must be abandoned for some more realistic policy aimed at building up media consumption.

Idealizing the Indigenous

One indigenous form of communication that is not difficult to idealize is African art. Traditional arts transfer well to radio and television, and pro- grams featuring them are extremely popular with African audiences. Wheth- er, on balance, African arts benefit from their introduction into the modern media is not clear. In their original setting these art forms have an instrumen- tal character. They are performed or displayed at given times and at given places for: stated purposes—to accompany rites of passage, high points in the agricultural cycle, investitures, and other vitally significant ceremonial occa- sions. The modern media, by contrast, demand performance on an arbitrary cue, according to an entirely different rhythm, which has no intrinsic mean- ing. This wrenching of art away from the event that gives it meaning may drain it of authenticity and significance; however, perhaps the wider stage and the extended audience provided by the new media may save traditional arts from eventual extinction or relegation to museums.

Unimaginative personnel policies and the fact that the popular arts have not yet become part of the market economy militate against the development of national talent. Popular singers, instrumentalists, and composers generally receive far less compensation than their mass appeal justifies. Broadcasters, reporters, editors, translators, scriptwriters, dramatists, novelists, and design- ers receive minuscule stipends for their work in the media. Future steps to professionalize creative and performing arts and to reward outstanding artists appropriately will do much to enhance the quality and amount of indigenous materials in the media.

Nationalizing the Sectional

The mass media are obviously of primary importance in helping to surmount tribalism and the lack of a sense of national identity. Equally obvious, the media offer no panacea, as the continuance of tribalism in such multilingual countries as the British Isles, Canada, and Belgium demonstrates. Mass me- dia, in the McLuhanesque sense of the term, hardly yet exist in much of Tropical Africa. Most people still identify primarily with a literal village rather than the metaphorical-paradoxical "global" village.

Nevertheless, one can already see effects of the media in the rapidity with which fashions in music, dress, hair style, slang, and political activism are diffused among the urban youth of Africa. The young, of course, are especially sensitive to such influences and consequently subject to the tensions that arise from the clash of old and new cultures. One of the most popular serious content items in both the print and broadcast media is the question-and-answer feature, much of which concerns the novel personal and social problems that arise at the cultural interface. Analysis of questions and comments by newly literate children in a vernacular newspaper illustrated the dilemmas such children faced in trying to reconcile school teachers with the traditional beliefs acquired at home (1).   These dilemmas are essentially urban. The larger dilemma of the urban-rural split remains, with the rural population tending to maintain its own sectional differences. Broadcasting policies are intimately involved in this dilemma because decisions have to be made as to which languages to use in broadcasting, where to locate regional and local stations, whose traditional arts to support, how news and information are to be gathered and disseminated. More localism rather than less seems essential to audience building, but the need for national image-building argues more for centralization.

Emphasizing the African

Table 3 indicates on the average 43 percent of the programming in African television came from foreign sources. African news media depend on foreign international news agencies and foreign international broadcasters for news, not only of other parts of the world but of Africa itself. We have commented on the reasons for this dependence—the combination of circumstances precludes the essential mechanism of syndication to work autonomously within Africa. As one way of emphasizing the African, some observers suggest cutting back on the amount of media services by eliminating imported programs. This tactic would run counter to the intrinsic logic of the media, however, whose high cost is justified in part by the factors of frequency of issue (in the case of the press) or continuousness (in the case of broadcasting). Broadcast facilities are designed for continuous operation. Intermittent use discards one of broadcasting's unique advantages, its instantaneous availability; it also represents a wasteful use of capital resources, because equipment continues to deteriorate whether used or not—in fact frequent turning off and on hastens deterioration. In any event, the schedules of most systems are already so fragmented as to suggest an urgent need for extension rather than reduction.

This consideration returns us to the dilemma of the choice among ways of institutionalizing the media. If the media are allowed to "cater [neither] to cheap entertainment nor commercialism," in Nkrumah's words, they must sacrifice much of the motivational power that builds mass consumership.

Other means must then be found to involve the audience. Nkrumah's regime was interrupted before there was time for his policies to be put to the test and to determine whether he was prepared to furnish means of audience-building other than mass-appeal programming. We do know, however, that Ghana television began operating commercially in 1967, within a year of Nkrumah's overthrow, and that in 1971 Ghana television imported 31 percent of its programming (27, p. 349). The imports included such standard examples of "cheap entertainment" as *I Love Lucy* and *Mod Squad*. Nevertheless, African stations have in practice succeeded better in "emphasizing the African" than was at first thought possible by foreign contractors and advisers. Foreign imports have helped build audiences—for African as well as for foreign programs; and they have given African producers a breather during which to prepare local programming. Internationally syndicatable programming from African sources, however, remains far in the future. *Lucy* can count on a long run.

REFERENCES

1. Ainslie, Rosalynde. *The Press in Africa: Communications Past and Present.* New York: Walker, 1967.

2. Browne, Donald R. "International Broadcasts to African Audiences," in Sydney W. Head (ed.), *Broadcasting in Africa: A Continental Survey of Radio and Television.* Philadelphia: Temple University Press, 1974, pp. 175–199.

3. "Can City Newspapers Speak to the Masses in the Country?" *African Journalist 4,* 11, Zurich (1972).

4. Eapen, K. E. "ZANA: An African News Agency," *Gazette,* 18 (1972), 193–207.

5. "Education Satellites," *Africa,* London (1974), 42–43.

6. Feuereisen, Fritz, and Ernst Schmacke. *The Press in Africa: A Handbook for Economics and Advertising,* Second Edition. Munich: Verlag Documentation, 1973.

7. Findlay, Joseph W. O., Jr. "The Sierra Leone Broadcasting Service," *SLBS Record,* Freetown, Vol. 1 of periodical published in Freetown, (1973), 1–14.

8. Ghana. *This is Ghana Television.* Tema: State Publishing, n.d.

9. Hachten, William A. *Muffled Drums: The News Media in Africa.* Ames: Iowa State University Press, 1971.

10. Head, Sydney W. *Broadcasting in Africa: A Continental Survey of Radio and Television.* Philadelphia: Temple University Press, 1974.

11. ———. "Content of Children's Letters to a Vernacular Newspaper," in Harold G. Marcus (ed.), *Proceedings of the First United States Conference on Ethiopian Studies.* East Lansing: Michigan State University, 1975, pp. 249–259.

12. International Telecommunication Union. *African VHF/UHF Broadcasting Conference.* Geneva: ITU, 1963.

13. ———. *African LF/MF Broadcasting Conference.* Geneva: ITU, 1966.

14. ———. *General Plan for the Development of the International Network in Africa.* Geneva: ITU, 1967.

15. Kenyatta, Jomo. *Facing Mount Kenya: The Tribal Life of the Gikuyu.* New York: Vintage Books, 1962.

16. Kibaki, Mwai. "Address at Seminar on the Press and National Development," *African Journalist, 4,* Zurich (1972), 3–5.

17. Mazrui, Ali A. *Cultural Engineering and Nation-Building in East Africa.* Evanston, Ill.: Northwestern University Press, 1972.

18. Mboya, Tom. *Freedom and After.* London: Andre Deutsch, 1972.

19. McGann, Tom. "Africa's First Color Television Network," *Combroad, 22,* London (1974), 32–33.

20. Morrison, Donald G., *et al. Black Africa: A Comparative Handbook.* New York: Free Press, 1972.

21. Mytton, Graham. *Report on the National Mass Media Audience Survey, 1970–1971.* Lusaka: University of Zambia, 1972.

22. Obote, Milton. "Language and National Identification," *East Africa Journal, 4* (1967), 3–6.

23. Pool, Ithiel de Sola. "Factors Contributing Towards Modernization and Socioeconomic Performance: Communication," in Peter Lengyel (ed.), *Approaches to the Science of Socio-Economic Development.* Paris: UNESCO, 1971, pp. 191–206.

24. Quarmyne, A. T., and F. Bebey. *Training for Radio and Television in Africa.* Paris: UNESCO, 1967.

25. Tickton, Sidney G. "Instructional Technology in the Developing World," *Educational Broadcasting Review, 6* (1972), 97–104.

26. United Nations. *Statistical Yearbook, 1972.* New York: UN, 1973.

27. United Nations Educational, Scientific and Cultural Organization. *Statistical Yearbook.* Paris: UNESCO, 1972.

CHAPTER 9

The Free Flow of Information—For Whom?

HERBERT I. SCHILLER

For a quarter of a century one doctrine, the idea that no barriers should prevent the flow of information between nations, dominated international thinking about communications and cultural relations. The genesis and extension of the free flow of information conception are roughly coterminous with the brief and hectic interval of United States global hegemony. In retrospect we can see that the historical coincidence of these two phenomena—the policy of the free flow of information and United States imperial ascendancy—was not fortuitous.

As World War II drew to a close, attention in the United States at the highest decision-making levels was already focusing on the era ahead. In 1943, two years before the war's end, it was clear that the United States would emerge from the conflict physically unscathed and economically overpowering. In the most general terms, the more articulate exponents of what seemed to be a looming American Century envisioned a world unshackled from former colonial ties and generally accessible to the initiatives and undertakings of American private enterprise. This enterprise would inevitably be dominated by the United States because accumulated advantages, not all of them war-related, would permit American business to flourish and expand into the farthest reaches of the world capitalist system. The limits that the very existence of a sphere under socialist organization put on this expansion were neither agreeable nor acceptable to a self-confident North American leadership.

It was an especially propitious time to extol the virtues of unrestricted informational and resource movements. The depredations of the Nazi occupation had traumatized Europe and a good part of the rest of the world. Freedom of information and movement were the highly desirable and legiti-

A version of this chapter, with a different title, appears in Herbert I. Schiller, *Communication and Cultural Domination* (White Plains, N.Y.: International Arts & Sciences Press, 1976).

mate aspirations of occupied nations and peoples, and real national needs could easily be confused with private business objectives.

Free information flows could not only be contrasted with the fascist mode of operations, but were associated also with the hope for peace shared by war-weary peoples everywhere. Palmer Hoyt, an influential American publisher, declared a few months after the war's end:

I believe entirely that the world cannot stand another war. But I believe as completely that the world is headed for such a war and destruction unless immediate steps are taken to insure the beginning at least of freedom of news—*American style*—between the peoples of the earth. A civilization that is not informed cannot be free and a world that is not free cannot endure (10, pp. 60–62).

The U.S. advocates of the easy movement of information capitalized heavily then on the experiences and emotions of people freshly liberated from fascist-occupied and war-ravaged continents. But accompanying the rhetoric of freedom were powerful economic forces employing a skillful political and semantic strategy.

THE OLD CARTELS

The decisive role played by the British worldwide communications network—both its control of the physical hardware of oceanic cables and its administrative and business organization of news and information—which held the system together, promoted its advantages, and insulated it from external assault, had not escaped attention in the United States. Against these finely spun structural ties the American offensive was mounted. Conveniently the attack could avail itself of the virtuous language and the praiseworthy objectives of the "free flow of information" and "worldwide access to news."

But there was no mistaking the underlying thrust. For years Kent Cooper, the executive manager of the Associated Press, had sought to break the international grip of the European news cartels—Reuters foremost, Havas, and Wolff. Cooper's book (5) described the global territorial divisions the cartels had organized and the limitations these posed for the activities of the Associated Press. As early as 1914 Cooper wrote, the Associated Press "board was debating whether the Associated Press should not make an effort to break through the Havas [French] control of the vast South American territory" (5, p. 41). He recalled: "The tenacious hold that a nineteenth century territorial allotment for news dissemination had upon the world was evidenced by each year's discussion of the subject by the Associated Press Board of Directors, continuing until 1934" (5, p. 43).

Cooper's indictment of the old cartels has an ironic quality today when United States news agencies largely dominate the flow of world information:

In precluding the Associated Press from disseminating news abroad, Reuters and Havas served three purposes: (1) they kept out Associated Press competition; (2) they were free to present American news disparagingly to the United States if they presented it at all; (3) they could present news of their own countries most favorably and without it being contradicted. Their own countries were always glorified. This was done by reporting great advances at home in English and French civilizations, the benefits of which would, of course, be bestowed on the world" (5, p. 43).

Cooper recognized too the significance of Britain's domination of the oceanic cables.

The cable brought Australia, South Africa, India, China, Canada and all the British world instantaneously to London on the Thames. . . . Britain, far ahead of any other nation, concentrated on the cable business. First it tied its Empire together. Then it stretched out and tied other nations to it. And in harmony with Victorian practices, the news that went through this vast network of cables gave luster to the British cause! (5, p. 11).

Cooper was not alone in seeing these advantages. James Lawrence Fly, chairman of the Federal Communications Commission during World War II, also drew attention to this subject:

Among the artificial restraints to the free development of commerce throughout the world, none is more irksome and less justifiable than the control of communication facilities by one country with preferential services and rates to its own nationals. . . . Great Britain owns the major portion of the cables of the world, and it is a fair statement that, through such ownership and the interlocking contractual relations based on it, that country dominates the world cable situation (9, p. 168).

This understanding of the power afforded by communications domination was not forgotten. It was manifest two decades later when the United States companies, with huge government subsidies, were the first to develop and then monopolize satellite communications.

The impatient United States press associations and government communications regulators found others in the country who recognized the advantages that worldwide communications control bestowed on acquiring foreign trade and export markets. *Business Week* summed up the business view by quoting approvingly a comment that had appeared at an earlier time in the London *Standard:* "It [control of communications] gives power to survey the trade of the world and . . . to facilitate those activities which are to the interest of those in control" (4, p. 41).

Of course, British power was not unaware of American interest in these matters. The influential *Economist* reacted tartly to Kent Cooper's expanding campaign in late 1944 for the free flow of information: The "huge financial resources of the American agencies might enable them to dominate the world . . . (Cooper), like most big business executives, experiences a peculiar moral glow in finding that his idea of freedom coincides with his commercial advantage. . . . Democracy does not necessarily mean making the whole world safe for the AP" (7, p. 88). (Nor did it mean, the *Economist* failed to add, retaining control for Reuters and British Cables.)

The public official most directly concerned with formulating and explaining United States policy in the communications sphere immediately after the war was William Benton, the assistant secretary of state. Benton, who was to become a United States senator as well as president of the *Encyclopaedia Britannica*, outlined the government's position on the meaning of freedom of communications, in a State Department broadcast in January 1946.

The State Department plans to do everything within its power along political or diplomatic lines to help break down the artificial barriers to the expansion of private American news agencies, magazines, motion pictures, and other media of communications throughout the world. . . . Freedom of the press—and freedom of exchange of information generally—is an integral part of our foreign policy" (21, p. 160).

A COLD WAR WEAPON

The economic aspects of the free flow of information policy certainly were no secret, though the media neither dwelt on the self-serving nature of its widely proclaimed principle nor made the implications of the policy explicit to the public. Instead, a remarkable political campaign was organized by the big press associations and publishers, with the support of industry in general, to elevate the issue of free flow of information to the highest level of national and international principle. This rallied public opinion to the support of a commercial goal expressed as an ethical imperative. Simultaneously it provided a highly effective ideological club against the Soviet Union and its newly created neighboring zone of anticapitalist influence.

Obviously a fundamental premise of free enterprise—access to capital governs access to message dissemination—would be intolerable to societies that had eliminated private ownership of decisive forms of property, such as mass communications facilities. Therefore, the free flow of information issue gave American policy managers a powerful cultural argument with which to create suspicion about an alternate form of social organization. It helped to weaken thereby the enormous popular interest in Europe and Asia at war's end for one or another of the varieties of socialism.

John Foster Dulles, one of the chief architects and executors of America's cold war policy, was forthright on this matter: "If I were to be granted one point of foreign policy and no other, I would make it the free flow of information" (10). This is a recurring theme in postwar United States diplomacy.

CHRONOLOGY OF THE FREE FLOW PRINCIPLE

Well before the war was over, American business had incorporated the free flow of information issue into a formal political ideology. In June 1944 the directors of the American Society of Newspaper Editors adopted resolutions urging both major political parties to support "world freedom of information and unrestricted communications for news throughout the world" (6, pp. 472–473). Subsequently both the Democrats and the Republicans adopted planks in their party platforms in which these aims were incorporated (12, pp. 404, 413). In September 1944 both houses of Congress adopted a concurrent resolution that followed closely the recommendations of the editors and publishers. Congress expressed "its belief in the worldwide right of interchange of news by newsgathering and distributing agencies, whether individual or associate, by any means, without discrimination as to sources, distribution, rates or charges; and that this right should be protected by international compact" (24).

Having sought and secured congressional endorsement of their aims, the directors of the American Society of Newspaper Editors, meeting in November 1944, then declared: "Most Americans and their newspapers will support Government policies . . . and action toward removal of all political, legal and economic barriers to the media of information, and that our Government should make this abundantly clear to other nations" (1). The group noted with satisfaction that the newly appointed secretary of state, Edward Stettinius, Jr., had announced "that the United States plans exploratory talks with other nations looking to international understandings guaranteeing there shall be no barriers to interchange of information among all nations" (14, p. 7).

At the same time the American Society of Newspaper Editors, in conjunction with the AP and UPI, announced an international expedition of a delegation to "personally carry the message of an international free press into every friendly capital of the world" (1). In the spring of 1945, while the war was still being fought, the delegation traveled 40,000 miles around the world, to 22 major cities and 11 allied and neutral countries, "on first priority of the War Department on Army Transport Command planes" (2).

While the private group of United States press representatives was making its international journey to marshall support for the free flow doctrine, the directors of the Associated Press "placed a fund of $1,000,000 a year at the disposal of Executive Director Kent Cooper to make the AP a global institution" (3).

In fact, as the war drew to a close preparations for the promotion of the free flow doctrine shifted from the national to the international level. With congressional and political support assured and domestic public opinion effectively organized, the free flow advocates carried their campaign vigorously into the channels of international diplomacy and peacemaking that were becoming activated with the end of hostilities.

UTILIZATION OF INTERNATIONAL ORGANIZATIONS

One of the first occasions that provided an opportunity for an *international* forum for espousing the free flow doctrine was the Inter-American Conference on Problems of War and Peace, convened in Mexico City in February 1945. Latin America, regarded for more than a century as a prime United States interest with European economic influence practically eliminated as a result of the war, was a natural site for testing the new doctrine in a congenial, if not controlled, international setting.

Predictably, the conference adopted a strong resolution on "free access to information" which was "based substantially on a United States proposal" (19, p. 21). The Western Hemisphere having been successfully persuaded of the merits of "free flow," attention turned to the rest of the world.

International peacekeeping structures were being established and the United States made certain that the newly created United Nations and the related United Nations Educational, Scientific and Cultural Organization (UNESCO), would put great emphasis on the free flow issue.

In the 1970s the United States often was on the minority side of the voting in the United Nations (on some issues in almost total isolation—e.g., direct satellite broadcasting). In the 1940s affairs were quite different.

Fifty states were represented in the first meetings of the United Nations in 1945, hardly more than a third of the membership 30 years later. Of the original 50, two-fifths were Latin American states, at that time almost totally subservient to North American pressure. The West European member states were economically drained, politically unstable, and heavily dependent on the United States for economic assistance. The few Middle Eastern, Asian, and African countries then participating in the UN, with a few exceptions, were still, in real terms, subject to the Western empire system. In sum, the United Nations in 1945–1948, with the exception of the USSR and the few East European states allied to it, was distinguished by an "automatic majority," invoked whenever its heaviest financial supporter and economically strongest member desired to use it. In this atmosphere the UN's endorsement of the free flow doctrine was hardly surprising.

The earliest proposals for the constitution of UNESCO, drafted by a United States panel of experts and reviewed by the State Department, prominently espoused the free flow of information as a UNESCO objective (22, pp. 5–7).

From the start UNESCO, with the United States delegation taking the initiative, made the free flow of information issue one of its major concerns. In its account of the *first* session of the General Conference of UNESCO, held in Paris between November and December in 1946, the United States delegation reported that it had proposed to the subcommission on mass communications that "UNESCO should cooperate with the Subcommission on Freedom of Information of the Commission on Human Rights in the preparation of the United Nations report on obstacles to the free flow of information and ideas . . ." (20, p. 17). In fact, a free flow of information section was created in the Mass Communications Division of UNESCO itself.

THE COURSE OF THE FREE FLOW DOCTRINE
IN THE UNITED NATIONS

In the United Nations similar initiatives were under way from the outset of that organization's existence, to stress and publicize the free flow doctrine. The UN's Economic and Social Council established the Commission on Human Rights in February 1946 and empowered the Commission to set up a subcommission on freedom of information and the press in June 1946 (17, p. 400). On December 14, 1946 the first General Assembly adopted Resolution 59 (1), which declared: "Freedom of information is a fundamental human right and is a touchstone of all the freedoms to which the United Nations is consecrated" (18, p. 439). The Assembly also resolved to authorize the holding of a conference of all members of the United Nations on freedom of information.

The United Nations Conference on Freedom of Information was held in 1948 in Geneva. It provided the international ideological polarization the United States' policy managers had expected of it.

The Conference's final act, embodying essentially the United States' views on free flow, was adopted by 30 votes to 1 (Poland, against), with five abstentions (Byelorussia, Czechoslovakia, Ukraine, USSR, and Yugoslavia). The Soviet proposal that the final act be signed only by the president and executive secretary of the Conference instead of representatives of all governments attending was not pleasing to the United States delegation. All the same, perhaps reflecting the uneasiness aroused by the Conference's overtly provocative character, the Soviet recommendation was unanimously adopted (23).

The conference represented, in the eyes of United States observers, "in the main . . . a victory for American objectives . . ." (26, p. 76). The (London) *Economist,* though generally approving of the work of the Conference, noted:

It was the impression of most delegations that the Americans wanted to secure for their news agencies that general freedom of the market for the most efficient which has been the object of all their initiatives in commercial policy—that they regard freedom of information as an extension of the charger of the International Trade

Organization rather than as a special and important subject of its own. And the stern opposition which they offered to Indian and Chinese efforts to protect infant national news agencies confirmed this impression (8).

UNITED STATES CULTURAL HEGEMONY—1948–1968

Efforts to gain wide international support for the free flow conception were at best inconclusive. But the two decades that succeeded the Freedom of Information Conference in 1948 saw the realization of the doctrine in fact, if not in solemn covenant. New communications technology—computers, space satellites, television—combined with a powerful and expanding corporate business system, assisted the push of the United States into the center of the world economy. Without public pronouncements, private, American-made media products and United States informational networks blanketed the world.*

THE NEW INTERNATIONAL MOOD

Largely as a reaction to the flood of American cultural material and the usurpation of national media systems that was required to disseminate it, a new mood with respect to the free flow of information doctrine became observable in the international community in the 1960s and 1970s. Besides the free flow view, there now appear frequent references to cultural sovereignty, cultural privacy, and cultural autonomy.

This shift of emphasis from the quantity to the consequences of the free flow of information may have arisen from the changed character of the international community itself. Since 1945, 85 new national entities have emerged to take place in the community of nations, most of them still in their early economic developmental period. The concern of these states with safeguarding their national and cultural sovereignty is evident. Then, too, the results of two decades' *de facto* free flow of information have not gone unremarked. As the Prime Minister of Guyane observed, "A nation whose mass media are dominated from the outside is not a nation" (1).

Finally, the possibility of direct satellite broadcasting from space into home sets without the mediation of nationally controlled ground stations, whether or not likely in the immediate future, has created a sense of urgency around the question of cultural sovereignty.

The Working Group on Direct Broadcast Satellites was established in 1969 "to consider mainly the technical feasibility of direct broadcasting from satel-

*See expecially the major symposia on "Cultural Exchange—or, Invasion" and "Forms of Cultural Dependency" in the Winter 1974 and Spring 1975 issues of the *Journal of Communication.*

lites" (15). It has met more or less regularly since that time, extending its range from the technical aspects to the social, legal, and political implications of direct satellite broadcasting.

So too, UNESCO, the strongest advocate of the free flow doctrine at one time, has veered noticeably from its former unquestioning support. In its Declaration of Guiding Principles on the Use of Satellite Broadcasting for the Free Flow of Information, adopted in October 1972, the cultural organization acknowledged that ". . . it is necessary that States, taking into account the principle of freedom of information, reach or promote prior agreements concerning direct satellite broadcasting to the population of countries other than the country of origin of the transmission" (15). The United Nations General Assembly supported this view in November 1972, by a vote of 102 to 1 (the United States cast the single dissenting vote).

Reactions in the private communications sector in the United States were predictably hostile and self-serving. Frank Stanton, for example, wrote: ". . . the rights of Americans to speak to whomever they please, when they please, are (being) bartered away" (13). His chief objection to the UNESCO document, he claimed, was that censorship was being imposed by provisions that permitted each nation to reach prior agreement with transmitting nations concerning the character of the broadcasts. Stanton (13) and those in agreement with him assume that the United States' constitutional guarantee of freedom of speech to the *individual* is applicable to the multinational corporations and media conglomerates whose interests they so strongly espouse. Yet more than a generation ago one writer asked:

Is freedom of the press to be conceived as a *personal* right appertaining to all citizens, as undoubtedly the Founding Fathers conceived it; or as a *property* right appertaining to the ownership of newspapers and other publications, as we have come to think of it largely today? (25).

But the national power behind this view is no longer as absolute or as fearsome as it was in 1945. A renewal of economic vitality in Western Europe and Japan, significant growth and expansion of the noncapitalist world, and, not least, the experiences of the last quarter of a century, have produced an altogether changed international environment.

When there is still an uneven distribution of power between individuals or groups *inside* nations, or *among* nations, a free hand to continue doing that which led to the existing condition serves to strengthen the powerful and weaken further the frail. Evidence for this conclusion abounds in all aspects of modern life—in race, sex, and occupational and international relationships. Freedoms therefore, which are formally impressive, may be substantively oppressive when they reinforce prevailing inequalities while claiming to be providing generalized opportunity for all.

Not surprisingly, individuals, groups, and nations are seeking means to limit the freedom to maintain inequality. Measures aimed at regulating "the free flow of information" are best understood in this perspective.

REFERENCES

1. American Society of Newspaper Editors. In *New York Times*, 29 November 1944.
2. ———. In *Editor and Publisher*, 16 June 1945.
3. Associated Press. In *Editor and Publisher*, 21 April 1945.
4. *Business Week, 87* (August 1945).
5. Cooper, Kent. *Barriers Down.* New York: Farrar & Rinehart, 1942.
6. Dulles, John Foster. Quoted in John S. Knight, "World Freedom of Information," *Vital Speeches, 12* (1946), 476.
7. *Economist.* Quotation in "Charter for a Free Press," *Newsweek*, 11 December 1944.
8. *Economist*, 1 May 1948, 701.
9. Fly, James Lawrence. "A Free Flow of News Must Bind the Nations," *Free World, 8, 2* (August 1944).
10. Hoyt, Palmer. "The Last Chance," in John S. Knight (ed.), *Vital Speeches, 12* (1946).
11. International Broadcast Institute. *Intermedia, 3* (1972), 1.
12. Porter, Kirk H., and Donald Bruce Johnson. *National Party Platforms 1840–1964.* Urbana and London: University of Illinois Press, 1966.
13. Stanton, Frank. "Will They Stop Our Satellites?" *New York Times*, 22 October 1972, Section 2, pp. 23, 39.
14. Stettinius, Edward Jr. In *Editor and Publisher*, 2 December 1944.
15. UNESCO. "Declaration of Guiding Principles on the Use of Satellite Broadcasting for the Free Flow of Information," *Spread of Education and Greater Cultural Exchange* A/AC, 105/109.
16. ———. *Report of the Working Group on Direct Broadcast Satellites of the Work of its Fourth Sessions.* A/AC, 105/117. Annex 1, 22 June 1973.
17. United Nations. Resolution 2/9 of June 21, 1946. *Economist and Social Council Official Records, 8* (1946).
18. ———. *Yearbook on Human Rights for 1947.* Lake Success, N. Y.: United Nations, 1949.
19. United States Dapartment of State. *Report of the United States Delegation to the Inter-American Conference on Problems of War and Peace.* Mexico City, Mexico, February–March 1945. Department of State Publications (2497), Conference Series (85). Washington: United States Government Printing Office, 1946.
20. ———. *Report of the United States Delegation with Selected Documents.* First Session of the General Conference of the United Nations Educational, Scientific and Cultural Organization, Paris, November–December 1946. Washington: United States Government Printing Office, 1947.
21. ———. *Department of State Bulletin, 14,* 344 (February 1946).
22. ———. *Proposed Educational and Cultural Organization of the United Nations.* United States Department of State Publication 2382. Washington: Government Printing Office, 1945.
23. ———. *Accomplishments of the United Nations Conference on Freedom of Information.* Documents and State Papers, 1, 3 (June 1948).
24. United States House of Representatives. Nineteenth *Congressional Record* 8044:58.

25. Vance, Earl L. "Freedom of the Press For Whom?" *Virginia Quarterly Review, 21* (Summer 1945), 340.

26. Whitton, John B. "The United Nations Conference on Freedom of Information and the Movement Against International Propaganda," *American Journal of International Law, 43* (January 1949).

PART II

New Directions

CHAPTER 10

Conflict and Resolution in Sweden

IVAR IVRE

Although radio and television in Sweden belong to the public sector, Sveriges Radio has been given the form of a private corporation, in which shares are owned by the press, industry, commerce, and what might be referred to generally as the "popular movements."* Sveriges Radio was given the judicial status of a private corporation for two reasons: When Swedish radio was inaugurated in 1925, groups who had previously wanted to engage in broadcasting were to be given representation on its board of directors. Because of judicial circumstances peculiar to Swedish law, the total incorporation of the service into the public sector was seen to have certain undesirable consequences: Employees would have the status and accountability of civil servants; decisions of the management would be subject to appeal; and all correspondence and internal papers of the enterprise would be classified as public documents (4, p. 110). The corporation is financed via receiver license fees as fixed by Parliament.† Only through Parliament's authority to determine annually the portion of license revenues made available to the corporation can the state be said to exercise continual, although indirect, influence over programming. All other means by which government might directly influ-

---

*Typical of these movements (*foldrörelser*) are temperance and evangelical movements (from the 1860s forward), the consumer cooperative movement, adult education federations, and the labor union movement (all founded in the closing decades of the nineteenth century). Peculiarly Scandinavian circumstances, among them a rather sparse and homogenous population, have permitted these organizations to retain their local, grassroots democratic character while growing to nationwide stature.

†The present license fee is Sw.cr. 220 (roughly $50) for radio and black-and-white television. For color television there is an additional fee of Sw.cr. 100 ($20). Each license covers all such receivers in the household. The number of radio and television sets in Sweden is consequently much greater than the statistics given here. As of December 1973 the number of combined radio and TV licenses was 2.74 million. Of these, 0.68 million were for color TV. The number of licenses for radio alone amounted to 0.26 million.

ence the content of the broadcast media are prohibited by the statutes governing the activities of the corporation. The three documents of the statutes—the Radio Act, the Broadcasting Liability Act, and the Agreement between the Government of Sweden and Sveriges Radio Aktiebolag—have been in effect since July 1967.

The Radio Act sets forth the conditions for Sveriges Radio's sole rights to broadcast, the monopoly status of the corporation. Two stipulations are of particular interest: The right to monopoly "shall be exercised impartially and factually," and furthermore, "no authority or other public body may examine in advance or prescribe the advance examination of radio programmes." Neither may any authority prohibit any broadcast "on account of content."

The Broadcasting Liability Act gave Sveriges Radio the same status as that enjoyed by the press in terms of criminal and civil liability for the content of broadcasts. There shall exist within Sveriges Radio a number of program supervisors who bear liability for any violations of the regulations governing freedom of the press, just as newspaper and magazine publishers and editors are liable for the content of their publications. Only one case has been brought to court since this legislation has come into effect, however, and it was dismissed.

The Agreement with the state has the character of a civil contract between two parties. Guidelines for broadcasting are most clearly expressed in this document, which may be characterized as an interpretion of the Radio Act. The Agreement formulates in general terms "the demands and expectations placed on broadcasting by the government" (5, p. 112).

Observance of the Radio Act and the Agreement with the state is controlled by a special organ, the Radio Council, which consists of seven members appointed by the government. All are more or less directly associated with the political parties or influential organizations and interest groups and are well-known and prominent in their field. All criticism and complaints about programs broadcast over the air related to the content of the Radio Act and the Agreement fall under the jurisdiction of the Radio Council. In addition, the Council itself can initiate postbroadcast inspection of programs. The Council may not, however, engage in prior censorship.*

The management of Sveriges Radio is the province of its board and the Director-General, appointed by the board. The duties of top management have long been basically administrative, but since the advent of the two-

---

*See also my article "Sveriges Radios massmedieforskning" (Mass Media Research at Sveriges Radio), in *Radio och tv möter publiken* [Radio and TV meet the People], Stockholm, 1972. The present discussion has been expanded and elaborated on some points.

channel system the board has shown a growing interest in matters of program policy.

The board has 13 members and 12 alternates. The government appoints the chairman and five members and five of the alternates. Five members and five alternatives are appointed by shareholders in proportion to their share in the corporation: the "popular movements," three members and three alternates; the press and private enterprise, one member and one alternate each. In 1971 this board of 11 members and 10 alternates was expanded by the addition of two members and two alternates, to be appointed by the employees of the corporation via their union.

The system, which came into being in 1968 together with the new regulations, implied two significant changes. First, the influence of the "popular movements" or major interest groups was increased. Their share in the corporate capital increased from 40 to 60 percent, with a corresponding increase in their representation on the board. The share controlled by the press and its representation was reduced by the same proportion, from 40 to 20 percent. The share controlled by private enterprise remained unchanged at 20 percent. Stated simply, these changes meant that strong well-established interest groups in Swedish society were given a strengthened position in the management of the corporation. Second, the new rules of procedure gave program production personnel within the corporation a greater measure of independence. In practice this meant that the authority of the director-general was reduced in comparison with the previous structure.

The arrangement created a two-channel television system with the motto "internal competition in stimulating contest." Apart from some coordination to prevent collisions of similar program content, each channel was free to define its own program output. The system, unique to Sweden, contained "many mutually contradictory features," as Karl-Erik Lundevall, then assistant director-general, characterized it (5).

His anxiety turned out to be warranted. The resulting problems constitute the reason for increasing participation in program political matters on the part of top management. This increased participation came to limit to some extent the newly gained independence of the channels. The authority of the director-general was reinstated. The drift toward change was confirmed in new rules of procedures for the corporation, effective in 1973, which replaced the rules in effect since 1968, in which paragraph No. 2 had heralded the principle of "internal competition": "The organization [of the corporation] shall be characterized by considerable independence for the units of program production (channels) in the aim of allowing freedom of maneuver and independence, variation and stimulating internal competition in programming." This paragraph does not appear in the new rules of procedures. This latter document defines the "main function" of program production units as being to "work under the direction of management as operative units with considerable independence and [to] produce programming in accordance with the goals, guidelines and directives given by management as well as the annual project plans, and within the bounds of the budget."

REGULATIONS AND OBJECTIVES OF PROGRAM POLICY

Of the three main documents governing radio and television broadcasting in Sweden, the Radio Act and the Agreement between the State and Sveriges Radio contain the stipulations of greatest importance for program production, and thereby for the broadcasting system as a whole. Of the various regulations stated in the documents, we here treat those that fall into the categories of *goals of programming* and *norms*. The programming goals stipulated in the Agreement concerning standards of content and quality are rather vaguely and ambiguously formulated. In the words of the Agreement, programs shall be "diversified in character and content . . . (and) provide good diversion and entertainment, with due regard for differences of taste." They shall further "satisfy different interests," such as religious, musical, dramatic, artistic, literary and scientific interests, as well as "the special interests of minority audiences." All this, "to the extent practicable" (2).

It has been said that these programming objectives are expressed so generally that they may be interpreted in practically any way. On one point, however, the goals of programming are stated more clearly. The Agreement states that considering "the central position of sound radio and television in the national life . . . [it follows that] the Corporation is required, *inter alia*, to disseminate, in suitable form, information on current events as well as information on important cultural and social issues, and to encourage debate on such issues."*

Thus, the duty to inform and orient is clearly stated. Implementation, however, must be regulated in some respects due to the "central position" of the media. The stipulations of *impartiality* and *factuality* in the Radio Act thus become norms not only for news and news commentary, current affairs, and forums for debate, but also, where applicable, for the program output as a whole.

When these norms were treated in the Agreement, a third condition was attached. Impartiality and factuality "shall be applied having regard to the requirement that extensive freedom of expression and freedom of information

---

*See also my article "Sveriges Radios massmedieforskning" (Mass Media Research at Sveriges Radio), in *Radio och tv moter publiken* [Radio and TV meet the People], Stockholm, 1972. The present discussion has been expanded and elaborated on some points.

shall obtain" (2). Hereafter, I refer to "impartiality" and "factuality" as norms, while "freedom of expression" and "freedom of information" are designated as freedoms.

The set of governing norms is thus somewhat equivocal. Two primary norms are mitigated by a third stipulation demanding deference to two freedoms. Because these freedoms are not mentioned in the Radio Act, however, they are to be looked upon as subordinate to the norms concerning impartiality and factuality. Nevertheless, they are to be observed. The reference in the Agreement to the conflict between norms and freedoms reflects an awareness that broadcasting must necessarily be the subject of some controversy. From the point of view of mass communications research this pattern of sought-after balance and ever-present conflict seems well suited to a discussion of the structure and functions of the communications system.

Before pursuing this discussion, however, a summary of the extent and character of television programming is appropriate. The summary (Table 1) is confined to the programming of the two channels during the period July 1972–June 1973.

By international standards Sveriges Radio's television transmission time is quite modest—92 hours per week for the two channels combined. By the same comparison—with the exception of other Scandinavian television systems—the amount of informative or otherwise serious programming may be regarded as considerable. The conflicts of confidence or trust have been provoked mainly by programs in categories 1–3, but also to an increasing extent by content belonging to category 4. Programs for children and young people have become increasingly controversial in recent years, treating issues previously considered appropriate only in adult programming—for example, the war in Indo-China, hunger in various parts of the world, relations between rich and poor nations.

AN ATTEMPT AT FUNCTION ANALYSIS

In his analysis of the American commercial system of mass communication Melvin DeFleur advances the hypothesis that the enormous output of popular entertainment programming is the factor that "maintains the equilibrium of the system." The *commodity* the distributors-networks (or producing units) sell to the *financial* backers, usually advertisers, is the *attention* of the mass audience, the attention of potential consumers. This attention is attracted by the vast entertainment output. A lesser output of such programs implies less attention; less attention, less advertising revenues; and less advertising revenues, growing dysfunction within the system (1, pp. 165–170).

Swedish radio and television are noncommercial; the audience finances

Table 1 Program Output of Swedish Television During the Year July 1972–June 1973: Total Output, Output per Channel, and Output per Category of Program Content.

Program Categories	TV1		TV2		Total	
	Hours/Week	%	Hours/Week	%	Hours/Week	%
1. Culture, science	4.4	9.2	3.2	7.1	7.6	8.1
2. Politics, economics, current affairs	4.5	9.3	5.1	11.6	9.6	10.4
3. News (excluding sports)	5.4	11.3	4.7	10.5	10.1	10.9
4. Sports, hobbies, leisure activities	5.5	11.4	5.1	11.5	10.6	11.5
5. Religion	1.1	2.4	0.3	0.7	1.4	1.6
6. Theatre and film	7.3	15.1	9.1	20.6	16.4	17.7
7. Children's and young people's programs	3.9	8.2	5.3	11.8	9.2	10.1
8. Music	2.1	4.4	1.1	2.5	3.2	3.5
9. Entertainment	8.5	17.8	8.6	19.4	17.1	18.6
10. Miscellaneous announcements, shorts, programs for immigrants[a]	4.3	9.0	1.4	3.1	5.7	6.2
11. Adult education	0.9	1.9	0.4	2.0	1.3	1.4
TOTAL	47.9	100.0	44.3	100.0	92.2	100.0

[a] Programs for immigrants—mainly Finns—constitute the largest subcategory in Category 10 with 2.4 hours/week, all broadcast on TV1.

Source: Sveriges Radios Arsbok, 1972–1973

programming by the payment of receiver license fees. Despite this direct economic relationship between the channels and the audience, the commodity attention is of secondary importance to the maintenance of the system.

Precisely because the system in noncommercial, observance of the norms has great importance for the function of the Swedish system. By way of analogy to DeFleur's analysis, the commodity of trust in the observance of the norms corresponds to the commodity attention in the American system. A striving for impartiality and factuality must appear to be the guiding light for program production. If public trust in this effort erodes, the whole system is shaken. The structure of the Swedish monopoly system, however, implies that the trust commodity is not so much that of the mass public as of the trust of groups capable of directly or indirectly exerting influence in the political system.

A Model of Trust

Lindblad (3, 4) has developed a model to demonstrate "how Sveriges Radio is governed." This model has been adapted and developed in Figure 1 to illustrate the function of trust in a system like Sveriges Radio.

POWERS OF GOVERNMENT. The government and parliament establish the societal goals for program production. Decisions at this level may change both programming goals and the structure of the corporation. Alleged breaches of the Broadcasting Liability Act are decided in the courts.

THE CORPORATION AND ITS EMPLOYEES. Top management consists of the board and the director-general. The two-way arrows indicate the constant and mutual influence occurring between management and employees. In a situation of normal trust their interpretations of the societal goals will

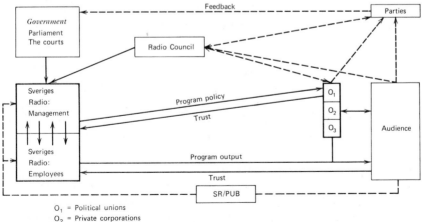

O₁ = Political unions
O₂ = Private corporations
O₃ = Religious and temperance organizations

Figure 1   How Sveriges Radio is governed.

hardly diverge. The employees' interpretation of these goals will undoubtedly be influenced by a professional ambition to extend the bounds of the freedoms of expression and information. Management tends to be influenced by its ultimate responsibility for ensuring that the norms of impartiality and factuality are observed.

THE AUDIENCE AND ORGANIZATIONS. One might argue that interest groups within organizations belong in the box labeled "audience" because they represent members of the audience at a higher level of aggregation. By separating them in the model we wish to point out that the expectations of and trust in the program production apparatus on the part of the general public is not of the same character as that of organized interest groups—even though these may claim to speak in the name of the public at large. The function of trust on the part of organized interest groups is more closely related to the execution of program policy, while that of the general public is more related to program output. In other words, the audience at large is more interested in the extent to which programming fulfills the goals of "good entertainment," "diversified in character and content," etc. Organizations, corporations, and interest groups are more concerned about how impartially and factually political, economic, and social problems and conflicts are treated in programs, particularly if their own spheres of interest are involved.

A somewhat heavier line, the "trust" line, has been drawn between Sveriges Radio's management and the cluster of interest groups to point out the community of interests existing by virtue of the fact that all, or nearly all, of the members of the board are directly or indirectly associated with these groups. The double role of board member and interest-group member is assumed to work for two reasons. First, members of the board are not bound by a fixed mandate; rather, they are expected primarily to see that programming is produced in accordance with their personal interpretations of the stipulations of the Agreement and the Radio Act. That these interpretations may be colored by their political interests or other experience is considered desirable, which fits the ideal of representative democracy. That their interpretations may also be mutually contradictory is also considered an essentially democratic feature—such conflict is seen to ensure a balance of interests in the decisions of the board. That this double role does in fact work is evidenced by the fact that nearly all of the decisions of the board are reached without having to put them to the vote.

Actually, this consensus is quite natural. The task of representative democracy in a decision-making body such as the board of Sveriges Radio is the maintenance of the present system—that is, self-preservation. Consequently, in cases of controversial programming the board is potentially able unanimously to stress the importance of observance of the norms. Government might otherwise intervene and alter the structure of the corporation. A similar course of action on the part of the board might have been achieved had the same interest groups utilized their connections with the political parties (see the feedback line). Such an intervention would then be considered desirable in the name of the public service philosophy—"radio and television in the service of the 'public'"—which is the ideological cornerstone of the system (2, pp. 117–120). In such cases the interests of the general public are seen to have been served as well via their representatives in the political system. The model also includes a feedback channel between the public and the parties as a symbol of the direct relationship between voter and politician assumed in systems of representative democracy.

A two-way link has been drawn between the audience and organized interest groups. Individuals quite often vent their displeasure or dissatisfaction via the organizations to which they belong. Thus they contribute to the latent dissatisfaction with program policy that might be existing within the organization.

According to our analysis, however, the interest of the broad general public may be assumed to focus on the programming goals. Thus their trust or confidence in the program output has other components than that of organized interest groups. One may say—with DeFleur—that this trust is expressed in terms of *attention* and *appreciation* or, to use another idiom, in terms of registered *uses and gratifications*. Variations in this attention and appreciation due to the composition of the program output have been traced in the audience measurements conducted by the corporation, for example. Consequently, the model includes a feedback channel between the audience and the Audience and Program Research Department (SR/PUB), only a portion of whose research has to do with audience measurement.

RADIO COUNCIL. The channels between the Radio Council and the parties and organizations, respectively, are two-way channels. This indicates the integration of the council into the system via, among other things, the political affiliations, of its members. The council avoids statements and verdicts that may have the character of precedent to avoid, in turn, program censorship. Thus Sveriges Radio itself must interpret the findings of the council. The Corporation is not compelled to adhere to the findings of the council, and possibly the interpretation of Sveriges Radio's management will differ from that of the council. If this interpretation is more strict than that of the council, no problems will arise. If, however, it should be more lenient and if its application in program output can be perceived as defiance of the interpretation of the council, a schism may develop, which may ultimately be resolved by the findings of an arbitration committee appointed by the government. No such conflict has yet occurred or is likely.

Conflict of Ideologies

The fall of 1971 appears to have been a critical period that can serve as an example of a "crisis of confidence" in the broadcasting system. Labor and private enterprise (as opponents on the labor market) were subjected to a frank and, to some extent, one-sided critique in a series of five programs. Another series in eight parts undertook a nearly total reevaluation of the history of the Swedish labor movement from its beginnings in the 1880s to the present, including 40 years of practically unbroken Social-Democratic government. Because this reevaluation adopted a clearly Marxist-Leninist point of view and was expressed in highly professional but strongly personal programs, the series was politically and socially controversial.

The situation was further inflamed by an incident that occurred in an entertainment program with radical political overtones. One scene in the program depicted the signing of the first comprehensive agreement between the employers' association and organized labor in 1938, an event considered a milestone in the history of the Swedish labor movement. The signing of the contract was depicted as having transpired during a party and the signatories as so intoxicated that they nearly confused the contract with the innkeeper's bill. The presentation might have been acceptable except for the fact that the leader of the Swedish Trade Unions Congress depicted in the sketch was widely known to have been a life-long teetotaler.

The five programs on the labor market were not brought before the Radio Council, but the other two were. The Council found both in flagrant violation of the impartiality and factuality norms. Even before the decision of the council was handed down, the Board of Sveriges Radio issued a unanimous statement reiterating the responsibility of the program personnel to see that "impartiality and factuality in program production be strictly observed."

The conflict reflected an increasingly apparent power struggle between two ideologies of broadcasting. In terms borrowed from Siebert, Peterson, and Schramm's "four concepts of mass communication" (6) and adapted to the Swedish context, these may be labeled the professional and group-oriented ideologies respectively (see Fig. 2). Both ideologies claim to serve the interests of the public. The differences between them are clearly apparent, however, in their answers to such questions as, "Who should have authority over the channels?" "Whose interests should be served?" and "What should programming strive to provide or achieve?"

The new radio and television structure gave increased influence, through increased representation on the board of the corporation, to adherents of the group-oriented ideology. This increased influence may have given rise to expectations of increased influence over programming as well. Such expectations ran a collision course with the expectations inspired by the new independence granted adherents of the professional ideology. This consensus with respect to the norms is an essential feature of what might be called the old professionalism. Discrepancies between the interpretation of management and that of professionals were quite minor. In the new broadcasting system,

Ideology	Who should have authority over the channels?	Whose interest should be served?	What should programming strive to provide or achieve?
Group-oriented	Representatives of political parties, organizations and interest groups	Established groups in society	Information about and a positive image of society as it is
Professional	People working within radio and television	The desires of the public; development of the media	Diversified program output; independent, critical views

Figure 2   Conflicts between group-oriented and professional ideologies.

however, such discrepancies became both greater and more frequent. One might well speak of a new professionalism.

This tendency was enhanced by the fact that the number of employees was greatly increased with the addition of a second television channel. Within the channels alone, some 400 new positions were created between 1968 and 1972. A corps of employees whose median age even previously was quite low was expanded by more than 50 percent with, on the average, even younger professionals. Members of this corps were quite naturally influenced by the change in ideological climate occurring in the late-1960s.

As far as the group-oriented ideology is concerned, observance of the norms of impartiality and factuality is one of the cornerstones of radio and television. When Lindblad (4), himself a proponent of this ideology, analyzed the two ideologies, he—symptomatically enough—failed to take note of the freedoms of expression and information. For the professional ideology, however, these freedoms constitute the cornerstones and binding of the profession.

The statistics regarding the Radio Council's treatment of formal complaints alleging violations of the Radio Act and the Agreement with the state provide some empirical measure of how the conflict between these ideologies affects program output as well as interpretations of this output. The number of complaints to the council increased from 228 in 1970 to 794 in 1973. However, many of these complaints fell outside the competence of the council, and organized campaigns against certain types of programs, often involving the distribution of form letters to be mailed into the council, inflated the statistics. Nevertheless, cases acted on by the council increased from 160 in 1970 to 554 in 1973.

The proportion of programs found to violate the stipulations of the Act and the Agreement increased from 12 in 1970 to only 19 in 1973. These reflect support of the efforts of the council to protect the freedoms of expression and information, albeit only on the condition that employees of the corporation or other program personnel engaged by the corporation refrain from taking a stand or actively engaging in the controversy. The council considers such behavior the improper exploitation of a right to expression primarily intended for program participants external to the corporation (i.e., advocates in one or another respect). With respect to the monopoly media, radio and television, the public's "right to know" may not be utilized by the media professional in his desire to advance his opinion.

Rules of procedure established in 1973 for Sveriges Radio marked an advance of the group-oriented radio and television ideology. When the agreement between the state and Sveriges Radio expires in 1977, a parliamentary commission is expected to be appointed with a mandate to draw up new guidelines. The fact that it will be a parliamentary commission means that the group-oriented ideology will be well represented. But so, too, was the commission that laid the ground for the creation of the radio and television system.

REFERENCES

1. DeFleur, Melvin. *Theories of Mass Communication.* New York: McKay, 1970.
2. *Laws and Basic Regulations.* Stockholm, 1972.
3. Lindblad, Ingemar. "Nagonting om styrning av programverksamheten" ["About the Governing of Programming"], in *The Yearbook of Sveriges Radio 1971.* Stockholm, 1971.
4. ———. *Etermediernas varld* [The World of Radio and TV]. Malmo: Bonniers, 1970.
5. Lundevall, Karl-Erik. "Organisation for inre konkurrens" ["Organization for Internal Competition"], in *Sveriges Radio infor 1970-talet.* Stockholm, 1969.
6. Siebert, F., T. Peterson, and Wilbur Schramm. *Four Theories of the Press.* Urbana, 1956.

CHAPTER 11

Educational Television in Cuba

JORGE WERTHEIN

Cuban television was already well developed by 1959, with seven television channels and several repeater stations. Television programming was commercial, and coverage was limited to urban areas where the population represented potential consumers. Relative to population size, Cuba was ahead of all other Latin American countries in television communications.

Soon after the Revolution, television—as well as all other mass media—was nationalized. Channels and installations were reorganized to obtain broader and more effective coverage. The number of television channels was reduced to three: one nationwide; one covering five of the six provinces; and a third, *Telerebelde*, reaching nearly all of what was formerly Oriente province.

In 1959 the Radio and Television Commission was established under the Ministry of Education. An experimental project in educational television (ETV) was launched for primary school viewing. Teleclasses (with supporting written material) were given in science, mathematics, Spanish, social studies, and music. The teleclasses were broadcast daily, in one subject per day, from 6 to 6:30 p.m. on an open channel. A daily newspaper, the *Prensa Libre* (Free Press) published "Page for Study" every Friday, which outlined the main points to be covered and the activities to be shown by the teleclasses during the following week (1).

The Radio and Television Commission also developed teleclasses for use in junior high schools. The subjects were the same, adjusted to the level of the audience, and the classes were broadcast Monday through Friday from 6:30 to 7 p.m. The supporting written material, together with teacher's guides, was published in *Bohemia*, a widely circulated biweekly magazine, under the title "Lessons for Everybody." The latter included instructional aids for teachers and students, and illustrations and bibliographies relating to each broadcast.

A 1960 survey revealed that the teleclasses had an average audience of 200,000 persons, two-thirds of them teachers and students, and the remaining third adults who had no direct links with the existing educational system.

In 1961 the "Year of Education," the well-known literacy campaign was

131

initiated. Television, complemented by radio and supporting written material, was used intensely in the dissemination of literacy training programs, guiding students in their studies through explanatory classes that were broadcast daily from 2 to 4 p.m. (2). To dramatize the success of the literacy campaign, live coverage of the literacy workers and students was broadcast through television and reinforced by radio, newspapers, and magazines.

With the successful completion of the campaign, attention was shifted to adults who had just learned to read and write, as well as to those who had not yet completed primary schools.

Of the approximately 450,000 adults enrolled in the adult education courses, about 300,000 were reached by teleclasses developed for this level. The teleclasses were attended by many of the adult students in special classrooms, and were broadcast without interruption Monday through Friday from 5:30 to 6 p.m., during the period February 1962 to February 1964. Specialized courses for workers were broadcast on another channel.

In 1966 the National Television System was reorganized, and a Program Department was placed in charge of educational broadcasting. A new half-hour television program called "The Popular Technical Institute," focusing on increasing agricultural productivity, was broadcast three times a week, and was further developed over the next two years. Supporting written material was published in a daily newspaper with national circulation.

The "Schools to the Countryside" program also began in 1966. Some 20,000 junior high school students worked together with teachers and agricultural workers in the province of Camaguey. The program aimed at reducing the differences between city and country, establishing close bonds between the school and daily life, and educating the new generation in and for work. The following year the plan was systematically incorporated into the school program; at fixed times of the year junior high school students throughout Cuba went to the countryside for 45 days (3). Teleclasses were broadcast for the students in each of the courses for grades 7 to 13. The program was designed "to give special review lessons in every subject in the different grades, in a lively way, using film and dramatizations" (4).

The use of ETV was slowly increased and consolidated in 1969. Huge numbers of students had entered the primary level in the early years of the Revolution and this put great strain on the secondary level in 1969. The number of sixth grade graduates requiring schools and teachers was even larger, and the Ministry of Education found itself with insufficient means to meet that demand. Television and radio were urgently needed as systematic support for secondary school education nationwide. Thus began an average of six hours of teleclasses daily. Teleteachers were trained and control was established. In the classroom itself, more advanced students acted as monitors to clarify the material and help students benefit from the classes most advantageously (5).

The system of teleclasses has been coordinated by teams of specialists and technical aides at the Ministry of Education and the Cuban Broadcasting Institute (ICR), and has developed in close association with secondary school teachers. The Ministry of Education provided lesson plans, teachers, monitors, and control of educational content; the ICR provided writers, directors, script people, and special equipment and trained personnel in technical areas. Students, first in the classrooms, then in the countryside, and then in workshops, received teleclasses after the installation of 12,000 sets.

During the First National Congress on Education and Culture held in 1971, it was recommended that:

The mass media should help in education: the press, radio, television, and cinema can dedicate part of their resources to literacy campaigns, classes on TV, etc. The mass media should inform, educate, guide, and unite the people.

The First National Forum on Educational Television held in 1973 recommended that television should be used as a massive means of carrying out the pedagogical principles of the Revolution and that ETV programming should contribute permanently and systematically to the pedagogical, ideological, and political training of students.

At present ETV covers a small part of the junior high and pre-university educational system (grades 7 to 13). Twelve teleclasses per week are broadcast at that level, for a total of four hours. Seven teleclasses for teacher training are broadcast a week, for a total of three hours. ETV also covers the university level with programs created by students and professors, four per week for a total of two hours.

Undoubtedly, ETV has been encouraged in Cuba, but unlike its use in other underdeveloped countries, it has been closely coordinated with the educational system. ETV will remain one of the important aspects of the educational transformation of Cuba and, as Roberto Solís, Director of Educational Programs, stated,

The use of television in teaching is fundamental to our aim of achieving a steady improvement in education in our schools. It will also be indispensable for teaching at other levels, such as technical training, linked with a determined effort to raise the general cultural level and provide greater opportunities for everyone.

REFERENCES

1. Jimenez, Jesús García. *Televisión Educativa para América Latina.* Mexico: Editorial Porrua S.A., 1970.
2. Carnoy, Martin, and Jorge Werthein. "Cuba: Economic Change and Educational Reform, 1955–1974," Report to the World Bank, September 1975.
3. Solís, Roberto. "Educational Television in Cuba," *Educational Television International, 4,* 2 (June 1970).
4. Cuban Broadcasting Institute Internal Report, Cuba, November 1976.

CHAPTER 12

Mass Media Revolution
in Peru

HELI E. de SAGASTI PERRETT

The National System of Information, created by Peru's Revolutionary Government of the Armed Forces on March 5, 1974, represented a reorganization and centralization of the government's activities in the area of mass communications. As such, it was a culminating step in a process of interaction between political and communication systems in Peru, a process that had increased in momentum over the preceding nearly five-and-a-half years. Several key policy decisions between 1968 and 1974 reflect a developing view of the important role assigned to press, radio, television, and film, and the government's own part in ensuring that the media adequately fulfilled that role. These show one developing country defining and attempting to regulate and change the very nature of the symbolic environment presented by the media from an environment that potentially threatened the government's goals of transformation in other areas of national life, to one which would play a supportive, and possibly a leading, role in such transformations.

Revolution, as defined by the Revolutionary Government of the Armed Forces of Peru, is seen as a peaceful process of planned and legislated changes in economic, social, and cultural structures. The rationale for such transformation existed in the traditional poverty of the masses in Peru and the wealth and power of the elite. Government spokesmen emphasized that such internal symptoms of underdevelopment and domination were intimately related to the external condition of Peru's economic dependence and the associated social and cultural dimensions of such dependence. National institutions—including the mass media—were seen as perpetuating and maintaining inhumane inequalities.

"Revolution," then, came to signify a continued process of change that would result in an independent nation undergoing an accelerated process of development and where the large mass of the people came to have improved access to economic benefits and power. The impetus and direction of such changes would come from above, from the Revolutionary Government and the technocrats who advised it, but the mass of the people would collaborate in bringing them about.

This political philosophy motivated and directed changes in key areas of national activity in the first five years of the Revolution. Major laws were passed that were directed toward the transformation of education, industry, agriculture, and mining. The successful implementation of such changes required new attitudes and behavior patterns on the part of the Peruvian people. Often new values and new skills were needed. A new social and economic reality thus called for a new symbolic reality. It required mass media to cooperate in the provision of a supportive atmosphere for change. The result was a growing definition of the importance of mass media's task in these planned transformations: It would help in the creation of the cooperative, creative, nationalistic and humane "New Peruvian Man" who would help bring about the new society and would live in it.

When the mass media itself proved slow in accepting its new role, increasing political pressure was exerted on it to change.

MASS COMMUNICATION BEFORE THE REVOLUTION

When the Revolutionary Government of the Armed Forces came into power in Peru in 1968, it inherited a system of mass communications in which the press was reasonably well developed, radio had existed almost 50 years, television had existed about 10 years, and a struggling national film industry dated back approximately 30 years. It also inherited a system of media functioning that was essentially based on a capitalist model and was considered unsuitable to the new government's purposes.

As they existed at the time, these media were neither nationalistic nor development-oriented. The symbolic world was largely an imported world that showed assumptions, points of view, and images that threatened the government's political goals. The media's role in planned nonformal education was limited, and any educational effect it did have was likely to be neutralized by contradictions in the rest of the system.

Statements by government officials and change-oriented thinkers that were elaborated in the official communication channels illustrate the Revolutionary Government's dissatisfaction with the media. Such criticisms of the prerevolutionary control and operation of the mass media fell into six main categories:

1. The mass media were largely in private hands.

   • Of some 222 existing radio stations the state controlled five.

- Of 19 television stations the state controlled one.

- There was only one official newspaper.

2. The privately owned media were not distributed among the people; instead, a large proportion of the existing mass communication channels was in the hands of family monopolies.

    - For example, five family monopolies controlled between them more than 13 of the 19 television channels and 44 of the nation's 222 radio stations.

3. The national communications enterprises were often related to foreign interests through their banking, industrial, commercial, or agricultural activities.

    - This situation served to preserve Peru's material dependence on "imperialist" nations.

    - It served to protect foreign interests at the cost of national goals.

4. There was a high proportion of nonnational content in the mass media.

    - Such content focused attention on nonnational realities that were likely to be threatening to national goals.

    - It served to teach and impose foreign values, ideas, attitudes, and behavior patterns, threatening the national culture.

    - It was of little spiritual or educational value.

    - Its existence limited the development of national talent.

5. The mass media were overloaded with commercial advertising.

    - This advertising largely promoted foreign economic interests rather than national production.

    - It imposed foreign motivations, behavior patterns, and vocabulary.

    - It served to create false necessities, promoting unnecessary consumption.

6. The mass media did not serve the educational needs of the nation.

    - They had little to offer in terms of educational or cultural content.

    - The content they did transmit sometimes threatened the achievements of other educational institutions.

These criticisms provided the often-reiterated argument for change and the official rationale for increasing government intervention in the operation of the mass communication system.

MASS COMMUNICATION SINCE THE REVOLUTION

A series of government decisions made between October 1968 and February 1974 were critical for the control and operation of Peru's mass media.

In terms of the press (and to the extent that these applied to radio and television) there was the *Statute of Freedom of Press* and the establishment of state monopoly of newspaper importation. For radio and television the *General Law of Telecommunications,* which established norms for radio and television programs and publicity, and the government's consolidation of its control over television program production were most critical. Film was to be regulated by the 1972 *Law of Promotion of the Cinematographic Industry.*

The Press

The Statute of Freedom of Press of December 1969 and the associated Rules and Regulations of the Statute of Freedom of Press of January 1970 elaborated the general conditions under which newspapers and related periodical publications could be published under the Revolutionary Government and the legal limitations of freedom of expression. These injunctions on liberty of expression also applied to the editorial or informational programming of radio and television.

The Statute and Rules and Regulations are significant as an early embodiment of the Peruvian government's thinking about the relationship between political and mass communication processes, about nationalism, and about the freedom of the media. An educational role for the media was not as yet emphasized.

At this stage the government did not increase its role as impresario in the communications field. It did, however, define a part for the press to play in the political process both in terms of what it must and must not do.

Information from the "national public sector" was to be supplied only by its responsible organizations (Article 4).

Punishments were listed for the publication of official secret documents, editorials, articles, or stories that might be considered threatening to the "Integral Security of the State and the National Defense." Also punishable was the publication of any information that would be considered an attempt against the monetary or economic stability of the country (Article 27). Yet the press had to give immediate and prominent publication to any Official Communications from the "Power of the State." Infractions were punishable (Article 26).

The government's concern for nationalism in the media was reflected in its restriction against foreign ownership of the press. The press that was already privately owned was left in private hands, under the condition that the individuals involved would be Peruvians, resident in Peru (Article 10).

Freedom of expression was defined by the Statute as subject to the law. In understanding this early government attitude toward freedom and responsibility, two facts are significant: the right of freedom of expression as defined in the Peruvian Constitution (Article 63) and the activity of the Peruvian press in the first year of the new government not only to withhold support for government policies, such as those aimed at transformations in mining and agriculture, but sometimes to criticize openly acts such as the nationalization of the Internal Petroleum Company interests. The Statute itself refers to cases of "slanderous defamation" that had been occurring in the name of liberty of the press (1, p. 8).

The result was that freedom of expression was defined as existing within the limits established by the law. Such limitations were "respect for the law, the truth and the moral, the exigencies of the Integral Security of the State and the National Defense, as well as the safeguarding of personal and family intimacy and honor" (Article 2). Subsequent criticisms pointed out the wide range of interpretation left by the terminology of the Statute and its by-laws.

With respect to enforcement of the legal limitations on liberty of expression, the law clearly stated that prior censorship would not exist (Article 3), from which official information was excepted (by Articles 4 and 26). For the most part what was expected was self-regulation on the part of the media, with the press showing a responsibility to the policy goals of the government and not threatening the stability of the political system. Should such controls fail, the government, through the Statute and associated Rules and Regulations, had set up a list of infractions and their punishment, by fine or imprisonment, usually of the director of the publication or of the author of the offending article (Article 27).

In November 1971 the Peruvian government's potential for leverage on the press was enlarged. Three closely connected events served to place newsprint in the hands of a state monopoly. The creation by law of the National Enterprise of Industrial Commercialization (ENCI) reserved for the state the commercialization of those industrial products that were fundamental to the nation's economic activities. Another law reserved for the state the importation of products that were fundamental. Finally, a Supreme Decree reserved for the state the exclusive importation of newsprint (not produced in quantity in Peru), which placed a monopoly over this product in the hands of ENCI.

The reaction on the part of some of the Peruvian newspapers clearly demonstrated that they saw these laws reflect a new turn in government thinking about freedom of expression. The potential of such legislation in terms of economic leverage on newspapers is indeed obvious: Newsprint control has been a measure frequently used around the world to establish government control of the private press. However, in the first years of the Revolutionary Government's power there exist no known cases of their actual use of this leverage. While newspapers in other parts of the world suffered from the effects of the paper shortage, no Peruvian newspaper was prevented from publishing because of a lack of this basic product.

Radio and Television

The General Law of Telecommunications of November 1971 was a long-awaited measure which had been anticipated by considerable expectation and speculation. It had been preceded by a campaign on the part of some of the media against government control. This law embodies the Revolutionary Government's thinking at the time about control and operation of radio and television. (It also treats other telecommunication services.) Like the Statute of Freedom of Press, it came about as a direct consequence of dissatisfaction with the past performance of radio and television.

The "Considerations" which precede the articles of this law clearly outline the government's view of the important task of these media in the revolutionary process and the role of the state as key planner and impresario in ensuring that they fulfill that task. The substance of arguments for the law follows:

1.   There should exist norms in agreement with the general communications policy of the Revolutionary Government in regard to the activities of the media of telecommunications.

2.   Telecommunications should help promote the socioeconomic development of the country.

3.   The existing capitalistic nature of the mass media in Peru did not allow the achievement of the Revolution's educational and cultural goals.

4.   It is the "duty of the State, for reasons of national security and social interest, to orient, control and supervise the services of telecommunications in all their aspects, when signals are generated in the national territory" (2, p. 9).

5.   It is necessary to assure the planned development of telecommunications.

6.   The telecommunications worker should share in benefits.

The Telecommunications Law was in many ways a more extreme step than the Statute had been, but it reflected some of the same tendencies. Here we discuss the importance of the law for radio and television in terms of the Peruvian Revolutionary Government's approach to state control, nationalism, freedom of expression, and the educational task of the media.

The General Law of Telecommunications strengthens the state's control and power of intervention in radio and television's activity either through direct managerial action or through its legal-bureaucratic-military functions (Ministries and the United Command of the Armed Forces, for example).

The law created a third kind of communications enterprise, the "Associated State Enterprise," in which private interests were associated with state ownership, to be expropriated in the case of commercial television in a minimum of 51 percent and in the case of commercial radio in a minimum of 25 percent. The only kind of television enterprises permitted were the Associated State Enterprises and public enterprises. For radio, Associated State Enterprises and "public enterprises" were joined by private enterprises (Article 16).

Also evident was a concern for a wider distribution of privately controlled radio and television, restricting monopoly control (Article 17). Thus private property in the telecommunications area, while limited, was not completely destroyed, in harmony with the general political philosophy and industrial policy of the Revolutionary Government.

Although this law strengthened the position of the state in radio and television and underlined its role as a key planning body, complete state control was not established. Furthermore, much of the actual mechanics of state control, orientation, and supervision were left unspecified by the law, possibly assumed to operate through normal industrial relations.

The state control of radio and television was justified by the Revolutionary Government for reasons of "national security" and because they are "media of massive education" (Article 15).

In accord with the general nationalistic stand of the Revolutionary Government of Peru and with the Statute, the General Law of Telecommunications further emphasized removal of foreign influences from mass communication processes.

Peruvian nationality and a minimum residence on national territory were made a prerequisite for exploitation of radio and television services by private individuals (Article 41). Peruvian nationality was also made a prerequisite for almost all radio and television professionals, with very limited foreign participation only under specifically stated conditions.

The law limited the percentage of foreign produced programs (up to 40 percent) excluding programs of educational, scientific, cultural, or sporting interest from this percentage limitation (Article 22). All commercial publicity is to be nationally produced. The actual percentage of publicity allowed is also defined (Article 19).

The law also defines some restrictions on freedom of expression in mass communication through radio and television in addition to those already defined by the Statue of Freedom of Press where this applied to radio and television.

Use of telecommunications media "against the security of the State, the public order, morality and good habits" (Article 3) was prohibited. As in the Statute, these legal limitations are broadly defined and thus can potentially be interpreted in accord with political convenience.

In the case of war of "national emergency as declared by the Executive Power," the United Command of the Armed Forces would take direct and immediate control of the telecommunications services. In the case of regional or local emergency, such control would be taken by the Ministry of Transport and Communications in coordination with the former executive body (Article 7).

All radio and television stations were obligated by law to transmit "messages of national interest" so defined by the Executive Power (Article 20). The obligatory transmission of Official Communications had already been defined by the earlier press Statute.

The General Law of Telecommunications also emphasized the state-guided educational task of radio and television in the revolutionary process, although pure entertainment was not forbidden. Sixty minutes daily of each station's time was to be available to the state for cultural and educational programs created or supervised by the Ministry of Education (Article 21).

The state assumed indirect control of all educational broadcasting because all educational programs were subject to the approval and control of the Ministry of Education. All "educational" radio or television stations were obligated to present "educational programs of social interest" in agreement with the directives of the Ministry of Education.

Thus the General Law of Telecommunications stressed the role of the Revolutionary Government of the Armed Forces as a key planner of mass communication processes in radio and television and also as an impresario (associated with private interests) in this area of communications.

Although through the General Law of Telecommunications the Revolutionary Government had taken an active role in the planning of radio and television operation, in one sense the law was an unfinished formulation. Although it stated that the content of programs and publicity would have to be in agreement with the norms set up by the Ministry of Education, it did not specify such norms. The Supreme Decrees No. 05-Ed/72 and No. 06-Ed/72 filled this gap in the planning of radio and television content. According to official statements, these Decrees were to contribute to the creation of "a new Peruvian man within a more just and humane society." Their orienting principle was the Revolution's increased emphasis on, and enlarged vision of, the process of education. The General Law of Education, which had been passed between the time the Telecommunications Law was enacted and the stipulation of these norms, had presented a reform of the whole existing national educational system, placing emphasis on learning outside the schoolroom. In this task the mass media were seen as playing an important role (1).

In spite of the declared emphasis on education, the general view of the function of mass communication through radio and television programming was in terms of information, education, culture, and healthy recreation. Leisure time was to contribute to the "integral perfection" of the Peruvian people. The overall tone of the norms was that of humanism and nationalism, with a general orientation toward the limitation of potentially negative influences of program content (especially those of violence and sex). Special attention was paid to police news, quiz programs, and children's programs in an attempt to increase their positive contribution to educational processes. No particular type of program was forbidden expressly by law, although some of the norms were later used as arguments to eliminate or restrict certain types of programming.

The norms for publicity in radio and television (which, according to the General Law of Telecommunications, had now to be entirely produced in Peru) were based on the same considerations as the norms of programming. Again the overall tone was set in terms of human values; nationalism; and to a lesser extent than in the case of the norms for programming, on the role of content in the educational process. There was also a stress on commercial ethics, on the promotion of national production, and on the media not encouraging unnecessary consumption.

The government did not attempt to change the essentially capitalistic role of publicity in the mass media. It tried through the norms to reorient the content to bring it more into accord with the political philosophy and its goal of structural changes.

The importance of the norms was not so much in strengthening of state control in radio and television (which the General Law of Telecommunications had already done) but in showing how the government defined and expected to ensure an *adequate content* for radio and television. Such content was *not* left to the responsibility of media patrons or management but was to exist under state control, orientation, and supervision. Content that was "adequate" would be national, humanistic, and education-oriented—that is, content that would encourage the changes in values, attitudes, and behavior patterns so essential for the success of the desired structural changes of the Revolution. The emphasis was on radio and television's role in reeducation of adults and particularly on the "revolutionary" education of the new generation.

With the enactment of the General Law of Telecommunications, the norms for radio and television programming and publicity, and with the Revolutionary Government in a controlling position, changes in radio and television message content were expected to become visible. However, as the periods of grace established by law (90 days for programming and 60 days for publicity) expired, very little had changed. Except for increased political content, such as speeches by government officials and propaganda for policy objectives such as literacy, agrarian reform, reevaluation of women, and so on, the radio and television messages remained almost as nonnational, alienating and frivolous, as before. Even the so-called "national" programs were sometimes not completely national either in origin or in the behavior and value patterns they presented. The lack of changes underlined by national intellectuals and social critics came also to be officially acknowledged in statements by government leaders.

The question asked was why, when in theory everything should have changed, in practice scarcely anything had changed. Instead of reflecting a broadcasting revolution that would help and encourage changes in other areas of national life, mass communication messages continued to threaten their success. What was the cause? Who was operating a "counterrevolution" through mass communication when theoretically this was now impossible?

Attention soon came to focus on the production of television programs. Although the government's General Law of Telecommunications and complementary norms had ensured its control and regulation of television diffusion, the lack of adequate state-controlled facilities for the production of television programs threaten the effectiveness of such measures.

The outcome of such thinking was the creation of the Associated State Enterprise of Audiovisual Production of Peru (TELECENTRO) on January 31, 1974. TELECENTRO was another mixed enterprise in the mass communication field with a 66 percent ownership of shares by the state.

This new measure, through which the Revolutionary Government consolidated its role in the mass communication field, was presented by the government as a measure in accord with general government policy objectives in this area and a response to the necessity of state control of television programming—a measure to bring about a real change in Peruvian television.

Some of the general objectives to be reached through this policy were to:

1. Increase the percentage of national programming
2. Increase the general emphasis on education and information in television, although not to eliminate entertainment altogether
3. Give television programming a more nationalistic orientation
4. Give Peruvian artists more direct participation in Peruvian television
5. Obtain better planning of television time in the two main channels so that programming be "complementary"
6. Give the Peruvian public in general a more active role in televised mass communication processes

Film

Although film production—a few producers struggling against innumerable financial and technical odds and with no established distribution channels—

had existed in Peru for many years, before 1968 it was virtually nonexistent as an industry. The Revolutionary Government attempted to rectify this situation through the *Law of Promotion of the Cinematographic Industry*. The law, unlike many cinematographic industry promotion laws of other countries, applies not only to full-length film, but to all kinds of film production.

The promotion of the national film industry was argued in dual terms: the educational and cultural role of film and the general industrial development of the country.

The law is oriented toward developing a national film industry of high technical quality that can compete with foreign films on the national market and eventually open new markets outside Peru. Such national cinematography was defined as the use of national directors, artists, producers, and technicians; filming principally on national territory; use of a national script and national languages; and the preservation of national cultural values. So that such production could be developed, financial incentives were established. Support was provided for distribution of films that complied with the criteria of nationalism; had a high cultural, social, and artistic value; and met acceptable technical standards. An obligatory system was established.

The governing body placed in charge of the promotion of the national film industry and the selection of the qualifying films was the Cinematographic Promotion Commission, set up by this law.

However, in the first five years of the power of the Revolutionary Government of the Armed Forces in Peru, its thinking about film showed some general differences from expressed views of the role of the press or broadcasting. The government adopted a relatively passive position except in its encouragement of a national film industry. Otherwise it left film to operate as it had in the prerevolutionary years, with very few limitations or restrictions and without a clear definition of film's educational, cultural, or political role. Censorship of film was minimal. At this time the Board of Supervision of Films, an autonomous body created in 1947, continued to classify and censor films and fix their hours of exhibition, much as it had done before 1968. The declared policy of the board was not to cut scenes, although the board was authorized to do so by law. In its role of prohibitor of films for exhibition in Peru, it vetoed only a small percentage in these years.

Although no major changes in the operation of film censorship were legislated between 1968 and 1974, there were indications that the Peruvian government felt film policy did not reflect the desired structural transformations or the newly stressed educational role of the mass media. Thus, beginning with the nomination of a commission to investigate a new censorship law, a process was set in motion to plan future changes.

The first few years of power of the Revolutionary Government of the

Armed Forces of Peru established an important trend in the mass communications area. As the urgency of mass media's task of support in the implementation of planned and legislated changes in other areas of national life increased, change in the media themselves came to be seen as imperative. When the media showed their resistance to desired changes, the government assumed for itself the right of an increasingly active role in defining and ensuring a "revolutionary" and socially responsible media. As a result, the press; radio and television; and to a lesser extent, film, all received political attention. There was a marked growth in government planning and management of mass information systems over the years.

In the case of the press, emphasis was placed on a responsible definition of liberty of expression, while leaving it to operate in private hands but with potential government, economic, and legislative leverage available. In television, and to a lesser extent in radio, the government saw itself more in an impresario role in both production and diffusion. It also defined itself as indirectly responsible for control, supervision, and orientation of program and publicity content. Film does not seem to have been considered so important as press, radio, or television and was originally dealt with as a national industry that needed to be developed, only later coming to be defined more in relation to educational, cultural, and political goals. In these information-planning activities the Revolutionary Government of the Armed Forces of Peru demonstrated its realization of an important fact that some other developing countries have forgotten: For changes to be successfully implemented in other areas of national life, the mass media have to cooperate.

REFERENCES

1. Benevides Correa, Alfonso. *La Verdadera Libertad de Pressa.* Lima: Oficina Nacional de Informacion, 1970.
2. *Ley General de Telecommicaciones, No. 19020.* Lima: 1971.

CHAPTER 13

Elite Control and Challenge in Changing India

KUSUM SINGH

The trouble of our times is that we have forgotten to say "no" to injustice.
Jitendra Singh, *Seminar* (January 1969)

The Indian power structure consists of a loose industrialist-landowner-politician-executive alliance that builds on and partially supersedes the older caste system. Many leaders of this alliance are highly ambivalent toward the officially proclaimed goal of socialism.

On the whole, the development of the past two decades has been astonishingly slow, and whatever economic development has occurred has been achieved at the expense of the poor (1). Illiteracy is still near 72 percent. The persistent tendency to overinvest in higher education and to underinvest in mass education adversely affects both equity and long-run growth. Not only does the educational system continue to serve the interests of the upper and the middle classes, but industrial development is geared to providing consumption goods for these strata. Emphasis on economic growth through industrialization and urbanization has led to increasing dependence on foreign aid which in turn has tended to become self-perpetuating.

Intellectuals play a key role as intermediates and communication links between the rulers at the top and the masses at the bottom. The bureaucratized modern state must use ideology, and for this it needs intellectuals to create bonds of loyalty; they are specialists in communication, and through their use of mass media they are in a position to influence elite and nonelite alike.

Indian society is not a "mass" society in the Western sense. Newspapers, radio, and television are essentially oriented to an elite so that the term *mass media* hardly applies. The rural masses still pursue a traditional communication network based upon personal relations, while the educated urban elite communicate through the media. There is also a cleavage between communal groups so that within a religion, tribe, or culture there is an almost autonomous communication system whose isolation is reinforced by regional or linguistic distinctiveness. The point is that there is no single system of communication in India.

Absence of a common language creates linguistic barriers and makes unification of culture infinitely complex. There are 14 major languages and some 800 dialects, and linguistic frontiers do not correspond to state boundaries— several languages may be spoken in any one state or even within a village.

Considerable social and political havoc has resulted from the debate over using Hindi as the national language, and even today it arouses such strong sentiments that any rational solution has eluded the government. There has never been a common language the elite share with the people. Previously not only was there a gulf between written and spoken language, but knowledge itself was jealously guarded in an esoteric language by the brahmanical intelligentsia in a caste-conscious society. Not until the British rule were the elite driven by necessity to find a common language in their effort to oust the British from India. Even after the British departure the elite needed a medium of communication to enhance their control across the country.

Ironically, English was the only cultural medium the elite shared, but it happened to be the language of the British rulers. This perpetuated the schism between the Indian elite and the people. Gandhi's pragmatic solution was to develop Hindustani, a combination of Hindi and Urdu, which was simple enough to be understood by a peasant. Unfortunately, Hindustani survived only as long as Gandhi; the drive for "pure" Hindi is rapidly turning the national language into something as unintelligible to the mass of the people as English has always been.

The manner in which Jawaharlal Nehru and Mahatma Gandhi tackled the problem of communication showed remarkable understanding of the Indian situation. At a time when radio and television were not available to the freedom fighters and newspapers were of little use to the many illiterates, Gandhi succeeded in identifying himself with the common people and spoke a language that was so authentically Indian that Nehru remarked:

. . . some of Gandhi's phrases sometimes jarred upon me—thus his frequent reference to Rama Raj as a golden age which was to return. But I was powerless to intervene, and I consoled myself with the thought that Gandhiji used the words because they were well known and understood by the masses. He had an amazing knack of reaching the hearts of the people (11).

Nehru himself was more ambivalent toward the masses. He confessed to being deeply moved by the people's affection but at the same time wished to escape from them. His ability to sway the crowd aroused the autocrat in him and partially satisfied his "will to power." And it may have created the notion among the elite that ordinary men and women would voluntarily submit to the power and influence of so-called superior intelligence.

PRESS

The Indian press played a significant role during the freedom movement, and even today it is the most important forum for the expression of public opinion. According to Gandhi, the objectives of the press should be: ". . . to understand the popular feeling and give expression to it; another is to arouse among the people certain desirable sentiments; the third is fearlessly to expose popular defects." The press in India was until recently the only medium not under the direct control of government and in a position to evaluate critically the implications of national policies.

The relations between the private press, the government, and business leaders clearly highlight the problem of control versus freedom. The greatest threats to the freedom of the press come not only from the restrictions imposed by the government but also from a hardening of the ownership pattern which results in tighter control and less freedom for journalists. In 1954 the first Press Commission reported as the most obvious instance of bias that the bulk of newspaper owners and publishers were persons who believed strongly in the institution of private property. Consequently, they encouraged expression of views and news that favored the status quo while censoring contrary views and news. The production of a modern newspaper requires such a large investment of capital that the enterprise can more easily be taken up by capitalists.

This pattern of ownership continues to be almost the same. The government did attempt to diffuse the ownership of newspapers and its separation from big business, but loopholes remain in the legislative process.

While the English language newspapers have thrived and grown in circulation, the smaller newspapers published in regional languages have been perpetually on the brink of financial ruin. The government's policy has been to support them through advertisements and newsprint subsidies so as to counterbalance the English newspapers which are seen as wielding a "political and social influence in the course of national affairs far in excess of what mere circulation figures might indicate" (10).

National emergency was declared in June 1975, followed by strict press censorship. "I abhor censorship," maintained Indira Gandhi, but she added that it had become necessary because "newspapers were spearheading the campaign against the government and undermining the self-confidence of our people." Before this action, however, the Indian press had been constrained less by Indira Gandhi than by its own editors and reporters. The central problems of India—poverty, hunger, population growth, landlord exploitation, caste conflict—have usually been ignored by the Indian press.

FILM

The film industry in India is an example of both direct and indirect control and perhaps has done the most to generate a revolution of "rising expectations." Moreover, the cinema is the only medium in India that can claim to be truly a "mass medium"; it is believed to be the largest single factor responsible for breaking down the regional and cultural barriers between people of different states. Yet, despite their popularity, films are confined for the most part to urban and semi-urban centers. In 1972 there were only 4700 permanent cinema halls and 2600 touring units (12).

The film industry is privately owned and functions in a highly competitive environment. It presents an interesting cross-section of the country by way of bringing together talent from all its regions. Film plays an important role in India and has an exceptionally powerful hold on the people. Because of a polyglot market Indian sound films are produced in more than a dozen languages, and rarely is a film made without its quota of songs and dances. India is second only to Japan in the number of films produced each year.

Indian theatres are required to exhibit an approved informational film at every show, and because private industry is not interested in documentaries and newsreels, the government has established a large public sector to produce them. In addition to being the chief producer of documentaries, newsreels, and children's films, the government sometimes ventures into feature production, for example, *India '57*, in collaboration with Roberto Rossellini. After Satyajit Ray's fabulous success with his first film *Pather Panchali*, the government instituted a Film Finance Corporation in 1960 to provide financial assistance to film producers.

However, the compulsory screening of short educational films in cities where the audience is literate and reads newspapers is less important than taking them to remote inaccessible villages that do not even have electricity. This is supposed to be done by the audiovisual vans of the central and state information agencies, but how many vans are available or whether they can reach remote villages is not known.

The legal framework within which Indian censorship works has a firm and explicit constitutional base that has given the government censorship powers that are almost impossible to challenge. In 1952 Dr. Keskar, then minister of information and broadcasting, saw himself as custodian of the illiterate masses and defended censorship with these words:

Films in Indian languages are meant for and seen by the mass of the people, most of whom are not educated. . . . Now, the mass in any country is to some extent conventional, has certain prejudices that cannot be helped. An intellectual or educated audience can forgive or even appreciate unconventional themes or ideas put on the screen. The same cannot be said of the bulk of the people. I am afraid this fact is conveniently forgotten. . . . Unfortunately, government cannot forget it because it is elected by the mass of the people and it has to take into consideration their feelings and sentiments.

In other words, strict censorship is defended as the will of the people, although there is no effort to find out what these "feelings and sentiments" are.

The most puzzling aspect of the Indian film industry is that the public sector is extremely centralized, while the private sector is extremely fragmented. More important, the public sector is dependent on the private sector's popularity to reach the mass audience. The film division has, no doubt, produced some remarkable documentaries on development and on the national heritage of India, but the brutal realities of poverty, unemployment, and disease familiar to the people are not shown in the government films.

RADIO

Radio transmission to the general public is provided entirely by All Indian Radio, a public corporation in the Ministry of Information and Broadcasting with headquarters in New Delhi and branches all over the country. According to government figures, radio covers about 70 percent of the country and 80 percent of the population with a medium-wave service (6). Each station broadcasts in the regional language. The News Service Division operates on a national basis, with correspondents at home and abroad and material from the major domestic and foreign news agencies. Because all stations can be operated as a cluster using a telephone hookup, major national events are covered over national networks.

The centralization of authority has made broadcasting a routine function of the state with little opportunity for media professionals to exercise initiative and responsibility. In a country as vast as India—with its many languages, diverse cultural patterns, and distinct regional needs—for a broadcasting system to work under a tight central control with departmental rules and regulations is self-defeating.

The first attempt to establish two-way contact between villagers and planners was the experiment of Radio Rural Forums in 1956 started in Poona in collaboration with UNESCO (8). It was based on the Canadian farm forum project. A radio forum, which is a listening-cum-discussion-cum-action group of village leaders, provides regular feedback reports of decisions and questions of clarification to the broadcaster. It made a promising start and by 1965 the number of forums had increased from 900 to 12,000, but the forums reached only the more advanced rural populations, leaving the others intact. The study on Five-Year Plan Publicity notes: "Certain features of the general composition of membership of the Forums deserve notice. It shows a fairly high preference for the more advanced sections of the village community, with the small farmers, landless cultivators, artisans, craftsmen and women having only a token inactive membership" (7).

TELEVISION

There appears to be no plan for the development of Indian television, which began in 1959. The government has hesitated to act because it is not sure how much of the country's scarce resources can be justifiably committed to television when the potential of a far less expensive medium like radio still remains to be exploited fully. The recent spread of television across the country shows, however, that it is too powerful and exciting an instrument *per se* to be ignored by the ruling elite, especially because it represents a symbol of "modernity," adding prestige to a developing country.

Television requires large investments which cannot be justified without systematic assessment of the widely assumed value of it as an educational medium. According to the government's estimate, the lowest cost of a 19-inch receiver in India is about Rs. 2300/ ($350), which includes taxes but not antenna cost, which is another Rs. 125/. The government claims that production of receivers is keeping pace with the yearly demand—which was said to be around 100,000 in 1974.

Despite claims of turning TV into a genuine mass medium by installing a large number of community sets, the fact remains that there are no provisions for such a scheme in the Fifth Five-Year Plan. The new TV stations in the state capitals, the augmentation of the existing TV station at New Delhi, and a number of relay TV stations more or less exhaust the total amount allotted for TV expansion.

The official estimate of television penetration is 3 percent (Delhi, Bombay, and Srinagar TV stations taken together), which is expected to rise to 16.8 percent after the implementation of all the Fourth Plan TV projects. But such "coverage" means simply that the signal is available; it by no means guarantees either the availability of programs or of receivers. Most of the interest and concern among the government officials, technicians, and scientists ("soft planners" like media professionals do not usually participate in high-level decision-making) focuses on the technicalities and feasibility of TV expansion and development.

Because the Indian government was unable to make a large investment for television installation and training of technical staff, it sought to collaborate with the United Nations and the United States. In 1967 an Experimental Satellite Communications Earth Station (ESCES) at Ahmedabad was completed with help from the International Telecommunications Union and the United Nations Special Fund. In the first phase of a National Satellite Communication (NASCOM) project, India collaborated with NASA of the United States and used its ATS-F Satellite to beam educational-instructional TV programs to approximately 5000 villages in different parts of the country for a period of about one year. The government plans to follow with a full scale nationwide system that will cover all of India's 570,000 villages by means of a domestic satellite system (13).

The India-US TV satellite broadcast experiment is the first to provide direct television broadcasting from a satellite into small village receivers without the need for relay stations on the ground (4). However, the satellite carries one national program instead of regional programs in different languages; again, the main objective of reaching the people is lost.

DEVELOPMENT AND ELITISM

The operational dynamics of India's communications institutions are related to the nature and structure of elitism; communication problems, therefore, reflect the complexity of India's sociopolitical system, which appears to be paralyzed between elements in the government demanding "socialism" and those urging the adoption of the "western model" by transplanting institutions and techniques from developed countries. The majority of the "westernized" intellectuals have gained great authority and prestige over the indigenous classes. Their preoccupation with professionalization has further alienated the intellectual elite from their own country.

The consequences of this state of affairs have seriously distorted the growth of mass communications in India. There is a great lag between the Indian demands on the mass media and the capacity of the mass media to meet them. The needs and compulsions of national development have provided new opportunities for the growth of the media, but the biases of the elite hamper creative utilization of the new opportunities. The elite allegiance to "modernity" has led to a failure to harness traditional channels of communication more directly, while mass media are still developing. There is an excess of talent in highly technical and specialized spheres, while folk forms and drama are unappreciated and relegated to an inferior status. Distribution of scarce resources among the communications media is often based on the priorities of professionalization, which may conflict with genuine needs of the country. Myrdal rightly points out:

The need in underdeveloped countries is not primarily for a large number of high-flown statistical theoreticians, which might seem beyond what can be rapidly provided. What is needed is well-trained persons who have substantive knowledge about conditions in underdeveloped countries and the critical ability to formulate questions about the material that are adequate to social reality in these countries. They should know how to direct their observations effectively and in addition have an elementary knowledge of sampling techniques and a few other simple statistical methods (9).

But the Indian system works by "benevolence and tokenism" and is likely to resist any shift of mass media investments from developed urban areas to rural underdeveloped ones. Objections would be raised to the so-called lowering of professional standards and technical excellence which have for so long been carefully nurtured to cater to sophisticated audiences in the cities.

However, the problems of mass communication apply equally to other institutions in the country. India cannot ignore modern techniques, but at the same time there are enormous possibilities for creating indigenous methods and techniques that can be mastered and improved upon by persons without a high level of training. At present even the small number of highly qualified persons are frustrated by the inadequate utilization of their skills. To attempt modernization at the intermediate level of technology in the present stage of development is neither feasible nor desirable; therefore, the already qualified technicians should be given an incentive to open new small units in rural areas with the active participation of the local people. Again this depends on how determined the government is to achieve self-reliance in investment, foreign exchange, and technology.

Rural participation of over 80 percent of the population is, perhaps, far more significant to national development than all the "modernization" and development that has been taking place in the large urban centers. Landowners in the villages, moneylenders, and local officials present a formidable combination of power and prestige—and they are often the most reactionary elements in national life. They use development as a way of enhancing their own authority and ensuring people's dependence; more important, they cannot be ignored by the ruling urban elite because of their political power in delivering the rural vote. It is surprising, indeed, how hard some of the *panchayat pradhan* (council presidents) work to isolate the poor from "distinguished" visitors. In any case, the "outsider"—who is usually a government official—is not eager to make direct contact with the people, but is merely interested in passing on information to an "authority" so that he may leave the village as fast as he can and return to the shelter of his desk job in the city.

The rural elite decide what kind of information is to be disseminated in the villages and what kind is to be suppressed; even community radio sets have not radically changed the information flow because the government radio is usually in the courtyard of a member of the *panchayat* (village council). News travels faster but the rural elite are still the first to have it. To reach this rural population the government must allow the mass production of inexpensive radio sets so that even an ordinary farmer could afford to buy one to listen in his own home with his family and friends. The development of the transistor may change the power structure in the villages and transform old communications patterns.

The mass media can do little unless "hooked into" that interpersonal network that enables people to bypass the traditional rural elite. In the Indian villages organized pressure from below is particularly lacking and therefore the role of the "intermediaries" is of some significance. There have been cases of many Naxalite revolutionaries (intellectuals and young students mostly from well-to-do families) who went out into the villages and worked and lived with the poor. Little known and less appreciated were the efforts of young media professionals who organized a cooperative and designed television courses for exploited workers in Uttar Pradesh.

The ruling elite will not risk disturbing the status quo by inquiring too deeply into what communication is doing to achieve national goals. Therefore, official egalitarian ideals result in greater social and economic disparities; pretending to legislate large-scale institutional reforms, but not implementing them, has bred deep cynicism, distrust, and uncertainty among the people about what actually comprises the established law. This has created further resistance to development.

Apparently no developing country with limited resources can afford to give complete freedom to its mass media; rather, the aim is to define areas in which the media can operate economically and efficiently. A problem arises when strict control is justified on the ground that a transitional society like India's cannot indulge in the luxury of criticism because it endangers national solidarity and integrity. The media professionals are therefore carefully instructed to structure content according to what the political elite consider the most effective way of meeting the national goals. Therefore, the mass media are controlled not simply by written law or decree, but by the unwritten constraints of a small political bureaucracy.

The elite argue that because broadcasting makes large demands on public revenue, government control is essential. As a result, the Director General of All India Radio is constantly queried on the most trivial matters and is at the beck and call of the Minister of Information and Broadcasting. As we move down the hierarchy from the DG to deputy DGs and then to the station directors, the standardization and regimentation is even more apparent; the trappings of power and the "mystique of authority" impel creative persons to function as bureaucrats rather than as media professionals. Greater emphasis on technical and managerial skills has led to dependence on administrative plans and to maneuvering for a higher status in the hierarchy of the all-powerful, domineering administrative service.

PLANNING

No communication strategy can succeed without defining political and economic goals explicitly and implicitly. Democratic planning under a parliamentary democracy has been defined as "democratic persuasion to bring about participation and cooperation of all; democratic planning—involving all groups from the villages to the National Government—at all levels; and the use and strengthening of democratic institutions to administer and speed development" (5). My analysis indicates that development planning of the past two decades is characterized by centralized planning based on the assumption that because the intellectual elite possess knowledge and expertise, they should devise effective strategies for the illiterate masses. The critical issue here is that the Indian mass media have little chance of growth unless there is radical structural change in the administrative system as well as a change in the values and attitudes of those who run the media. This is evident from the inadequate appreciation of the creative role of communication media in national programs such as education, family planning, and farming.

Indeed, the intellectual elite in India have adopted a technological fetishism and believe that more technologically sophisticated media will solve problems such as agricultural underproduction and overpopulation. The technological view of birth control—as expressed by the Khanna Study (14), for example—glibly assumes that the need for population control is self-evident; therefore, if the Indian people are properly "motivated" and given access to contraceptives, the problem will be solved. Little effort is wasted on acquiring feedback to determine how people view their own life in terms of family size. And all this takes place in a country where children are the only security in the absence of old-age pensions or unemployment insurance.

In the highly personalized culture of India face-to-face communication is particularly important. No other formula or plan can account for the vast variety of human factors in different villages spread over the country. To use technical assistance in major cities to train professional personnel is one thing, but quite another to absorb such personnel at the village level. Working at the village level requires special skills for which the media professionals are not trained. Even more important, they require special incentives to work in the villages. Instead, they often experience official pressure for quick results which may compel them to resort to expedient methods (use of power or show of authority), when perhaps a slower method would produce more lasting results with better understanding and good will.

The purpose of this argument is to emphasize some fallacies in repeated statements that failure of many government schemes and programs is due to traditional attitudes, ignorance, illiteracy, poverty, and general apathy on the part of the people. Obviously, the elite need to revise their view of the development process and to change their traditional attitudes toward social and economic stratification; most important of all, development is not only a matter of "stages of growth" but is also related to greater equality in income, health, and other facilities.

Many of the problems of the media intellectuals stem from the relentless bureaucratic culture that persists in India today. They are caught between the conflicting pull of the formal ritualism of the past and the rationalistic methods of the future, resulting in a paralysis of creativity. The media professionals themselves complain that some of the best minds in the country are worn out by administrative and organizational chores, leaving no time or energy for creative work. The assumption seems to be that those with some authority and power must necessarily be the intellectual giants; craving of government recognition is deeply rooted in most intellectuals. Indeed, the government makes a better bureaucrat of an intellectual than it does of a so-called professional bureaucrat or, for that matter, of a politician.

To presume that the media intellectual "chooses" a lifestyle is unrealistic; more often the lifestyle chooses him, and he at best attempts to rationalize his position according to the degree of identification he seeks from it. Not only does he exercise no personal choice, but external pressures create inner conflicts as to his role in society, resulting in ambivalent stands on crucial issues. Because he is not in a position to act on his beliefs, he will fuss over petty matters of form rather than risk being bogged down with substance. Perhaps this is why he fits so well into the bureaucratic culture, where status hierarchy is clearly defined and rigid rules and procedures relieve him of the painful process of making the right decision for the right reason. The easier and safer course is for the media professional to wear the garb of "modernity" and talk in terms of modern technology, attend seminars and international conferences, and expect a logical rise in status as he moves up from radio to television and then to satellite—and remain as far removed from the people as the astronaut is from the earth.

REFERENCES

1. Adelman, Irman, and Cynthia Taft Morris. *Economic Growth and Social Equity in Developing Countries*. Stanford: Stanford University Press, 1973.

2. Barnouw and Krishnaswamy, cited in *Indian Film*. New York and London: Columbia University Press, 1963.

3. Dube, S. C. "Communication, Innovation, and Planned Change in India," in Lerner and Schramm (eds.), *Communication and Change in the Developing Countries*. Honolulu: University of Hawaii, East-West Center, 1967.

4. Frutkin, Arnold W. "Space Communications and the Developing Countries," in Gerbner, Gross, and Melody (eds.), *Communication, Technology and Social Policy.* New York: Wiley, 1973.

5. India Government, The Planning Commission. *The New India—Progress Through Democracy.* New York: Macmillan, 1958.

6. ———, Ministry of Information and Broadcasting. *Radio and Television: Report of the Committee on Broadcasting and Information Media.* New Delhi, 1966.

7. ———, Ministry of Information and Broadcasting. *Report of the Study Team on Five Year Plan Publicity.* Faridabad: Government of India Press, 1965.

8. Mathur J. C., and Paul Neurath. *An Indian Experiment in Radio Farm Forums.* Paris: UNESCO, 1959.

9. Myrdal, Gunner. *The Challenge of World Poverty.* New York: Pantheon Books, 1970.

10. Nair, L. R., cited in "Private Press in National Development: The Indian Example," in Lerner and Schramm (eds.), *Communication and Change in the Developing Countries.* Honolulu: University of Hawaii, East-West Center, 1967.

11. Nehru, Jawaharlal. *Toward Freedom.* New York: John Day, 1941.

12. Taylor, Charles Lewis, and Michael C. Hudson. *World Handbook of Political and Social Indicators,* 2nd ed. New Haven: Yale University Press, 1972.

13. *The Times of India. Directory and Yearbook,* 1972.

14. Wyon, John B., and John E. Gordon. *Population Problems in the Rural Punjab.* Cambridge: Harvard University Press, 1971.

CHAPTER 14

Broadcasting in Malaysia

DONALD L. GUIMARY

Broadcasting in a developing nation, especially one with sizable multiracial and multilingual audiences, can be an awesome task. Such is the task that confronts Malaysia. Its population of more than 11 million is composed of about 47 percent Malays, 34 percent Chinese, 8.5 percent Indians and Pakistanis, with the balance a mixture of other races. Since gaining independence from England in 1957, the Malays have held political power. The Chinese, however, own or control 98 percent of the nation's businesses and industries.

From 1948 to 1960 an "Emergency Period" involved warfare using British troops to combat communist guerillas. Some are still active, especially since the fall of South Vietnam in April 1975.

After the Emergency Period, the new Malay government felt the three races could exist harmoniously. But on May 13, 1969 riots between the Malays and Chinese erupted in which more than 1000 persons were killed. This was a pivotal point for the nation affecting all levels of society. The government adopted policies designed to prevent future conflicts and racial discord. These measures have a significant impact on broadcasting as well as on other mass media.

In 1971 the Malaysian government adopted its Second Malaysian Plan and its New Economic Policy to restructure society both economically and socially. The measures involve the "eradication of poverty irrespective of race and the modernization of rural life." Traditionally the Malays tend to live in rural *kampongs* (hamlets in the jungles) and have not been regarded as economic achievers. The Chinese, however, generally prefer urban living and have the reputation of being both educationally and economically motivated.

To modernize the nation and to bring more Malays into urban areas, the Second Malaysian Plan included having the Malays obtain 30 percent ownership of businesses and industries by 1990. This means that government preference would be given to Malays (at the expense of Chinese and Indians) in terms of employment, scholarships, loans, and so forth. The measures included broadcast programming as well as employment policies at Radio-Television Malaysia (RTM), the government broadcast facility.

The Greater Malay language, Bahasa Malaysia, was designated the national language, and all students are required to pass language examinations at all educational levels. This also applied to government employment policies including RTM. The government adopted a national slogan, *Rukunegara* (Pillars of the nation) which comprises belief in God and loyalty to the King, the nation, the Constitution, to the rule of law, good behavior, and morality. These principles are (or should be) reflected in all broadcast programming.

To prevent criticism the government amended its Sedition Act to prohibit any public discussion in the mass media and in Parliament of four sensitive issues: the special position in society of the Malays, the national language policy, the rights of citizenship, and the special positions of the sultans and the King.

RTM owns and operates all broadcast facilities. The formal objectives of RTM are:

1.   To explain in depth and with widest possible coverage the policies and programs of government to ensure maximum understanding by the public

2.   To stimulate public interest and opinion to achieve changes in line with the requirement of the government

3.   To assist in promoting civic consciousness and fostering the development of Malaysian arts and culture

4.   To provide suitable elements of popular education, general information and entertainment

RADIO PROGRAMMING

There are four domestic radio networks: National, Blue, Green, and Red. In addition, an overseas radio network, Suara Malaysia, broadcasts in Indonesian, English, Mandarin Chinese, Arabic, Thai, and Tagalog (Filipino).

The National Network broadcasts 24 hours a day, seven days a week. Its programming is composed of 57 percent entertainment, 24 percent information and education, 9 percent instructional programs for classroom use, 7 percent news, 3 percent drama. Music and songs for listeners of all races are carefully selected, but all programs are presented in Bahasa Malaysia.

The Blue Network broadcasts 87 hours per week and carries seven news bulletins in English daily. This network also relays news in Bahasa Malaysia from the National Network twice daily. Programming is 15 percent news, 65 percent entertainment, and 20 percent information and education. Radio plays and short stories embody principles of Rukunegara. To encourage the use of the national language the program "Learn a Word a Day" in Bahasa Malaysia is also aired.

The Green Network transmits 94 hours and 20 minutes weekly in Mandarin, Cantonese, Amoy, and Hakka—all Chinese dialects. Its programs consist of 58 percent entertainment, 20 percent news, 11 percent information and 11 percent education.

The Red Network is directed toward the Indian audiences. The main broadcast language is Tamil, although music in other Indian languages such as Telugu, Hindustani, and Malayalam is also carried. The Red Network is on the air 86 hours and 30 minutes per week. Content is 11.6 percent news, 9.4 percent educational, 8 percent information, 68 percent entertainment, and 3 percent "other."

The Overseas Network carries 56 hours per week. Most of the overseas programming is in Indonesian (56 hours); 17½ hours are in English; 14 in Mandarin, seven each in Thai, Arabic, and Tagalog.

TELEVISION

Television service was inaugurated in 1963. Channel 2 began in 1969. TV Malaysia moved into its new headquarters, known as Angkasapuri, on a 33-acre site in Kuala Lumpur in 1969.

Channel 1's programming is mainly designed for the Malay population, with the majority of its broadcasts in Bahasa Malaysia. Slightly more than half of its programs are locally produced; the balance are foreign productions and commercial advertisements.

Programming consists of 53 percent information and (nonclassroom) education, 25 percent entertainment, 13 percent news, and 9 percent drama.

Channel 2 is aimed primarily at the urban audiences. It is on the air 27 hours weekly, and 40 percent of the programs are imported productions. Information and nonclassroom education constitute 48 percent of the total; 46 percent is drama; news is 2.5 percent; and entertainment consumes 3.3 percent.

Television news is offered at 9 p.m. on both channels, RTM's prime time. Channel 1 offers news in only Bahasa Malaysia. Channel 2 presents the news in Tamil, Mandarin, Bahasa Malaysia, and English.

Readers, not commentators, are employed on Television Malaysia, as in England. News items are edited and presented in keeping with Rukunegara. RTM's official booklet states:

In presenting the news and other reports every attempt is made by the staff of the News Division to promote the principles of Rekunegara, the New Economic Policy, and the Second Malaysian Plan. The primary aim is to support efforts to build a united Malaysian nation through goodwill, solidarity and racial harmony.

The general pattern of presentation is to show film clips of the prime minister or some government functionary at an official function. This is then followed by reference to a lesser official. Documentaries or investigative in-depth features are not aired. RTM uses the wire service of Bernama, also a government national news service, which also subscribes to the principles of Rekunegara.

TV Malaysia uses imported television productions primarily from the United States, England, and Japan. A week's schedule for Network 1 (May 27–June 3, 1974) lists the following programs from the United States: "The Magician," "Rin Tin Tin," "Dusty's Trail," "Merrie Melodies," "Wrestling Forum," "Make Room for Daddy," "Partridge Family," "Here's Lucy," "Bonanza," "The Brady Bunch," "The Untamed World," "The Virginian." These programs appear to be easily understood by rural audiences in the kampongs.

Network 2 tends to offer more "sophisticated" programs since this network is aimed at urban audiences. For the same time period the following imported programs were aired: "The Wild, Wild West," "Marcus Welby," "Owen Marshall," "The Bob Newhart Show," "Laramie," "Bewitched," "The Name Game," "Disneyland," "Kreskin," "The Carol Burnett Show," "My Three Sons," "Cannon," "Mannix," "Streets of San Francisco," "Kojak," and "Hawaii 5-0." Some observers believe that TV Malaysia offers such "law and order" programs to emphasize the importance and efficiency of law enforcement activities.

Given the racial diversity of the nation, planning programs to satisfy Malay, Indian, Chinese, and other audiences is undoubtedly a difficult assignment. TV Malaysia receives from 100 to 200 letters per week. One common complaint, printed in the *Sunday Mail* published in Kuala Lumpur, concerned the language issue: "From the Indians and Chinese come requests for more and better films. Why can't TV Malaysia give us more Tamil, Hindi, and Chinese films? Why can't they (RTM) screen the more up-to-date feature films? Why must there be so many interruptions when these films are shown?" (The films are usually shown after 7 p.m. and then interrupted for the Mandarin news at 8 p.m. and at 9 p.m. for the news in Bahasa Malaysia.)

TV Malaysia's policies on programming for its audiences vary with its various audiences. Information Ministry Parliamentary Secretary, Shariff Ahmad, explained, "We are more concerned with the rural areas—in the kampongs, rubber estates and the new villages. These are people whose working day begins at about 5 a.m. or 6 a.m. or earlier. They are also unfortunate in that they lack other recreation amenities. The townsfold can go to a movie or look for entertainment elsewhere. . . . We estimate the rural people go to bed around 9:30 p.m. and the feature films are primarily for them."

Educational television was launched in 1972. ETV telecasts are in Bahasa Malaysia in science, mathematics, civics, geography, and English at both the elementary and secondary schools. Nearly all of the almost 8000 schools have been equipped with television sets. The United Nations Development Project has been instrumental in providing both funds and equipment and personnel for instruction TV. But not all teachers have been adequately prepared for using TV in the classrooms. And in some of the rural areas schools may be equipped with television sets but lack electricity and must depend on portable generators for power.

What can be said of all this? First, Radio-Television Malaysia is probably unique in its multilingual operations. Employees are required to be at least bilingual or in some cases trilingual. Second, RTM is obviously a vehicle used to further government objectives, the most important being racial harmony and nation-building. Third, as a consequence, freedom of expression simply does not exist. With increasing student demonstrations, rumors of rice shortages, occasional racial clashes, the conflict between Malaysia and the Philippines over the Jolo Islands, and the increasing guerilla activities, Malaysia has been described as a tinderbox. Yet none of these events is discussed on Radio-Television Malaysia.

Rukunegara remains the yardstick by which all program content is measured. If Malaysia is able to achieve its goal of national development and racial harmony, the measures might well be worth the effort.

CHAPTER 15

The Price of Progress in Thailand*

DIANA LANCASTER

A monk in a yellow robe climbed into a sermon chair and for three hours sat talking and giggling for the entertainment of about 1000 villagers sitting below him on the concrete floor. A few months later, heralded by vans with loudspeakers, a filmshow drew much the same audience to the triangle of rough grass just outside the same temple compound. On both occasions there was free entertainment which gave pleasure to a mixed audience of young and old, farmer, trader, and professional. But with the impact of the moment, the similarities ended. The sermon stayed alive through the ensuing year in the social life of the small farming community in northern Thailand. Snippets were recalled with laughter whenever groups formed and the tapes I had made were requested over and over again for funeral wakes, housewarmings, and working parties. The film failed to make its point and was quickly forgotten.

Films had prestige in the area, but they were expensive. If they were shown privately for a wedding, an ordination, or a housewarming celebration, the hosts could afford only disjointed, browned snippets, either silent or in foreign languages. Otherwise there were "pay films" twice a week or shows put on by traveling medicine salesmen about three times a month during which the "commercial breaks" were usually longer than the showing period. But the first film I mentioned was a government sponsored show—a full-length color feature as good as a "pay film," with no selling breaks. This analysis, which uses the sermon for contrast, suggests why, despite its initial advantages, a well-produced health propoganda film might have misfired.

*For 18 months between 1970 and 1972, I lived in a village suburb of Chom Thong, Chiengmai, 60 kilometers southeast of Chiengmai city in northern Thailand. My research, funded by the London Social Science Research Council and a grant from the London-Cornell Project, was focused on relationships between local entertainment patterns and social change.

165

Research that concentrates on the fragile and always changing boundary areas where two different systems of lifestyle come into contact is liable to fall between the boundaries of disciplines. The literature is sparse in discussions of entertainment that take into account interaction between specific art forms and their audiences as well as the effects on associated types of entertainment and on the lives of the audience at times not simultaneous with the individual event. Social scientists have concentrated on aspects of community organization; literary critics have analyzed specific art forms; and communications specialists have been concerned with messages and people. One pioneer who attempted to straddle all three sets of relationships was James L. Peacock who, in *Rites of Modernisation,* explored a popular urban theatrical spectacular in the context of social change (in Surabaya, Java). He suggested ways in which this one form of entertainment contributed and generated motifs by which the audience guided themselves through a transition period from a rural community orientation towards an urban, nationalistic, and "progressive" attitude. He described the drama as a kind of "x-ray" machine, revealing aspects of the social life not immediately apparent "on the ground." He also noted that the drama itself was a type of action that could influence the social change: Members of the audience were exposed to a period of "thinking modern" during the shows when they practiced unfamiliar patterns of reaction.

Both in their entertainment systems and in the problems they are having to face as developing industrializing nations, Indonesia and Thailand have much in common. James L. Mosel (6, p. 184) emphasized a similar point about the political socialization of Thailand—that education into modern political roles was more likely to be made effective through audience participation in the way things were said through the mass media than by attention to what was being said.* In "Communication Patterns and Political Socialization in Transitional Thailand" he wrote:

In transitional societies the mass media system is the great secondary political socializer. In such societies a discontinuity arises between the political culture into which the child is inducted through socialization and the role demands of a modern political state. The strategies of action and the "calculus of power" learned through enculturation tend to be incompatible with, or at least nonsupportive to, the skills and attitudes required for political development. Under these conditions the learning of modern political roles must in part come from later adult experiences with the mass media system since this is a major purveyor of modern influences. As an agent of political socialization the mass media system teaches its political lessons not only through the information it disseminates but also through the *way* in which poeple participate in the system.

*Mosel (6, p. 184) acknowledges Gregory Bateson as influencing his understanding of "deutero-learning."

In this chapter the examples of a film and a sermon throw into relief two different systems for classifying and evaluating events which are coming into contact as "progressiveness" gains acceptance as an ideal in a formerly conservative rural community.

SYSTEMS OF ENTERTAINMENT

One advantage of talking in terms of system is the reminder that each part affects every other and that only in relationship to each other do parts of a system have meaning and the possibility of interpretation. The recognition of subsystems in human social interaction has given social scientists courage to isolate and explore particular sets of relationships concerned with kinship, economics, politics, language, and religion. Here I am proposing that there is also value in treating those events loosely lumped together within a particular culture under the heading of "entertainment" as a "system." In the same way people must learn to manipulate kin, economic, and political relationships to contribute to and benefit from their cultural environment, so they must learn the appropriate responses to their entertainment system. The filmmakers made a gross misjudgment about the type of entertainment system their target audience (in rural Thailand) belonged to, and they triggered responses other than those they obviously aimed for.

Another advantage of labeling abstract sets of relationships as systems is that various types can be visualized conveniently through analogies in the physical world. A sentence from Gregory Bateson's essay "A Reexamination of 'Bateson's Rule'" in *Steps to an Ecology of Mind* inspired a helpful device for referring to the two systems of entertainment. He wrote: "We note then that, in biological systems, the step from radial symmetry to bilateral symmetry commonly requires a piece of information from the outside" (3). Attempts to map relationships between the multiplicity of entertainment forms in the Thai system had suggested to me the radial symmetry of a jellyfish, but when I needed to compare the more highly specialized forms of the West, they slotted more tidily into the hierarchically arranged, segmented symmetry of the ant. This discussion deals, indirectly, with the "outside information" that might be effecting the transition from one system to the other.

The jellyfish of rural Thai entertainment is built about three spines: movement, music, and words. Each of its art forms is related to those about it in the same way as the spokes of a wheel. The spokes reach out to embrace every social occasion according to a carefully formulated pattern of "appropriateness," and they feed back into and draw nourishment from a hub which distills a theatrical interpretation of those forms. The most sophisticated and intelligent way to appreciate a system of this kind is not to look for a starting point in order to trace a developmental pattern, but to be aware of as much of the total area as possible at the same time. (See Figures 1 and 2.) A tremendously wide "surface area" of entertainment system was exposed about five times a year when there were major fairs lasting three, five, or seven days. Besides the Ferris wheels and shooting booths and exhibitions and food and trinket stalls of the fairground, it accorded with Thai tradition to include within its more elaborate celebrations multiplicities of the kinds of attractions that Western audiences prefer to isolate from the distraction of competition. For instance, at school fairs and municipal fairs two rock bands might be playing different songs on adjacent stages; three films were being screened concurrently; Thai-boxing was drawing crowds to the center ring; a

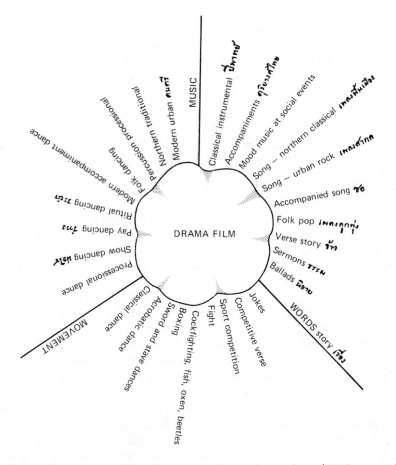

Figure 1   Radial relationships of Northern Thai entertainment forms (jellyfish system).

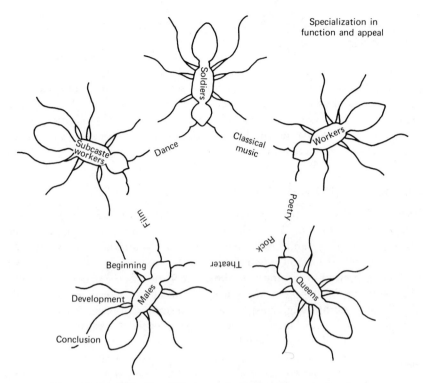

Figure 2   Specialization of Western entertainment forms (ant system).

drama with introductory "floor show" was beginning on another stage; and perhaps a beauty contest, a singing competition, and five-aside football were all cramped into a moderate-sized field.*

There was no way of sorting the tangle of noise and activity back into separate events each with its own beginning, middle, and end. For the local fairgoers sequential development was of no interest—plots in films and drama held no surprises—but that details of every production be scanned was important. Because no single pair of eyes could take in the full panorama, the solution was to combine in groups of from five to seven people, each one at an angle looking over the shoulder of another to cover the whole 360 degrees. Cues about what was going to happen next were built into each kind of show so that when the xylophone beat "curtain up" for the drama, or the leading lady was about to go into the popular "crying scene," groups surged towards that end of the field; when a local hero began to get a thrashing in the boxing ring or it was time for the comics on one of the film screens, the groups

*For a full description of a classical Thai celebration with a rich complement of competing attractions, see Simmonds (9).

dragged in that direction. An audience was never composed of single units—always groups.

Significance was in details that multiplied complexity in the overall pattern of entertainment. Appreciation went across subsystems (forms) of words, movement, and music to choose for comparison flourishes in costume, styles of singing, a movement to express a mood of a stereotyped character, jokes, the appearance of different leading ladies. Artistry was in elaboration within limits known by everyone who had learned the entertainment system rather than in attempts to extend those limits.

ENTERTAINMENT AND THE SOCIAL SYSTEM

At no point was entertainment cut adrift from the everyday social life of the village where I studied. One of the most often quoted maxims was, "Brothers and sisters (younger and older) help each other"—and help was most obviously given in the form of support at times of crisis and rejoicing. Neighborliness was expressed in visiting, and times when the whole village gathered for celebration at the temple or even at a private house were thought to be the times of greatest blessing. To sponsor an entertainment was a certain way to earn merit for advancement in the Buddhist cycle of rebirths, and to be present was valuable. Everybody gained, including deities from the 32 heavens. In opening invocations for singing and dramatic performances and before recitals of instrumental music there were traditional formulae that invited the gods to take pleasure in what was to be offered and to come down and give blessing by their presence. Their pardon was asked for any mistakes. Because the gods were the guardians of entertainment and social well-being depended on participation, entertainment was in no way trivial or escapist. Rather than competing categories, work and entertainment were complementary duties.

Key designs in the structure of the entertainment "jellyfish" were relatively fixed to support elaboration. Points of anchorage began with the social occasion: There were only certain entertainment forms suitable for each type of occasion. For instance, at a housewarming a film was appropriate or a type of reciprocal singing accompanied by pipers during which a man and a woman extemporized verse but wove their way through instruction on the traditionally correct procedure in courting, for building a house, and in taking proper gifts on proper visiting occasions. At a funeral wake, long poems of struggles between the underworld demons and local heroes were recited to soothe the spirit of the dead; there was a special gambling game, local instrumental music, and a particular form of bawdy joke. More knots tied a particular verse form to a kind of song and a way of producing a special kind of voice that was appropriate to its melody. Some tunes were so rigidly associated with moods and moments that reactions were as predictable as Pavlovian reflexes: When funeral drums sounded in the distance, some of the local girls showed me the hairs rising on their arms. A song from drama at the point when the heroine is grieved with a parting was played at the moment flames began to burn a corpse. Dance steps were taught as if they had an "alphabet" of verbal meanings, and dance gestures in drama were indelibly associated with a stereotyped character and his contribution to the staged pattern.*

The range of what was "given" left little scope for individual inventiveness, but as with the audience, the individual was not considered to be a particularly important unit. Expertise had value, but the most important qualification for any performer was that he go through a major ceremony called "respecting the teachers" (a version of an annual ceremony for all Thai school-children and university students). This had an almost magical value: Several older actors and leaders of drama troupes told me that they had been performing for some years before they decided to make entertaining their career. The performers had seen the necessity of finding a teacher (living or dead) to whom they could make appropriate offerings at an annual ceremony and before each performance "so that they should not forget" the verse, dance, or music.

While every performer publicly acknowledged the active guidance of traditional masters, within his or her particular specialization there was scope for excellence. For instance, actors were typecast—one girl always played the leading lady, another was the demoness, one elegant, long-nailed male played the hero and another was the bandit/demon/country yokel/comic. Within their own roles they were free to improvise—nothing was written down. The leader sometimes gave detailed direction about the sequence of scenes, but even if I asked an actor while he was in the wings waiting to go onstage, he did not know which piece they were playing. There were many favorite stories, but even those could be built on characteristic interactions between sets of roles with improvised episodes of fighting, abduction, parting, infatuation, courting, treachery, and reconciliation.

Originality had no place in the scheme; a gift for recombining elements distinguished leaders of entertainment. One actor told me that in 12 years leading a troupe, he had never put on the same play twice. He juggled old stories, adapted radio plays, renamed the characters from other shows he had seen, and based some new productions on events from his own and his friends' lives. He was not boasting creative authorship, but the skill of a "wright." His authority was from a proper ceremonial relationship with the teachers, and the proof of that proper relationship was in his continuing success.

---

*Morton (5) wrote about attitudes toward Thai music and its subordination to requirements of the social occasion.

Sometimes in the opening invocations for performances it was difficult to distinguish deities from teachers. The offerings provided for each were similar, and both represented the whole context of performer, audience, work, entertainment, and harmonious social intercourse. Sometimes the term *teachers* included all those whose long lives had given them understanding of the proper way things should be done so that they knew as much of the design of the "jellyfish" as had already been found pleasing and could protect the society from snagging on ignorance. Days in the year were reserved for taking presents to old people and asking their blessing. Respect for age was shown through forms of greeting and in words used to address old people. Compounds where very old people lived gained prestige as much as if people of high status or much wealth lived there. The right of individuals to bear these tokens of esteem was confirmed by the Buddhist system as it was interpreted at the village level. Merit was earned through a hierarchy of socially approved acts, and people who had proved themselves worthy through these acts (in a present or previous life) were rewarded with long life, wealth, or high status. Old people had the authority of understanding acquired through a long life, and they had the long life because they were worthy. That they should be given respect and obedience was natural and logical. (At least while their slowly learned skills were relevant; now the sharp youngster with technical skill, money to spend, and a Honda motorcycle has to learn a different world from his grandfather.)

Formal instruction in monasteries and schools had until recently relied on rote learning. Students with accurate memory retention, rather than those who attempted to reason, were rewarded with scholarships. Because pronouncements of anyone with teacher status (clerical or lay) came from those their society had endorsed as worthy, they were necessarily admirable and, in every way that mattered, correct. Less privileged members—young, poor or unordained—were in no position to show disrespect by contradiction. In fact, the tendency was more to express positive gratitude for the gift of the teacher's experience by taking little presents to teachers and giving tokens of respect to those whose wisdom and worth gave them high office.

ENTERTAINMENT IN A SERMON

When the monk climbed into his sermon clair he came in the dual role of teacher and expert. As a teacher, he came to deliver the special sermon ordered for the New Rice ceremony; as an expert, under constraints that forbade him to alter one word of the holy scriptures set for recitation, he came to enrich the villagers' appreciation of their patterns of social interaction.

The holy scriptures were one of the Triple Gems of Buddhism. The stories of the former lives of the Buddha were told in words that were sacred and known to the congregation of the faithful. Usually a sermon was read—either intoned according to set rhythms or recited as prose—from behind a screen in the most holy building of the temple complex. A scattering of old ladies and fewer old men wearing formal black and white sat on the floor listening, their palms together in the gesture of reverence. But this monk, who was an artist, transformed the ritual into an explosion of gaiety. The words of the set sermon he presented without deviation, some sung and some spoken, and for these the regular sermon-goers joined their palms; but he raided the conventions of every other entertainment form to pack those words like treasures in a pirate's chest.

Attending sermons was a way to accumulate merit, for which the older people had a more urgent appetite than the younger ones, but actually listening to sermons was more unusual. Catch-phrases in Pali cued the congregation on proper responses, but in between there was no objection to chatting, smoking, chewing, taking soft drinks, and eating. Sermons were not preached in the Western sense of one man telling another what to do. They were long ballads about former lives of the Buddha, encapsulating morals and parables and precepts. Portions were chosen from any part, each as edifying as another; sections were repeated in different settings; and the words were often distorted or in languages unfamiliar to the congregation.

The particular sermon I am using was given on an occasion that permitted more than usual license. Tradition allowed that the presentation concluding the day of celebrations for the New Rice could be lively to the point of bawdiness, and on this occasion a big crowd of all ages came to hear the famous monk. The proper story was a favorite; it told of Prince Wesandorn, the earthly shape in which the Buddha demonstrated the virtue of generosity to such extremes that his citizens banished him and Indra had to intervene personally to prevent him giving away his wife to Brahmin beggars. In the most popular section an ugly greedy old Brahmin courted and acquired a pretty young wife, who then turned into a scold and forced him to beg Wesandorn's two children for servants.*

By skillful use of the relationship between art forms, the monk not only managed to keep for three hours the attention of an audience that usually split along age and occupation lines to seek amusements, but he provided a means by which his quips and quotes would be related to every kind of gathering through the ensuing year. He broke into art forms clearly distinguished from each other and occasion-specific, but through his artistry the

---

*Rajadhon (8) gives the history of this particular sermon. He notes that it was traditional for the reciter to display his wit, "and additions of his are thrown into the recitation which sometimes borders on drollery and vulgarity. The orthodox people frown."

"inappropriateness" that could easily have given offense was absorbed. Instead, when each of those art forms was next used, it reminded people of his whole sermon.

To a certain extent the monk was aware of the shape of the entertainment system and that his manipulation was deliberate. He had received training at a government-sponsored center where particular attention was directed to learning the niceties of different local rhythms, tunes, vocabularies, and "voices" that went with the enormous variety of forms. He was a monk of the high *Maha* grade and was one of the "missionaries" encouraged by the government to travel to more remote country areas as part of a national unification campaign. From the evidence of the sermon, his brief would seem to have been twofold—to "give honor" to local customs so that people far from Bangkok might also feel themselves to be part of Thailand and to strengthen the impression that the Buddhist monkhood was vigorous and concerned, because Buddhism and the Monarchy seemed to symbolise Thailand in many areas the government feared threatened by insurgency. On four occasions during the sermon the monk got laughs at the expense of what he called communists. (In drama and sketches and local mythology, communists had heavy eyebrows like demons, Chinese eyes, and an appetite for the bodies of the innocent to use as manure on their fields.)

Both these objectives contradicted the role of monk. By definition, a monk was without secular ties. Strict rules of conduct minimized his social contacts, limiting the pattern of his eating and visiting so that it was out of alignment with that of the rest of the community. He was forbidden to listen to radio, songs, or music or to watch films, drama, and dancing. He should neither have known nor cared about the more intimate details of domestic life—the language of the marketplace, the little tricks of one-up-manship, or the rich vocabulary of abuse that could counter the impression (carefully fostered through centuries) that the monkhood was remote. Traditionally, the monkhood, another part of the Triple Gem of Buddhism with the Scriptures and the Buddha, was as far removed from the commonality as it could be, and the reverse of what the village people understood by "vigorous" (or Bangkok intellectuals by "relevant"). Without doing violence to what lingered of these ideals, the monk had to show the teen-agers that Buddhism was as up to date as they were—even quoting popular songs banned from the radio for their suggestiveness—while reassuring the more conservative that the world had not changed since the days when their now dying courting verses were new and daring.

The monk's raw materials were the unalterable words of the sermon and those entertainment forms proper to occasions suggested by them. For instance, one scriptural sentence mentioned the old Brahmin and his pretty wife. This gave the monk an excuse to spend nearly an hour describing the whole irregular courtship and even more bizarre wedding ceremony. These were occasions when cheeky flirting verses in the flowing rhyming patterns older people remembered were appropriate and to show off the clear high voice of chant used for serious declamation, which he cut off after one tantalizing sentence to grumble an aside and growl into the heavy thump of folk-pop used in contemporary courting. He involved the whole audience in the wedding ceremony by mentioning names similar to those of local dignitaries, pretending one was making announcements (with pompous exaggeration) and another singing a teaching song which used, instead of its own ancient specialized vocabulary, snippets of the most precocious jargon of the swinging set.

The monk mimicked each style, tantalizing with his skill so that each time he composed himself to demonstrate a different form, neighbors had just time enough to turn to each other with smiles and say, "Ah, he sings melodiously," before he scrambled the rhythm, the sound, the sense, and the context to nosedive into another pattern. For a few moments he let the old people enjoy the joke of nonsense words filling the rhythm of a teaching song, then he mixed the anguished sighs of disappointed love from a Bangkok song with his own contrary advice. Before the more affluent teen-agers with whom this mode was popular had sorted out the true from the tease, he was parodying a pop song about a girl who was cured of opium addiction—by taking heroin.

One melody for a teaching song was named after a hero in literature who was the pattern for romantic gallantry. When that tune began with the opening "*Phra Lo* was walking in the forest . . . ," people could sit back and expect a list of the fragrant orchids of the woodlands and then glimpses of the beginning of an ideal courtship with a pure and elusive damsel—but not in the monk's version. "*Phra Lo* was walking in the forest . . . the fragrance of rice wine wafted along and made him want to drink some. When he began to drink, his wife came along to stop him, but he pulled her ears. She was so angry she pulled what she could . . . (he clamped his mouth closed and continued the tune almost strangled with giggles) . . . until the man almost died." Then he shifted into drama and the nasal singing style that went with it, but he also took the parts of the five differently pitched drums that accompanied the opening chorus and the gongs that punctuated each line. His timing was so perfect that each crazy gong-beat noise made the audience hold its breath anticipating for just longer than was comfortable so that they burst with the kind of helpless laughter I normally heard only from children.

Perhaps the northern Thai system of entertainments was unusual because of the multiplicity of forms and the strictness with which each was associated with particular styles of presentation and occasions. Because, for instance, one line from a bawdy joke had the power to evoke the whole context of a cremation wake (the only time suitable for that style of joke), the monk could condense the entire social life of the village into three hours. A teaching song parody took the audience to an ordination or a housewarming, a dig at the tricks of some stingy housekeepers led into the weekly procession to the temple when families took special food offerings to the monks, a quip about mini-skirts moved to a rock concert where a line-up of 12 to 15 girls wiggled in abbreviated cha-cha-cha to every number, or to the frequent fairs where more lasses in minis sold 3-minute dances for five cents a time.

ENTERTAINMENT THROUGH FILMS

Live performers could throw their hooks into different areas of the jellyfish system to anchor their own contribution more firmly, but it was more difficult for "frozen" acts. Films gained in popularity as their integration in the entertainment complex gave them significance. For a Japanese film the audience at the open air cinema was mostly children encouraged by the low five cent admission fee. The promoter could fill the arena at 10 cents a head for an Indian, most Chinese, and some American films, but his best gates were for the more energetic Chinese fighting films, the most recent American Westerns, and Thai films. If the feature were a Thai film recently released in Bangkok, it was advertised for 15 cents to begin at 7 p.m.; in practice the price was raised to 20 or even 25 cents, and the start was usually delayed until 9:00 so that the potential audience could decide to fetch or borrow more money. (This was in an economy where 50 cents a day was a living wage.)

Films were assessed according to much the same criteria as fairs: If there was variety and excellence within each variation, the film was praised as "fun." If a production lacked the proper proportions of dancing and singing, clowning and fighting, and appropriate characterizations of pretty, wealthy girls, heroes groomed in country style but obviously of superior status, pathetic clowns and bad guys sufficiently dark and virile, it was "not fun," or even boring. The normal run of health propaganda films to reach this northern village was cheap blatant cartoons showing worms like tree trunks boring through bared toes or animated germs with evil grins turning the drinking water neon red. But the film that triggered this analysis had all the necessary elements to make it "fun." During the showing and the next day, the audience admired the leading lady and the dancing and expressed sympathy for the clown helplessly infatuated with the schoolmistress.

The health message was in the plot of the film. The story opened in a setting that was familiar to all the audience. It was a village in a relatively remote area similar to their own. What was perhaps not so obvious was that these scenes of dark wooden interiors, where a woman was dying in childbirth despite the ministrations of a disheveled midwife, revealed an inferior life ruled by dirt and superstition. The action began when a young doctor and his nurse-wife behaved according to a theme popular in literature but less discernible in life—they returned to the village that had nurtured them to pass on the benefit of their learning. The plot hinged on their efforts to promote an awareness of basic hygiene and nutritional values against opposition from more conservative elements. They set an example by keeping chickens for eggs and growing vegetables and finally succeeded in getting village cooperation to build a water tower. Dream sequences made the excuse for including singing and dancing, and the concluding victory party celebrated the reincorporation into village harmony and neighborly goodwill of all the converted "bad guys" who had opposed the scheme. They were reintegrated at a wedding when the leader of the reactionary faction finally married the pretty schoolmistress. This film was the most coherent, logical, smooth Thai production I saw in two years. The comfort with which I appreciated this film should have alerted me: I had not learned the "jellyfish" system of entertainment, but the "ant" system. When I could recognize the purpose of some specialized form of entertainment and relate to its message, the form was justified and I was edified. The audience around me had different expectations—and they saw a "different" film.* Their training was to evaluate and enjoy the film as entertainment. Had they expected instruction—about how to live longer, how to cut medicine bills and how to give the family more energy for work—they would have received it with gratitude from some person with the authority of high status.†

Expectations were further confused (from the point of view of the film's promoters) by the way the show was advertised. Many of the older people in the village could neither read nor understand the central dialect of the Thai language, so films were always advertised through loudspeakers on vans as well as on a bulletin board in the town. When the girls in my household heard the van, they went to the compound fence to listen and came back reporting that there was a "communist" film and all "communist" films were good so we should go. It became apparent that *communist* in this context was a shorthand description for government sponsored anti-insurgency propaganda film shows. The crew of the advertising van had picked out as the strongest selling point in the program for the whole show (which always included a number of shorts as well as the main feature) a news clip about brave Thai

---

*I am using the term *different* in the sense formulated by Karl Mannheim (4). Of course, the film, dogmatically speaking, was the same, but from our respective viewpoints it was a logically different object for the villagers and for me.

†James N. Mosel (6) about the Thai: "They seem to view information and knowledge as an economic commodity possessing a certain social utility, and its quality, i.e., validity, is dependent upon the craftsman who made it, or more specifically, the social status of the information's source" (p. 227).

soldiers—the inevitable Tiger regiment—killing evil communists in Vietnamese forests.

One of the girls in my household had learned some of the central dialect in her three years at school, so she had taken upon herself duties as my interpreter in situations where I was expected to respond to the northern dialect. We had been to many films where the dialogue was not fixed, but spoken in the northern dialect by a "mouth man" (who might or might not have seen a script or heard a version with sound), and she had the habit of giving me a running commentary. Before I learned better, I used to demand a sequential explanation, asking, "Why that?" and "What then?" Courtesy in the Thai tradition, and particularly towards superiors, operates according to the same inclusive principles as the entertainment system: A guest of high status cannot be wrong so that if she demands translation of a story that had not previously been apparent, a story should be supplied. At the health film I realized my error. This time I understood the dialogue better than my interpreter, but she continued to give me a scene-by-scene interpretation. The film, for her, documented a communist takeover, showing how an ordinary village like ours had been made clean and prosperous through obedience to its new leaders.

The "ant" approach is the one Aristotle approved for the Western world— in drama productions were complete if they had a beginning, a middle, and an end, but could not be classified with true drama if they were merely episodic.* Traditionally, the idea, the information, the excitement for the West has been generated through a series of either/or choices. The jellyfish tradition finds its excitement in recombinations generated in greater richness through a both/and approach which makes the use of *no* socially objectionable. Neither my nor her interpretation of the health film was correct—both were valid, but both were inappropriate.

ECOLOGY OF THE ENTERTAINMENT SYSTEM

Confusion was built into the initial decision to promote a specific message using an existing entertainment form as a vehicle. (Possibly this format was more readily understandable to a board of assessors providing money—either from foreign investors or sophisticated urbanites in Bangkok.) The choice was probably governed by factors other than those immediately relevant to the

---

*In *Poetics* (2) Aristotle wrote: "Of all plots and actions, the episodic are the worst. I call a plot 'episodic' in which episodes or acts succeed one another without probable or necessary sequence. Bad poets compose such pieces by their own fault, good poets to please the players; for, as they write show pieces for competition, they stretch the plot beyond its capacity, and are often forced to break the natural continuity."

impact of the message on rural audiences, because a more efficient method would have been to use speakers with local authority to give straight instruction. But once the form had been chosen, the filmmakers were faced with the major problem of where to put the message.

In a Thai film, as in a sentence there are pauses, words, rhythms, and stresses contributing towards its being received in an appropriate way. Episodes, like words, followed a certain predictable sequence, but they were not designed to support an entire long message of "if this happens, a specific reward follows." When the filmmakers attempted to thread a segmented plot through an episodic art form, they had to make choices to emphasize some sequences and impoverish others. To bring out the story of the young doctor and his fight against entrenched conservatism, they had to play up the serious scenes as if they had more significance than the scenes showing regional dances, a chicken "ballet," clowning, a shadow play, and singing, which had to be shunted into dreams, flashbacks, and stream-of-consciousness sequences instead of being given their full value in the structure.

Once the production was skewed by the need for a coherent Western plot, a series of other distortions followed. For instance, in characterization a system of stereotypes linked drama, jokes, stories, films, sermons, and some songs. Cross-category comparisons could ignore the entertainment form and recognize a character for whom there was a set pattern of expectations.* The distinctions were most clearly set out in popular drama because characteristics were emphasized with costume and appropriate styles of delivery for speeches, songs, and movements.

Appearances were important. The hero had to be handsome and the heroine pretty, but strictly within their own style. The lead characters were highborn and therefore elegant, refined. The male lead had delicate features—a pale skin, arched eyebrows, and often long painted nails. The leading lady's most moving moments came when she was parted from her loved or family, so she had to be tender, rather fragile, and skilled at producing tears on demand. The villains represented the untamed; they were vigorous, robust, and self-seeking. In popular drama they were often in league with or part of the underworld where lived heavy-browed dark-skinned demons who violated the careful rules of the upper worlds. The villains and heroines were in constant rivalry (sometimes successfully) with the world of gods and were

---

*Peacock (7, Ch. 5) comments that the Indonesian dramas are assemblages of "prefabricated" components rather than productions designed to sustain threads of interest that build into a single climax. He quotes support from Clifford Geerz and Edmund Leach who have noted for other parts of Indonesia and Burma that relationships between components of the same genre or category (whether in building a village, a temple complex, or a "show") carry more interest than relationships between categories.

usually defeated, but not annihilated, in the last scenes by the superior magic of the hero (acquired from his teacher either through years of abstinence and practice with formulae or with the help of a quick-witted "clown" friend).

Sometimes the real hero was not altogether clear because a distinction between good and bad did not apply. Totsagan (Ravana), King of the Demons, the 10-headed abducter of Sida in the Thai version of the *Ramayana,* was never permitted to be killed or even to seem to be vanquished on the stage. Girls in my village thought him more handsome, more virile and more desirable than the pure, dull, and properly effeminate hero, Rama.

In the sermon the official hero was the Buddha in his incarnation as Prince Wesandorn, but he, meek and generous, was pushed out of the story by Chuchok the ugly old Brahmin, unattractive in every way, except by his persistence and selfish energy he won a pretty girl, married her, and took Wesandorn's children as servants. In the health film the categories were confused. The doctor-hero was a rugged Western hero, not the usual smooth-cheeked "nice boy." His adversaries, though properly dark and earthy, were given a less honorable status than their stereotype deserved. By their actions, which were in character, such as setting their fighting cocks to upset the hero's carefully reared hens, the filmmakers meant to brand them as bad. Their final overthrow was meant to be a triumph of good over evil in the tradition of Western cowboy films where law and outlaw are given positive and negative values. But the imbalance initiated when a plot was squeezed into a film form disturbed the whole moral ecology of the entertainment universe.

If the filmmakers had wanted to make their point effectively—that the faction fighting health improvement had been bad—they should have killed its leaders. Bandits and wild characters of the forest were often given the title "Tiger" in Thailand, but so were good soldiers fighting for their country. The villagers held both in high respect and often felt more in sympathy with the fierce outlaw who lived by his wits than the tamed city dweller who went against him with the guns of the law. If, however, a "tiger" were killed, that was proof that he had been bad and lacked sufficient merit to stay alive. Some sense of neatness, appropriate neither to the film nor to the conventions of drama, prompted the filmmakers not only to attempt to label the defeated faction as bad, but to reintegrate it into the community by letting the leader marry the pretty schoolmistress. This humanitarian squeamishness destroyed the force of their argument. That the bad man was rewarded with the girl was confirmation that he had been right all along. (My informant explained to me that the "communist" had married the girl "because communists are very clever.") The moral universe of the dramatic tradition was as much a system as the entire complex of entertainment forms. It was inadvisable to tamper with one of its elements without anticipating reverberations in every part of the structure. While the filmmakers might have been sensitive to government policy, which was unsympathetic to much of the world-view supported in the northern entertainment system, they were naive in expecting to sneak in a teaching that directly contradicted it. The system, with its emphasis on appropriate forms for appropriate occasions, with every character keeping its place and style within that form, was dramatizing the message, "People are born into a system where each has his place, his behavior, and his end. The only fitting reaction is to know your own place relative to the others and to keep it without interference."* The filmmakers were taking a risk when they said, "You can cheat destiny and ruin the entire organization by acting out of character and allowing to live a type that should more properly die."

I did not find one person who saw the film who was aware that there was a message related to health and hygiene. On the way to market the next day, I asked the girl who had been my "interpreter" what she would like for lunch. She asked for a local food, her regular favorite, that had no nutritive value. I reminded her of the film that had shown the value of eggs and vegetables. She replied that she did not remember that part, but she would have eggs because I said they were good, and I was "older and had knowledge."

TRANSITION BETWEEN SYSTEMS

In this girl and her friends of the same generation, both the "ant" and the "jellyfish" systems claimed attention. She had been born into the village and educated into its entertainment system, learning the appropriate appreciation of social relationships, artistic values, religion and kinship obligations. But also in her generation the national education system had become effective in giving her instruction in reading and the central Thai dialect. She began to have difficulty understanding her grandfather's dialect and the local stories, music, songs, and drama that gave him pleasure. Instead, she used the central language for access to rock and pop music from Bangkok; she read stories of urban life in recently available magazines; and she traveled on the new hard-surface roads to the city, even coming into contact with me, a foreigner, who took her to Bangkok.

*Benedict R. O'G. Anderson (1) discusses the same kind of "moral pluralism" for the world of *Wayang,* Javanese puppet shadow theatre. Morality there is achieved in the fulfilling of one's own appointed function: there is no way of defining "appropriate behavior" until one knows for whom it should be appropriate. The *Wayang* characters each display the values and behaviors appropriate for different human types—values that might be in sharp contradiction to each other but demonstrate that there is a respected "niche" for every type.

The government was aware of this transitional stage in rural areas and approved the approaches of both the film and the sermon, yet these approaches were contradictory. The monk exploited the traditional northern entertainment system, encouraging agility in making cross-category comparisons; he tied firmly together the film and pop-song culture of the young people with the stories, verse forms and specialized vocabularies of the grandparent generation. This kind of world view, and the context of Buddhism in which it was given, emphasized community values over the importance of the individual, a static social structure, and a view of time that neutralized the urgency of development—seasons and "proper times" were as carefully worked into its scheme as people and roles.

While this approach flattered the villagers and reassured them that the rhythms of their agricultural background were still relevant, there could be dangerous consequences for a government committed to nationalism and development. Nationalism was undermined because the villagers were inclined to identify "horizontally" with peasant neighbors in the Shan states, Laos, and Burma rather than with the city folk and sophisticated Southerners with the political boundaries of Thailand; development, modernization, and industrialization all needed to use individuals cut loose from hampering kinship and village loyalties and with a sense of time moving in one direction. The health film, in dramatizing a political struggle to get a water tower built and in showing trends of progress, such as a decreasing infant mortality rate and a village increasing in prosperity, was preaching interference—saying that the system should be changed, saying that time was an enemy and competition could be productive.

Thailand, as a developing nation, needed both these approaches. The Northerners could be expected to care about Thailand only if they felt themselves to be a respected part of the country, but they had to be persuaded to put the claims of the nation before those of their smaller communities. The two entertainments I chose to compare demonstrated this dual concern, but perhaps the outcome gave a false impression: The "jellyfish" might win a few more battles, but it will certainly lose the war to the "ant."

Without destroying the whole system, there is no way to introduce purpose into a jellyfish, whereas ants operate with machine-like efficiency at specific tasks. The ant is goal-oriented and suitable for industry; it can reorganize its environment for its own comfort. The slow-moving jellyfish makes minimal demands. Although the West is becoming aware that it is destroying its own resources by the short-term "ant" approach, the impetus of its technological advances, particularly in communications, is already weighting the balance against other systems in rural areas. During the lifetime of the present students in that northern Thai village, radio, film, records, and television have been introduced and begun to usurp the place of the live entertainer. The need to fill an exact timeslot with material that will appeal to a sponsor, the government, and as many city and country people as possible immediately imposes constraints on the media. Their items have to be structured with a beginning, a middle, and an end, like much of the foreign material already broadcast. Soon people in rural areas will have to adjust their way of listening and watching to appreciate the single bold points emphasized in developmental productions. They probably will come to believe that the individual rather than a community of people is the significant unit. They probably will take their prosperous place in the developed world. But the price for that place will have included their cultural heritage and identity.

REFERENCES

1. Anderson, Benedict R. O'G. *Mythology and the Tolerance of the Javanese.* Ithaca, N. Y.: Cornell University, Southeast Asia Program, 1965.
2. Aristotle. *Poetics,* in Frank A. Tillman and Cahn Steven (eds.), *Philosophy of Art and Aesthetics.* New York, Evanston, and London: Harper & Row, 1969.
3. Bateson, Gregory. *Steps to an Ecology of Mind.* New York: Chandler, 1972.
4. Mannheim, Karl. "A Review of George Lukas' Theory of the Novel," in Kurt H. Wolff (ed.), *Karl Mannheim.* New York: Oxford University Press, 1971.
5. Morton, David. *Journal of the Siam Society, 58,* 2.
6. Mosel, James N. "Communication Patterns and Political Socialization in Transitional Thailand," in Lucian W. Pye (ed.), *Communication and Political Development.* Princeton, N.J.: Princeton University Press, 1963.
7. Peacock, James Lowe. *Rites of Modernization; Symbolic and Social Aspects of Indonesian Proletarian Drama.* Chicago: The University of Chicago Press, 1968.
8. Rajadhon, Phya Anuman. "Thet Maha Chat," *Thai Culture New Series, 21* (Bangkok).
9. Simmonds, E. H. S. "Mahorasop in a Thai Manora Manuscript," *Bulletin of the School of Oriental and African Studies, 30,* 2 (1967).

CHAPTER 16

Some Issues in Nigerian Broadcasting

FRANK OKWU UGBOAJAH

The Nigerian Constitution gives the government exclusive monopoly in broadcasting. In 1976 the central government operated 18 strategically located radio stations. Most state governments have their own broadcasting authorities. Within a period of five years every state of Nigeria could operate its own daily newspaper and its own radio and television network.

What does this trend mean to the average Nigerian? Candon studied the audience of the Tanzanian press and found that most news presented goes to the literate person who knows the English language and lives in the city, and the majority of Tanzanians who speak Swahili and live in the rural areas remain out of touch (1). This situation is also true of Nigeria where media-set ownership tends to be concentrated among the urban middle and upper classes.

In trying to bridge the knowledge gap in the communication of development issues, Nigerian mass media have resorted to increasing use of the 178 local languages.* Although English still dominates broadcasting, there has been a gradual increase of broadcast programs in various Nigerian languages. For example, the Nigerian Broadcasting Corporation in Benin, capital of the Bendel State of Nigeria, broadcasts the news in six indigenous languages—Edo, Igbo, Urhobo, Ijaw, Isoko, Itshekiri. Magazine programs and commentaries are also relayed in eight additional minor languages.

INNOVATIVE PROGRAMMING

Among the most popular innovative programs are request programs. The Nigerian Broadcasting Corporation's radio station in the East Central State

---

*Nigeria has only seven local language newspapers read by only two lingual groups, the Yoruba and the Hausa, and the readership is estimated at 2 percent of the population.

of Nigeria broadcasts 14 request programs in a week. Five of these programs are in Igbo, the local language. The programs are: "Umuaka Ekenenu" (Greetings to You Children), "Ekene Umunwanyi" (Greetings to You Women), "Ndewonu" (Greetings Everybody), "Ozi Ekene" (Message of Thanks), and "Ekene Ndi Ahia" (Greetings to You Market People).

The reason for the popularity of request programs is a desire for communicating to loved ones who are far away. The messages are of condolences, of love, of congratulations, for recuperation, and for general encouragement.

Listeners are much involved in these programs. During my study of one station a listener had traveled from a provincial town about 60 miles away to the site of the station to protest to the head of programs that his requests had not been relayed for three consecutive times.

The "Umuaka Ekenenu" beamed to young people of primary school age is very popular. This magazine program creates a young persons' forum where questions, which are sent in from all parts of the country, are discussed by their peers. Questions received for two months in 1975 centered on politics, education, child rearing, and on general knowledge. One listener wanted to know why there is only a single woman commissioner in his state, whether this was because women are not well educated or that their parents had no money to train them. Another wanted to know why a child cries when it is born when nobody had beaten it. There was a question seeking to know why the sun gives heat when it shines and the moon does not.

Another popular magazine program broadcast in the East Central radio station is the "Ekene Umunwanyi." A panel of women discusses questions from listeners about marriage and love affairs. This program is strategic in that it can be used to discuss family health habits and problems.

An innovative agricultural program is "Don Manuma" (For Farmers). The producer has created a fictional farming village, and actors demonstrate the benefits of mechanized farming, introduction of new seeds and nutritional habits through the "village" drama. Research findings on agriculture and budget proposals of government on agriculture are simplified and composed into songs and proverbs.

NEWS AND LISTENER PARTICIPATION

Emphasis in Nigerian news broadcasting is on letting the people know about government development activities and telling the government what cooperative or community-based development projects or activities are going on in parts of the state. The broadcasting media in the country do indeed publicize and motivate cooperative efforts in rural development. Editors know that most communities emulate what other communities are doing, and by publicizing them the media generate competition and relate the efforts of these communities to government recognition for necessary financial assistance. Community leaders visit the station on the average of four times a month demanding publicity privileges. Some leaders go as far as offering community-sponsored transportation services to reporters and producers.

I have conducted a study of broadcast attention to four key issues (public execution, enterprises promotion, census taking, and corruption) that occurred in Nigeria in the period 1970–1974. Radio stations have given the issue of enterprises promotion more attention than the issue of corruption in public life which engaged much of the energy and attention of competitive media (newspapers and magazines) in the country (2). But there is no organized feedback for the Nigerian mass media. My interviews revealed that letters are neither analyzed in any systematic way nor used for decision-making. An official of the Nigerian Broadcasting Corporation complained that even when feedback from listeners is communicated to responsible authorities, complainants are sometimes traced and victimized by unscrupulous officials "for embarrassing the state government." This has affected broadcast feedback because the station does not want to jeopardize its listeners.

Radio officials in Benin, the Midwest State, suggested that the Nigerian Broadcasting Corporation train its correspondents and that radio executives tour the provinces themselves.

In summary, broadcasting in Nigeria is striving to inform as many people as possible in their local languages. Broadcasters are becoming more innovative as they create forums for the discussion of vital development issues, but they lag in the utilization of audience feedback and often suffer from bureaucratic interference.

REFERENCES

1. Candon, John C. "Nation Building and Image Building in the Tanzanian Press," *Journal of Modern African Studies, 5,* 3 (1967), 335–354.
2. Ugboajah, Francis Okuadigbo. "Communication of Development Issues In The Nigerian Mass Media: A Sociological Perspective." Unpublished Ph.D. thesis, University of Minnesota, 1975, pp. 263–284.

CHAPTER 17

TV's Last Frontier: South Africa

RANDALL HARRISON and PAUL EKMAN

In 1976, television came to South Africa. This marks an interesting milestone in communication technology. It signals the final phase of a major innovation, the spread of television to all the literate, urban, Western, industrial nations of the world. In less than three decades, television grew into a globe-spanning giant which commands the time, attention, resources—and frequently the concern—of every advanced society.

Television comes at a crucial point in South African history. Except for Rhodesia, South Africa is the last white-ruled nation in a continent of black societies. The white South African maintains control in spite of the fact that he is outnumbered by nonwhites four to one. In recent months, he has seen the once white colonial countries on his borders become independent black nations. Not only are these nations governed by blacks, but the societies are primarily socialist, with, as in the case of Angola, violent conflict between those oriented toward China and those backed by Russia.*

Into this scene, introduce a powerful new communication medium: television. How will it be used? For the student of communication, an intriguing question. For the South African, whatever his color, the question is of more than academic interest.

In this article, we will *(a)* explore some broad questions about the potential consequences of introducing television into a society such as South Africa; *(b)* summarize some of the main features of the new television service and how they got that way; and *(c)* examine some predictions about the future.

South Africa is unique among advanced economic nations in adopting

---

This chapter first appeared in the Winter 1976 issue of the *Journal of Communication.*

*This summarizes, of course, only a few of the complex issues facing South Africa. It does not probe the vexing problem of apartheid, South Africa's difficulties in the United Nations, recent diplomatic overtures toward Latin America, attempts to establish "homelands," or efforts toward detente in Africa. For a journalist's summary of the current scene, see Lewis (4).

television so late. The reasons for the long delay are apparently political, cultural, and economic. In South Africa, the pros and cons of television were perhaps more thoroughly debated than in any other adopting society.*

Across the political spectrum, television was approached with extreme caution. The party in power feared that the new medium would usher in an uncontrollable flood of "foreign" ideas, Western "decadent" thought as well as Eastern "communist" ideologies. Intermittently, the opposition parties were equally cautious; they feared that television would provide a powerful new medium of propaganda which would enable the party in power to consolidate and extend its rule.

The most outspoken opponent of television was a man in a key decision role, then Minister of Posts and Telegraphs, Albert Hertzog. He viewed television as an "evil black box" which would undermine morals and family life. He was joined by many Afrikaners in a fear that television would mean importing many British and American programs. Whatever the content, this was likely to erode the recently achieved broadcast parity between English and Afrikaans, making it ever more difficult to maintain the Afrikaans cultural heritage.† To this were added economic arguments. The introduction of television would require vast foreign investment, and the nation, it was argued, had more important development goals.

In 1968, through a shuffle of ministerial responsibilities, Hertzog was moved out of his crucial role as Minister of Posts and Telegraphs. His replacement came into office with the announcement that he had no preconceived ideas regarding television; there would be a thorough review of television's alleged "damaging influence" on youth and the cost factors of introduction. Subsequently, Hertzog broke with his own party to form the ultraconservative Reconstituted National Party, which has been notably unsuccessful at the polls. With Hertzog gone, the plans for a national television system began to emerge.

Rumors spread that the vast new SABC Auckland Park complex in Johannesburg would house television as well as FM facilities. In July, 1969, the first "moon-walk" further fanned pro-television sentiment. While the rest of the developed world watched the historic moment live on television, South Africans were forced to read news reports and see delayed newsreels.

In December, 1969, the government announced that a twelve-man commission would investigate and make recommendations about the future of television. This body deliberated for over a year and in March, 1971, sent its report to the Cabinet. In late April, the Minister of National Education

---

*The story of this long debate is covered more thoroughly by Orlik (5–7).
†South Africa has two official languages, English and Afrikaans. The latter is derived from seventeenth-century Dutch and is spoken by approximately 60 percent of the white population.

announced that the government would launch television, probably within four years' time. Subsequently, the official starting date for the full service was set for January, 1976.

The government also announced that initially there would be one bilingual channel split equally between Afrikaans and English. Television was to be in the hands of the South African Broadcasting Corporation, which controls all radio broadcasting in the country. Modeled originally after the BBC, the corporation is at present designed to be economically self-sustaining, but with a nine-man board of directors appointed by the government.*

Television test programming began in May, 1975, in Johannesburg. In July, Cape Town and Durban were added. Originally, the SABC indicated that test programs would be nothing more than a camera trained on "a goldfish in a bowl." Prospective buyers would be able to check reception in their area and tune their sets, but they would have little idea of the programming to come. The SABC quickly decided, however, that it was best to give at least a sample. Initially, viewers saw an hour of programming per evening, the next noon the same hour was repeated. In October, apparently stimulated in part by disappointing set sales, the SABC added time to its program schedule.

Finally, the full nationwide service was scheduled for inauguration on January 5, 1976. South Africans are able to see five hours an evening, with additional time on weekends devoted primarily to sports. The single SABC TV channel is bilingual; each evening, two and one-half hours in Afrikaans and the same amount in English are programmed.†

Given the prolonged struggle over the introduction of television, observers have wondered what would—and would not—be shown on SABC TV‡ and to what extent would television be politically independent from the government.

A leading business weekly, the *Financial Mail,* raised the issue of TV content and its control in a special supplement devoted to the new medium. An

---

*For radio, revenues come from both advertising and from licenses; an owner pays approximately $50 a year for each TV set he owns. Starting in 1978, television will be allowed to sell commercials, but advertising will be limited to 5 percent of total air time.

†South Africa has adopted the German PAL system and all transmissions are in color. Color sets sell for approximately $1400 and black and white sets run $600. The SABC estimates that by the end of 1976, 400,000 sets will be in use, but other sources are predicting a more conservative figure of 297,000.

‡Program content, by broad categories, is as follows: drama and dramatic series, 18 percent; sports, 12 percent; variety, 9 percent; news, 7 percent; and documentary, general and "actuality," 53 percent. The latter category includes music, children's programming, women's shows, and magazine format shows covering art, books, gardening, hobbies, and religion. South Africans are producing approximately 50 percent of the content themselves, with the other 50 percent coming from the United States, England, and Europe.

article entitled "Your Mind in Their Hands" carried the subhead: "Just how independent can SABC TV be? After all, government holds the purse strings." Elaborating on this concern, the magazine asked:

What will we see on SABC TV? Are the newspaper critics of the Corporation correct in suggesting that the fare will be dull, leaning toward the pedagogical? Worse, will news and views become a platform for government [National Party] propaganda—a criticism often leveled at some of the SABC's radio programmes, particularly "Current Affairs?" (1, p. 17)

On TV's political stance, the *Financial Mail* quotes SABC Director-General Jan Swanepoel as saying: "We are an independent organization. We are not dictated to by the government" (1, p. 17).

This led the *Financial Mail* to ask: "Is it then purely a coincidence that, to so many people, SABC policy appears almost totally in line with government policy? Do the SABC and the government fortuitously have the same standards, beliefs and ideologies?"

Swanepoel answered: "To some extent I think that may be true. To give an example, I don't think we could incite people to overthrow the government by undemocratic methods. I don't think we would be part and parcel of that, nor could we incite young people not to join the police force and fight on the borders. Yet there are people who do this."

This raises the question of whether SABC television would ever air the views, in a news interview or in a current affairs discussion, of someone who was against joining the police, or fighting on the border. "Yes," says Swanepoel, "I think we would do that—we have done it on the radio services."

The issue of SABC policies flared in January, 1975, when a staff directive was "leaked" to the press. It was from a TV producer of English magazine and children's programs and contained the note that "programmes should follow government policy, SABC policy and departmental policy." His superiors quickly disavowed the directive. But as the *Financial Mail* observes:

. . . the outcry it evoked serves to illustrate just how touchy and suspicious a large segment of the public is to the long-standing belief, mistaken or otherwise, that the SABC follows the party line. It is an issue constantly hammered by the English-language newspapers, by intellectuals of all races, the Opposition, by artists and writers, many of them Afrikaans-speaking (1, p. 17).

The publication continues:

The SABC hotly contests this. Rather, it sees itself as holding sacred . . . ideals that are similar to those of the government—that this is a Christian nation, that violent change is to be abhorred, that cultural and traditional values must be maintained. The boat may be rocked, but only gently; not capsized (1, p. 17).

To the question, "Does the Board of the SABC have specific contact with the nation's policy-makers?" Director-General Swanepoel asserts: "No, none whatsoever" (1, p. 18).

The journal concludes, "Nevertheless, it cannot be easy for a public body," such as the SABC, "to keep at arm's length from a government which is not exactly renowned for its tolerance of opposition or its patience with those who see things differently" (1, p. 18).

The question of political access to the medium, while a heated issue, is, of course, only one area of concern.

The *Financial Mail* supplement carried one article entitled, "Living with the idiot's lantern." The subhead read: "Who can assess the social, political and economic impact of TV on South Africans? It will probably be more significant than most people think" (1, p. 36).

Raising fundamental questions, the journal asked:

Just what is the nature of TV? Why is it feared in some quarters as a perverter of youth and the righteous? To what extent will the medium change the face of South Africa—its politics and prejudices? Its life style? And is this country ready for such a radical new influence? (1, p. 36).

A key concern is the potential impact on race and intergroup relations. Some South African academics feel the bilingual service will foster greater accord between the two white language groups, the English and the Afrikaners. The argument goes: The TV viewer will watch programs in the other language, even if he doesn't understand very well, because it's there in the home; this, in turn, will lead to greater understanding of the other language, and perhaps the other culture. At least one observer feels, however, that it may have the opposite effect. "It'll just be another source of irritation between the two groups," he predicts. "Some people will feel: why should I pay a full license fee when only half the programs are in my language?"

The predictions about race are even more complex. First, it is generally agreed that, given the high cost of sets, relatively few blacks will be able to purchase them. But some South Africans predict that there may be a very large black viewership in spite of this. Black domestics may see TV in white homes. Drinking places may have them. Extended family groups may share a common set. When a set does appear in a black area, there will be many more viewers per set than in white areas.*

The *Financial Mail* concludes: ". . . Blacks will see TV, whatever the limitations." On potential impact, they quote Tom de Koning, Chairman of the Communication Department at Rand Afrikaans University: "The greatest effect on the Blacks will be the raising of their cultural aspirations. They will see other Blacks with cars, houses, and so on and ask, 'Why can't I have that?' In a real sense there will be a 'westernisation' of Blacks because of television. And their political claims will escalate as a result" (1, p. 36).

Some predict that television will also have an impact on white attitudes. For example, a South African sociologist observes that "most white South Africans have never been exposed to a well-educated black." He predicts that

---

*Plans call for a second channel which will be devoted to black audiences.

intelligent, articulate nonwhites will appear on television and when this happens, white perceptions will begin to shift.

Closely related to this is the concern about the impact on leadership—and politics in general. The *Financial Mail* quotes de Koning as saying: "Television will completely transform our political system" (1, p. 39). As in other countries, there is a concern that the politician with a good TV image will have more appeal than the candidate who is more competent but less telegenic. At least one psychologist, however, thinks this is an exaggerated concern. He observes: "The South African, particularly the Afrikaner, is not much taken in by appearances."

A final, pervasive concern centers on the potential impact of television on anti-social behavior, particularly among the young. The 12-man Commission of Inquiry into Television, which recommended adoption to the Cabinet, concluded that television was not, *per se,* evil. The Commission was charged with investigating the "possible harmful effects which such a service may have upon the moral life of the nation, especially its youth." The Commission concluded that television itself "cannot be blamed for the way it is applied and controlled in a specific country. It is true that there are cases overseas where television is being used to the spiritual, cultural and moral detriment of the society." But the Commission viewed this as a "result of the permissiveness into which such a society has gradually degenerated, not a cause of the permissiveness" (1, p. 36).

As television was hitting the airwaves, the South African press was quoting the complete range of foreign "experts," from an American TV star, who was convinced seeing violence does not influence aggressive behavior, to an Australian researcher, who believes watching television interferes with basic brain functions. For the concerned South African, the foreign research evidence was being summarized in a new book, in Afrikaans, by psychologist Elizabeth Nel and sociologist J. M. du Toit.

Among South African researchers, it is possible to find a range of viewpoints similar to the spectrum found in Britain and the United States. A frequently expressed view, however, is the one given by de Koning: "Television shows people that aggressiveness solves problems, rather than more social approaches. Hence in questionable situations, with no clear-cut pattern of behavior called for, the unsure person opts for violence."

Researchers, such as de Koning, Nel, and investigators at South Africa's Human Sciences Research Council, are exploring the impact of television, in field experiments and in longitudinal studies.* Of course, the overriding

---

*We have outlined the potential and the problems of research in South Africa in an earlier manuscript (2). Subsequently, in cooperation with Robert M. Liebert, we have advised on research strategies, provided research materials, and have collaborated in television studies conducted in South Africa.

impact of television, particularly in the social realm, will be difficult to assess with any single experiment or any easy set of observations. But many observers think South Africa will provide useful lessons about television.

First, the nation has fully developed mass media systems except for television; it thus is very comparable to other advanced industrial societies. Second, it is introducing a complete, nationwide system all at once; diffusion is expected to be faster than in any previous TV adopter.

Third, the South Africans have announced their determination to prevent what they consider undesirable side-effects of television, and they are drawing on the accumulated research experience of the world for that purpose. Finally, South Africa is a relatively contained, "closed" system; it may be easier to trace out the consequences of television there than in any previous television society.

As television blinks its way into South African homes, the South Africans themselves seem to have four alternative hypotheses about the potential impact. One obvious hypothesis, of course, is that the introduction of television will make no difference whatever. This argues that social and political events have begun to unfold inexorably and a new communication medium, no matter how powerful, will do little to influence the direction or velocity of change.

A second hypothesis is that television will have a broad "accelerating" effect. Existing trends will speed up; new trends will suddenly emerge. This argues, for example, that seeing refugees from Angola, and hearing them interviewed, has a different impact than reading about it in a newspaper. This impact mobilizes opinion (or creates division). And that, in turn, allows leaders (or forces them) to move more quickly and in directions that would not have been possible otherwise.

The counter argument is that television will have essentially a "braking" effect. Three rationales have been advanced. First, the forces in control of the new medium are essentially conservative and they will use the medium to preserve rather than transform. Second, the new medium will be more entertainment than enlightenment; it will be a "circus" to divert the citizenry rather than "food for thought" to immerse the viewer in the issues of the day. Third, even when the events of the day are presented via television, the effect may be more narcotizing than mobilizing. Seeing Angolan refugees may foster non-involvement, just as some have argued that nightly TV coverage of the Vietnam war led to indifference. (Each of these rationales rests on an assumption which is sharply contested by some observers.)*

*For example, many feel that television will be used by the present government to dramatize the need for change. When, in June 1975, an SABC film crew went to the Ivory Coast to make a TV documentary, *Africa,* the continent's newsmagazine, speculated that the TV program would help "defuse" opposition to the detente policies of Prime Minister Vorster and would encourage South African tourism and investments in the multiracial Ivory Coast (see 3, p. 60).

A final alternative might be called the "complex, differential impact" hypothesis. It suggests that television's effect will be pervasive, but that in some areas the medium will stimulate change while in other areas it may inhibit and divert. Further, television's impact will differ, e.g., among whites and blacks, among Afrikaans speaking and English speaking, among the affluent and the disadvantaged, among young and old.

While the outcome is uncertain, some would agree with the *Financial Mail's* observation: "The innocent little Cyclops in the corner is really a powerful subverter. Were the Big Eye able to wink, it certainly would" (1, p. 39).

REFERENCES

1. "All you ever wanted to know about TV but were afraid to ask . . . ," *Financial Mail,* special supplement, 14 March 1975.
2. Harrison, Randall, and Paul Ekman. "Television in South Africa: The Research Paradox, Problem and Potential." Unpublished manuscript, Michigan State University and University of California, San Francisco, 1972.
3. "Ivory Coast: Vorster's TV Crew," *Africa, 48* (August 1975).
4. Lewis, Anthony. "South Africa: The End Is Inevitable But Not Predictable," *New York Times Magazine,* 21 September 1975.
5. Orlik, Peter B. "The South African Broadcasting Corporation: An Historical Survey and Contemporary Analysis." Ph.D. dissertation, Wayne State University, 1968. Ann Arbor, Mich.: University Microfilms No. 70–27, 042.
6. Orlik, Peter B. "South Africa: How Long Without TV?" *Journal of Broadcasting, 14,* 2 (1970), 245–258.
7. Orlik, Peter B. "South Africa," in Sydney W. Head (ed.), *Broadcasting In Africa; A Continental Survey of Radio and Television.* Philadelphia: Temple University Press, 1974.

Developments in Theory and Research

CHAPTER 18

Comparative Cultural Indicators

GEORGE GERBNER

Developments in communication have extended the human ability to exchange messages and have transformed the symbolic environment of human consciousness. Perhaps that most profound dilemma is that just as knowledge can be said to confer power, so power generates and uses knowledge for its own purposes. Social and institutional structures (governments, broadcasting networks, publishing houses, and educational institutions) have a steadily increasing role in shaping the symbolic environment.

Self-government can no longer be supposed to follow from the assumption that the press and other communication agencies are free. In a highly centralized mass-production structure of the kind characterizing modern communication, "freedom" is the right of the managers to decide what the public will be told. The question is whether further enlightenment can lead to liberation from the shackles of mind and body that still oppress mankind or whether liberation from those shackles can lead to further enlightenment.

That final issue divides modern societies and calls for evenhanded—if not necessarily detached—investigation. Capitalist and socialist, orthodox and revolutionary, pre- and postindustrial, and other types of societies vary in the solutions they promise and further differ in the performance they deliver. There is probably no area of significant social policy in which far-reaching decisions are made with so little reliable information about the actual state of affairs as in the sphere of the mass production and distribution of the most broadly shared messages of national cultures. This chapter is an attempt to provide a conceptual framework for the comparative investigation of media policies, content, and effects in different social systems and cultures.

Communication is interaction through messages bearing man's notion of existence, priorities, values, and relationships. Codes of symbolic significance conveyed through modes of expression form the currency of social relations. Institutions package, media compose, and technologies release message systems into the mainstream of common consciousness.

A version of this chapter appeared in George Gerbner, Larry Gross, and William H. Melody (eds.), *Communications Technology and Social Policy*. New York: Wiley, 1973.

How is this massive flow managed? How does it fit into or alter the existing cultural context? What perspectives on life and the world does it express and cultivate? How does it vary across time, societies, cultures? Finally, how does the cultivation of collective assumptions relate to the conduct of public affairs, and vice versa?

The questions designate three areas of analysis.* How mass media relate to other institutions, make decisions, compose message systems, and perform their functions in society are questions for *institutional policy analysis*. How large bodies of messages can be observed as dynamic systems with symbolic functions that have social consequences is the question of *message system analysis*. What common assumptions, points of view, images, and associations do the message systems tend to cultivate in large and heterogeneous communities, and with what public policy implications, are problems for *cultivation analysis*.

THE INSTITUTIONAL POLICY PROCESS

How do media managers determine and perform the functions their institutions, clients, and the social order require? What is the overall effect of corporate controls on the basic terms of symbolic output? What policy changes, if any, do in fact alter those terms, and how?

Mass-media policies reflect not only a stage in industrial development and the general structure of social relations but also particular types of institutional and industrial powers and pressures. Mass communicators everywhere occupy sensitive and central positions in the social network. They have suppliers, distributors, and critics. Other organizations claim their attention or protection. They have associations of their own. They have laws, codes, and policies that channel and constrain them. And they have patrons who, as in any industrial production, supply the capital, the facilities, and the authority (or at least opportunity) to address mass publics.

The systematic exercise of powers resides in institutional roles and in relationships to centers of power. A scheme designed to analyze this process must identify the roles, suggest some sources of their powers, and specify those functions that affect what the media communicate. Power and its application become relevant to this scheme as they shape what is being communicated to mass-media publics. (See Table 1.)

Types of Leverage and Typical Functions

Authorities possess legal powers to enact and enforce demands or impose sanctions upon communicators. Legislative, executive, judicial bodies, regulatory

---

*Much of the following is drawn from my chapter "Cultural Indicators: The Third Voice" in George Gerbner, Larry P. Gross, and William H. Melody (eds.), *Communications Technology and Social Policy*. New York: Wiley, 1973.

commissions, public administrators, the police, and the military may have such authority. Authorities may assume rights patrons ordinarily have and may impose sanctions, such as for seditious or criminal acts, that patrons cannot. Authorities may also depend on the support of communicators for much of their authority; the "regulated" have been known to regulate the regulators.

Patrons are those who directly invest in or subsidize media operations in exchange for economic, political, or cultural benefits. Their clients are the media that provide such benefits in exchange for discretionary patronage. Media patrons may be banks, advertisers, other corporate or civic organizations, religious or military bodies, political parties, or governments. The principal types of patrons and the major client relationships determine the role of media management in the power scheme of every society. The client relationship also affects the institution's approach to most issues and problems and permeates the climate of communicator decision-making.

Table 1 Major Power Roles, Types of Leverage, and Typical Functions Directing the Formation of Mass-Produced Message Systems

Power Roles (Groups)	Types of Leverage	Typical Functions
1. Authorities make and enforce legally binding decisions	Political and military	Arbitrate, regulate, legitimize power relations; demand service
2. Patrons invest, subsidize	Control over resources	Set conditions for the supply of capital and operating funds
3. Management	Control over personnel	Set and supervise policies; public relations
4. Auxiliaries supplement and support management	Access to specialized services	Provide supplies, services
5. Colleagues	Solidarity	Set standards; protection
6. Competitors	Scarcity	Set standards; vigilance
7. Experts (talent, technicians, critics, subject specialists)	Skill knowledge, popularity, prestige	Provide personal, creative, performing, technical services, advice
8. Organizations	Pressure through representation, boycott, appeal to authorities	Demand favorable attention, portrayal, policy support
9. Publics (groups created or cultivated (or both) by media)	Individual patronage	Attend to messages; buy products

Management consists of executives and administrators who make up the chain of command in the organization. They formulate and supervise the implementation of policies intended to fulfill the terms of patron and other power-group support. They engage and control all personnel. Management's chief functions are to cultivate client relations and to conduct public relations. From the management's point of view, the messages that the institution produces must serve these two functions.

Auxiliaries provide supplies and services necessary to management's ability to perform its tasks. They are distributing organizations, networks, agencies, and syndicates; suppliers of raw materials, talent, artistic properties, and logistical services; wholesale and retail outlets; related manufacturing and trade concerns, associations, unions; and the holders of patents, copyrights, or other property rights.

Colleagues are communicators whose status, sense of direction or standards, and solidarity with one another can exert leverage on the formation and selection of messages.

Competitors are other professionals or media whose claims on scarce resources or ability to innovate can force the institution to exercise vigilance and either innovate or emulate to maintain its relationships with patrons and publics.

Experts possess needed personal skills, knowledge, critical abilities, or other gifts. They are writers, editors, creative talent, technicians, critics, researchers, subject matter specialists, consultants, and others who can give (or withhold) personal services necessary for communication.

Organizations are other formally structured or corporate groups who may claim attention, protection, or services. They may be business, political, religious, civic, fraternal, or professional associations. Inasmuch as some sort of public visibility has become a virtual requirement for organizational viability and support, the competition for attention is intense. Large organizational investments in public relations via the media exert pressure on media content and make media dependent on freely available (and self-serving) organizational resources.

Publics are the products of media output—groups created and cultivated through the messages. They are loose aggregations of people who may have little in common. But the symbols they share cultivate a community of meaning and perspective despite other differences. Management's task of "public relations" is to develop this sense of community into material value for the institution and its patrons.

Institutional power is exerted through the leverage built into power roles. Authorities can apply political or police pressure; patrons can provide or withdraw subsidy; managements can hire and fire; auxiliaries can work overtime or quit servicing; colleagues can strike; competitors can raid, scoop, or corner the market; experts can refuse to serve; organizations can support, protest, or boycott; and publics can patronize or stop reading, viewing, buying, or voting.

While analytically distinct, neither power roles nor types of leverage are in reality separate and isolated. On the contrary, they often combine, overlap, and telescope in different configurations. The accumulation of power roles and possibilities of leverage give certain institutions dominant positions in the mass communication of their societies.

MESSAGE SYSTEM ANALYSIS

The most popular products of mass-produced culture provide special opportunities for the study of socially potent message systems. In these systems—popular fiction, drama, and news—aspects of life are recreated in significant associations with total human situations. An area of knowledge or the operation of a social enterprise would appear only when dramatic or news values (i.e., social symbolic functions) demand it.

The symbolic composition and structure of the message system of a mass medium defines its own synthetic "world." All that exists in that "world" is represented in it. "Facts" reflect not opaque reality but palpable design. Focus directs attention, emphasis signifies importance, "typecasting" and fate accent value and power and the thread of action or other association ties things together into dynamic wholes. The "world" has its own time, space, geography, demography, and ethnography, bent to institutional purpose and rules of social morality. What policies populate, actions animate, fates govern, and themes dominate this "world?" How do things work in it, and why do they change from time to time? These are questions of message system analysis.

The study of a system *as system* notes processes and relationships expressed in the whole, not in its parts. Unlike literary, dramatic, or political criticism, or in fact, most personal cultural participation and judgment, message system analysis observes the record of institutional behavior in message mass-production for large and heterogeneous communities. The reliable observation of that record of institutional behavior reveals collective and common rather than individual and unique features of public image formation and cultivation.

The analysis may record topics, themes, persons, and types of action represented in the material. It may touch upon the history, geography, demography, and ethnography of the symbolic "world." The symbolic population and its interpersonal and group relationships may be observed. Themes of nature, science, politics, law, crime, business, education, art, illness and health, peace and war, sex, love, friendship, and violence may be coded. The roles, values, and goals of the characters who populate the symbolic "world" may be related to the issues with which they grapple and to the fates to which they are destined.

Media content indicators tell us not so much what individuals think or do as what most people think or do something *about* in *common*. They will tell us about the shared representations of life, the issues, and the prevailing points of view that capture public attention, occupy people's time, and animate their imagination. They will help us understand the impact of communication media development and social change upon the symbolic climate that affects *all* we think and do.

CULTIVATION ANALYSIS

The distinctive characteristics of large groups of people are acquired in the process of growing up, learning, and living in one culture rather than another. Individuals make their own selection of materials through which to cultivate personal images, tastes, views, and preferences, and they seek to influence those available to and chosen by their children. But they cannot cultivate that which is not available. They will rarely select what is scarcely available, seldom emphasized, or infrequently presented. A culture cultivates not only patterns of conformity but also of alienation or rebellion after its own image.

The message systems of a culture not only inform but form common images. They not only entertain but create publics. They not only satisfy but shape a range of attitudes, tastes, and preferences. They provide the boundary conditions and overall patterns within which the processes of personal and group-mediated selection, interpretation, and image-formation go on.

Cultivation analysis begins with the insights of the study of institutions and the message systems they produce and goes on to investigate the contributions that these systems and their symbolic functions make to the cultivation of assumptions about life and the world.

Message systems cultivate the terms upon which they present subjects and aspects of life. There is no reason for assuming that the cultivation of these terms depends in any significant way upon agreement or disagreement with or belief or disbelief in the presentations, or upon whether these presentations are presumably factual or imaginary. This does not mean, of course, that we do not normally attach greater credibility to a news story, a presumably factual report, a trusted source, a familiar account, than to a fairy tale or to what we regard as false or inimical. It does mean that in the general process of image-formation and cultivation both "fact" and "fable" play significant and interrelated roles.

The "effects" of communications are not primarily what they make us "do" but what they contribute to the meaning of all that is done (or accepted or avoided)—a more fundamental and ultimately more decisive process. The consequences of mass communication should be sought in the relationships between mass-produced and technologically mediated message systems and the broad common terms of image cultivation in a culture. The principal "effects" of mass communications are thus to be found in the fundamental assumptions, definitions, and premises they contain and cultivate, and not necessarily in agreements or disagreements with their overt suggestions or in acting upon their specific propositions at any one time. Communication is the nutrient culture and not just the occasional medicine (or poison) of mental life. The most critical public consequences of mass communications are in defining, ordering, and presenting the issues of life and society and not just in influencing who will do what in the short run.

A culture cultivates the images of a society. The dominant communication agencies produce the message systems that cultivate the dominant image patterns. They structure the public agenda of existence, priorities, values, relationships. People use this agenda—some more selectively than others—to support their ideas, actions, or both, in ways that, on the whole, tend to match the general composition and structure of message systems (provided, of course, that there is also other environmental support for these choices and interpretations). There is significant change in the nature and functions of that process when there is change in the technology, ownership, clientele, and other institutional characteristics of dominant communication agencies.

Decisive cultural change does not occur in the symbolic sphere alone. When it occurs, it stems from a change in social relations that makes the old cultural patterns dysfunctional to the new order. In time (although not necessarily without special attention and effort) new cultural patterns restore to public communications their basic functions: the support of the new (existing) order and its adjustment to changing times.

The mass media—printing, film, radio, television—ushered in the modern world as we know it. Mass communication changed the production and distribution of knowledge. The traditional disciplines cannot fully and adequately address those problems of changing societies that require a new theoretical focus. New disciplines and new forms of inquiry emerge to confront directly what the established fields touch upon only in passing. One such new discipline is communications. It emerged largely in response to the need for assessing the dynamics of mass media in different societies and for understanding the issues and choices they pose for all societies. Large-scale international cooperative efforts are underway to study mass media in changing cultures in comparative terms, thus making critical contributions to knowledge in all participating countries. The conceptual framework presented in this chapter is intended to contribute to those efforts.

CHAPTER 19

New Variables
for Cross-Cultural Study*

ALEX EDELSTEIN

If one looks at the structures of organized societies, one is struck as much by their commonalities as by their differences. Urban and professional life across cultures are more similar than different.

Given these equivalencies and the potentialities for comparing related communications behaviors, one would expect that more cross-cultural mass communication research would have been carried out. What we have seen essentially have been studies of media exposure.† That "act" of media exposure, to borrow a term from Carter (3), is comparable across cultures. But what about the *nature* of the act? What is equivalent—or different—across cultures with respect to how individuals use and evaluate media content and sources?

The problems of new variables for cross-cultural research in mass communication, thus posed, is simply one of what to observe and how to observe it.

*I would like to express thanks to Dr. Neil Hollander, who, as a graduate student in the School of Communications, played an important role in the conceptualization and operationalization of this research and the conduct of field work in Yugoslavia. Other members of the University of Washington group included Dr. John Mathiason and Mr. Robert Laing, M.A. Mr. Laing made a trip to Yugoslavia in connection with this study. Members of the staff in Yugoslavia included Mr. Milo Popović, Director of the Institute for Journalism; Mr. Srdjan Sokolović; Ms. Liljiana Danoljić; Ms. Jelena Donovič; and Stephan Marajanović. Mr. Sokolović participated also in the Seattle phase of the study. This research was supported by granted from the National Science Foundation and the Division of Education and Cultural Affairs of the Department of State. In Yugoslavia the project was administered by the Federal Agency for International Technical Cooperation (FAITC).

†An approximation of efforts at comparative mass communication research may be found in works by Lerner (8), Rao (13), Rogers (14) and Rogers and Shoemaker (15), but the Lerner and Rao works are less structured and do not seem to make systematic comparisons. The Rogers studies are placed in the situational context, but cross-cultural comparisons are not made at the same point in time.

1	2	3	4	5
Equivalent Social Groupings	Equivalent Social Problems	Learn Think about Equivalent Problems and Solutions to These Problems	Utilizing and Evaluating	Media and Other Sources of Information and Advice

\\faced with/ \\and/

Figure 1   Paradigm of cross-cultural study of mass communication.

There should be many new variables, but we appear to have lacked concepts and methodologies.*

Our own paradigm developed out of an interest in how individuals use interpersonal and mass communication to become aware of social problems and to define and resolve them in their own minds (7). As a way of beginning our cross-cultural investigations in predominantly Western cultures, we wished to test the proposition that individuals who exposed themselves to mass communication commonly become aware of social problems, attempt to describe them in some way, and in some cases make "decisions" about what should be done to solve those problems. The paradigm was formulated as shown in Figure 1.

As we have suggested, equivalence is a key concept. In this paradigm equivalence in social groupings was achieved by comparing individuals of similar sex, education, and other characteristics.

Equivalence in social problems was achieved in the sense that each person was permitted to describe his learning and thinking about problems that were important to him personally. The equivalence existed in the importance that each problem had for each individual, not in the *substantive* nature of the problem—that is, the issue was whether each individual was importantly concerned with a problem, rather than with what any problem was in substantive terms. This kind of equivalence permitted us to deal with all problems as a single set of data rather than as a group of subsets (although with an adequate sample this, too, would be possible).

The learning and thinking element of equivalence incorporated "levels." We could compare individuals who were merely aware that a problem existed, as compared to those who understood the nature of the problem so as to be able to describe it more fully, leading in some cases to definition of alternative means of dealing with the problem, or being able, as well, to suggest "other proposed solutions."

*Harms (8) and Samovar (16), particularly the former, suggest some parameters, but they are not operationalized as concepts, nor is there emphasis on mass communication.

We then looked for variability in the ways in which respondents in several cultures utilized and evaluated media and other sources of information and advice. While the "act" of using media and other information sources was considered to be equivalent, the ways in which those sources were used and evaluated could be expected to vary.

CROSS-CULTURAL CONSIDERATIONS

Some substantial differences in cultural inheritance were, of course, evident in the two Yugoslav cities we selected. The most obvious precursory conditions were the pronounced ethnic characters of the two cities. Belgrade is distinctly Serbian; Ljubljana is overwhelmingly Slovenian, with only small Austrian, Italian, and Croatian presence.

Slovenia (as well as Croatia, Bosnia, and Vojvodina) was incorporated in the Austro-Hungarian Monarchy. Serbia, by contrast, was under the control of the Turks from the fourteenth century to the first half of the nineteenth century. In the Middle Ages, however, both were independent states with high standards of culture and civilization.

Serbia reached the apex of power and prosperity under the reign of Emperor Dušan in the fourteenth century. Yugoslavia was affected by the classical influences of Greece and Rome, the Byzantine Empire, and later Central Europe.

While Serbia and Slovenia felt different influences, the Balkan Peninsula, on the crossroads between Central Europe and the Near East, has always been a point of intersection of cultural and political influence.

Some of the cultural differences that exist today among the Yugoslav nationalities are produced by different levels of economic development. A report to UNESCO by Majstorović (10) noted that at the end of World War II the geographical and cultural map of the country displayed formidable disparities that, although notably alleviated from 1945 to 1969, were still fairly conspicuous.

Our data on levels of education in Belgrade and Ljubljana reflected these disparities. Belgrade showed a substantial number of respondents who had less than an eighth grade education. The data also reflected even more substantially another distinctive condition: such an overwhelming wave of migration into Belgrade from smaller towns and surrounding peasantry that sociologists have referred to it as the ruralization of Belgrade.

To contrast these Old World cultures with an equivalent city with a Western culture we chose Seattle, a city of about 500,000 founded not much more than a century ago. Seattle is essentially a late-nineteenth- and twentieth-century community, with a mixed ethnic character made up largely of Scandinavians, English, and Irish, with a compound of European, Asian, and Russian influences. A professional community with several universities, it is also a shipping and sophisticated manufacturing center, with the Boeing Company its largest employer.

Seattle is a sea and air transportation hub for Alaska and Asia. There is some affinity with Ljubljana in this respect, for although Seattle is remote from other areas in terms of miles, it is an active transportation center, and a good proportion of the literate population travels abroad. Ljubljana is in the same sense close to Central Europe and to Italy.

MASS-MEDIA CONSIDERATIONS

The question with respect to media equivalencies, as we posed it, was not whether one community offered greater or lesser varieties of media but whether an individual of a given education, age, knowledge, and so forth might find sources adequate to his needs. The question focused on the *use* and utility of media sources and content, rather than the number of media. Nonetheless, the three communities were in many respects comparable in the availability of local press, television, and radio.

Belgrade has four daily newspapers, two morning and two afternoon.* The morning dailies are *Politika,* with a circulation of 270,000 copies, and *Borba,* once a party newspaper, that now is a general daily of 31,000 circulation. Both newspapers cover a spectrum of world and local public, cultural, and social affairs. Of the two evening newspapers, *Politika Ekspres* has a circulation of about 207,000 daily, and *Vecarnje Novosti* has the largest circulation in Belgrade, some 379,000. Each of the evening newspapers carries a small amount of local, regional, national, and world news but emphasizes human interest and "amusement" content, which includes accidents, crime, sex, and personalities.

In Belgrade, the weekly magazine *NIN* is considered a part of the "press." It is published by *Politika* and devotes a good deal of space to local and world affairs, commentary, and the like. It is similar in style to the weekly magazines that are contained in the Sunday editions of American newspapers, but is more extensive in its coverage. *Illustrated Politika* has a circulation of about 25,000 weekly; it contains some general information but is popular in its appeal, resembling the afternoon daily newspapers.

Ljubljana has two morning daily newspapers, *Delo* and *Dnevnik. Delo* is in many respects the counterpart of *Politika.* With a circulation of roughly 93,500, it maintains correspondents abroad and in regions of Yugoslavia, giving wide coverage of foreign affairs and internal Yugoslav matters. *Dnevnik*

*Data were taken from (1, 2, 4, 11, 12, 17).

has a smaller circulation of 67,000 and resembles a local newspaper, carrying a modest degree of foreign and national news.

Ljubljana also has a number of weekly newspapers and magazines. *Tedenska Tribune* is a general-circulation Sunday news weekly, comparable to *NIN* in Belgrade, which contains political, social, and other news and commentary. *Tovaris* emphasizes internal problems of self-management, the economy, and similar topics.

Seattle has two daily newspapers, the *Times* and the *Post-Intelligencer*. The *Times* is an independent conservative afternoon newspaper, with a circulation of 230,439 daily and 288,257 on Sundays. The *Post-Intelligencer* is a Republican chain newspaper, with a Hearst national editorial policy, but which carries columnists and the news service of the *New York Times*. Its circulation is 182,192 daily and 242,490 on Sundays. Neither newspaper carries a great deal of world news; each probably is typical for its circulation size.

A mass-media factor of some importance is the geographical setting of Ljubljana. Unlike Belgrade, Ljubljana has easy physical access to Austrian and Italian radio and television by regular and shortwave radio and by VHF and UHF television transmissions. Added to this are cultural factors such as language commonalities (a great deal of Italian and Austro-German is spoken in Ljubljana) and the ethnic imprints from long-time Austrian influences and World War II occupation by Italy.

In 1967 a study of television in Slovenia showed that 27 percent of set owners technically could view Austrian television; 21 percent, Italian television; and 22 percent television from Zagreb, the capital of Croatia. This would not be the case for Belgrade.

At the time of this study, Belgrade had only one television channel. In the past year, it has added another, which is similar but more commercial in content. An estimated 80 percent of the population in Belgrade has access to television sets, either through ownership (about 60 percent) or viewing (another 20 percent).

In Seattle there are three network television stations: the CBS, ABC and NBC outlets. Each carries all of the network documentaries; special public-interest programs; and morning, early-evening, and late-evening news shows. In addition, each station attempts to do a full job of covering local news. Seattle also has an educational television station, Channel 9, which carries local discussion and public affairs shows plus the network offerings of the Public Broadcasting Service. In addition, those who subscribe to a cable service can obtain news shows from Channel 12 in Bellingham and Channels 2 and 6 in Vancouver, British Columbia (Canada), and Channels 11 and 13 from Tacoma.

There are 17 broadcast radio stations in Seattle, several of which are specialty stations that broadcast almost exclusively religious programs, news and commentary, or popular music. The news radio stations are primarily net-work affiliated, and some are on limited broadcast schedules. Stations from nearby communities are also received. News on radio typically consists of numerous short broadcasts, similar in pattern to what is broadcast on Yugoslav radio, but there is somewhat less news commentary than Yugoslav radio.

There are two major programs or channels on Belgrade radio. Belgrade I goes on the air at 4 a.m. daily and broadcasts until midnight. Belgrade II is on the air from noon to 9 p.m. the same evening. It is followed immediately by Belgrade III, educational radio, which broadcasts generally until midnight.

About every two hours Belgrade I and II broadcast short news shows, about five to 10 minutes in duration. The evening radio news shows run approximately 10 to 20 minutes. The two stations are similar, both covering a wide range of music, concerts, drama, and news content. Belgrade III carries serious music, discussions, and cultural programs.

Ljubljana I and II follow a similar format. However, there appear to be more listeners of foreign radio broadcasts. As is the case with television, more foreign sources are accessible to Ljubljana than Belgrade. Generally speaking, there is more television and radio coverage in Ljubljana than in Belgrade, including a better ratio of sets per household.*

The point that is to be made is not that there are discrepancies in media mixes—which are evident—but that content available through these sources may be equivalent *from the point of view of the individual who is attempting to cope with a particular problem.* While the Seattle media consumer might work across a range of television and radio stations for requisite content, the Belgrade and Ljubljana consumer would work within a more limited array of stations but could abstract from the broadcasts an adequate—from his point of view—range of topical treatments. This is the level at which "equivalence" might be postulated.

METHODOLOGICAL CONSIDERATIONS

We sought to develop observational methods that were unobtrusive and could be specified in situational terms.

By *unobtrusive* we meant that the observer would not give the subject any information, particularly any that he might use to "value" the object. Insofar as is possible, the subject should himself state both the object with which he was concerned and the values that he, himself, attached to it. By *specification* we meant that the subject should locate the problem in time and space—that

---

*Slovenian data came primarily from *Radio, 1967, Television, 1968* and *Slovendsdo Javno Mnenje, 1969* (18).

is, he should himself tell the observer what problem he was concerned with (at that time) and why it was important to him personally. Proceeding in this way, we developed an approach that was unobtrusive in content. We did not ask respondents to tell us whether they agreed or disagreed with what we thought about given problems; rather, they told us what they thought about a particular problem which they specified and described. Data were obtained on how individuals learned and thought about local and world problems. We are presenting the data for both as a means of demonstrating the varying utilities of communication for individuals for different "objects."

The data incorporate only one so-called independent variable—that of sex roles. The reason that this variable rather than education, age, income, or other demographic indicators was selected was that the growing emancipation of the intellects and capabilities of women is of great concern both to developing and to so-called highly developed nations.

THE NEW VARIABLES

Because with our methodology the individual was asked to tell us what problems existed, rather than imposing a given set of problems, a quantitative measure of salience was easy to apply. Each variable leads to a resultant variable. The more problems mentioned by the respondent—such as housing, pollution, transportation, traffic, recreation, and safety—the more salience was expressed toward community problems, leading to *New Variable 1*—number of urban problems named.

We also asked the individual which of these problems was "most important to him personally." We then asked "why this problem was more important to him than the other problems that he had named." Hence, *New Variable 2*— number of reasons why one problem was judged to be *more important than other problems*.

We also sought to categorize the nature of these reasons, or attributes. Several "qualitative" codes were derived from the work of Carter (3) and from our own earlier research. We could ask whether the respondent used a pertinence-type discrimination (i.e., compared two or more problems on the basis of a single attribute), used distinctive attributes for the one most important problem without reference to other problems, or used himself as an attribute. (He might say in effect that a problem was most important because it affected him personally.) These qualitative codes produced three additional variables: *New Variable 3*—whether the individual actually compared one problem to another on the basis of a single attribute—*New Variable 4*—whether the individual described his most important problem by means of distinctive attributes, *not comparing one problem to other problems*—and *New Variable 5*—

whether *without further description* the individual said the problem was important because it "affected him personally."

We then asked the individual what should be done to solve the problem. Note that the problem had been specified by the individual; we did not ask the respondent what should be done to solve problems which we ourselves would suggest. The result was *New Variable 6*—whether the individual had decided what should be done to solve the problem.

We also asked whether *any other* solutions had been proposed. This permitted the individual to give us any knowledge he had about solutions that he had considered at any level, or had been aware of at any time. Hence, *New Variable 7*—how many "proposed solutions" an individual might suggest.

We then asked the individual how he had learned about the problem. We did not ask whether the individual had learned of it through any of the media and ask for a "yes" or "no" response to our "suggestions." Hence, *New Variable 8*—volunteered sources of knowledge about a specific problem.

We next asked the individual to tell us which of the sources that had been named was most useful to him with respect to *that problem.* We did not ask which source was most trustworthy, most complete, or whatever. We merely asked which source *was most useful.* Thus, *New Variable 9*—which source of information about a specific problem *was most useful.*

We then could ask the subject the reason *why* the source specified was most useful. We could total the number of reasons he had given and obtain a quantitative measure of source utility. Hence, *New Variable 10*—number of reasons given why a source of information was most useful.

In addition, we could code *qualitative* attributes of sources. Essentially four attributes that described the utility of sources of information were derived from the volunteered responses: *New Variable 11*—whether the source of information about a specific problem was *trustworthy—New Variable 12*—whether the source of information about a specific problem was *convenient* (e.g., accessible)—*New Variable 13*—whether the source was useful because of its *content* (e.g., cognitive)—*New Variable 14*—whether the source was useful because of its *channel dimensionalities* (i.e., sight plus sound, time to reflect, etc.).

In previous studies by Edelstein (5–7) we had been interested in the *structure* of knowledge about solutions. We had asked subjects to cite reasons for and against their proposed solution. A person who had both positive and negative values for an alternative could be considered more complex in his knowledge than one who had only positive *or* negative values for the alternatives. Hence, *New Variable 15*—complexity of structure of *knowledge about alternatives.*

In our earlier research we also observed that some individuals proposed only "war" solutions, while others proposed only "peace" solutions. These individuals could be compared with those who proposed *both* war *and* peace solutions. These responses varied in dimensionality. Hence, *New Variable 16*—dimensionality of structure of *alternatives.*

In prior research we also extended the mass communication paradigm to interpersonal communication. Thus individuals were asked whether in interpersonal communication they had proposed a solution, whether the other person had proposed a solution, etc. Hence, *New Variable 17*—whether the respondent proposed a solution—and *New Variable 18*—whether the other member of the dyad proposed a solution.

We could also look into the *nature* of the solutions. Hence, *New Variable 19*—whether individuals offered *similar* or *different* solutions (i.e., *cognitive overlap*).

SOME DEVELOPMENT APPLICATIONS

The need for more comparable and productive research in developing countries guided our methodological innovations. In conventional methodologies (many of them applied in developing areas) individuals are often asked to demonstrate literacy with respect to problems with which they are not personally concerned. A general test of literacy may or may not, however, be relevant to any individual's search for competence with respect to a *particular problem*. But individuals who are interested in a problem may develop the literacy skills necessary to function in relation to *that problem*.

The actual use of all media (particularly print) by the less educated (and hence in most developing countries, most women) could be underrepresented, therefore, by this conventional methodological approach. *General* tests would be given where only *particular* tests were called for. Situationally appropriate methodology, we reasoned, should produce fewer artifactual discrepancies among educational, sex, and other groupings. This did not mean, of course, that *some real differences would not be present*.

SEX ROLES AS A DEVELOPMENT CONCEPT

Sex roles in most societies define what men and women are expected to do and tend to do in work and social settings. For example, patterns of restraint in certain societies attempt to limit what a man or a woman may do in an occupational or social role; in the same way, there are affirmative demands for behavior in given situations.

We felt that our three cultures could test these propositions. Hence, we expected that the communication behavior of women required to play more traditional roles, with consequent proscriptions and restraints upon behavior, would vary from the behavior of those in situations where they were permitted more occupational and social freedom. We recognized (as a subsequent analysis showed) that education was a significant force in reducing differentiation in sex roles, but a straightforward analysis would serve as a basis for observing the changes brought about by educational development.

We first compared men and women *within* communities and then compared men and women *across* communities. We reasoned that the culture that demonstrated the most internal discrepancies in cognitive and communication behaviors would reflect the most traditional values. The location and historical settings of Serbia, as compared to Slovenia, and the representativeness of the two cities of these cultures were highly suggestive of this hypothesis.

We tested cognitive and communication behavior with regard to two kinds of events—a local problem and a world problem. We reasoned that the role discrepancies should be most apparent at the level of world problems, where a higher level of education and more abstract forms of participation were demanded. Unlike directly observable local problems, world events may seem remote; to generate interest, a greater range of interest is required. Local problems could be observed personally by the individual, but many local problems were defined in terms of female roles, such as marketing.

Belgrade (Local Problems)

KNOWLEDGE AND DECISION-MAKING.   In Belgrade, the most traditional community, men were more engaged than women in several ways, but women did demonstrate that local problems were important to them. For example, men named significantly more local problems, provided more solutions to them, and compared one problem to another in formulating solutions. Women were as able to describe *why* a local problem was important and were much more likely to say that the problem was important because it *affected them personally*. Thus, men were aware of a greater range of problems, affecting more persons, and were more likely to propose solutions, whereas women saw the importance of local problems in personal terms and conceded that the solution might not lie in their hands.

USES AND EVALUATION OF COMMUNICATION.   The data above suggest that men are exposed to more sources of information. This was confirmed. Men cited a greater number of sources of information; men also reported more use of television, radio, the press (the greatest discrepancy between the two groups) and demonstrated more ability to evaluate information sources. Men also discussed local problems more with persons outside the family, both informally and at meetings.

The female sex role was observed in the following ways: Women reported as much contact with friends, more discussion with members of the family, as much *direct contact* with the problem (i.e., learning by personal experience); and reported that they wanted additional information almost as much as men.

In Belgrade male sex roles seemed to have an effect on knowledge, decision-making, and use of mass media and interpersonal communication. Women maintained friendship and family communication roles.

Ljubljana (Local Problems)

If our cultural hypotheses were sound, we might expect fewer differences between male and female roles and behaviors in Ljubljana because it is a less traditional society.

KNOWLEDGE AND DECISION-MAKING. As expected, the discrepancies between male and female behavior were not so sharp as those in Belgrade. Men did show, however, somewhat greater ability to name local problems and a significantly greater ability to provide solutions, but even these differences were smaller than those observed in Belgrade.

Men and women did *not* differ in their tendencies to compare problems as a basis for suggesting solutions, to see problems as important to oneself, and to cite reasons for the importance of the problem. (Fewer reasons were cited than had been mentioned in Belgrade, indicating somewhat less salience of local problems in Ljubljana than in Belgrade.)

USE AND EVALUATION OF COMMUNICATION. The lack of discrepancies between male and female sex roles in the definition and solving of local problems led us to expect fewer discrepancies in communications behaviors, as well. Our expectations were confirmed in almost every respect. Men and women cited approximately the same number of media sources. Within media, men and women used television and radio similarly. Men used the press significantly more than women, but the discrepancy was not great. Men and women also used friendships to about the same degree, referred to family contacts in about the same proportions, cited personal experience as often, and expressed an equal number of references to media utilities.

This pattern was repeated for interpersonal communication. Men and women engaged equally in discussions with other persons and expressed a similar desire for information.

The male-female role discrepancy seemed most evident in the amount of discussion carried out at meetings, to which women had the least access.

Comparing communications behavior cross-culturally in Belgrade and Ljubljana with respect to local problems, we found that males in Belgrade, compared to men in Ljubljana, used more sources of information, and within this, used television, press, and friendships more than women in learning about the nature of local problems. Belgrade men also discussed local problems more in meetings. Thus, men in Belgrade were more preoccupied with local problems than those in Ljubljana, an evident difference in orientation.

Seattle (Local Problems)

KNOWLEDGE AND DECISION-MAKING. If our cultural hypotheses regarding traditional male and female roles were tenable, we should expect there to be even fewer significant differences between men and women in their knowledge and solving of local problems. This expectiation was confirmed in an unexpected way in Seattle. There we found that women were able to name local problems more than men, but they were somewhat less able to suggest solutions for problems—the same condition that we had observed in Belgrade and Ljubljana.

Women, however, were as able to compare and to describe the nature of problems and provided even more attributes for problems than men, although the differences were not highly significant.

USE AND EVALUATION OF COMMUNICATION. Our expectations for media use and evaluation followed from our findings about knowledge and decision-making. We assumed that there would be few differences between men and women both in the number of information sources that they used and in the nature of those sources.

As hypothesized, men did not differ from women in the number of media sources of information, nor in the use of radio, newspapers, friends, interpersonal discussion, or discussion at meetings. There were, however, some expected differences in the greater use by women of television and the family as sources of information. Television is used more by women in Seattle, and the family is a more significant source of communication. Women and men had similar knowledge, but different decision-making capacities; media differences were attributable to the occupational and social role of women.

The comparisons across cultures were of interest. Seattle men and women cited more local problems and offered a substantially greater number of reasons why the problems were important. Interestingly, Seattle men and women found these problems less soluble.

The greater concern with important local problems was accompanied by greater use of almost all sources of information by both men and women and correspondingly less dependence upon "personal experience" or personal observation. Both men and women in Seattle cited a greater number of media sources and used all the media more as information sources. They did not, however, engage more in interpersonal communication or discuss problems more at meetings, nor did they express more need for further information.

In general, our expectations for cross-cultural differences between sex roles were confirmed. As we had speculated, the within-culture differences in Belgrade were greater than the cross-cultural differences.

Belgrade (World Problems)

Because Belgrade was identified as the most traditional community, we expected more discrepancies between male and female roles than in Ljubljana and Seattle.

KNOWLEDGE AND DECISION-MAKING. Much as we had expected, men named more world problems, proposed more solutions for them, and compared one problem to another as a way of describing them. Women, however, were able to suggest more reasons why a problem was important. This implied that while women concerned themselves with fewer world problems, they learned more about them. Yet they proposed fewer solutions. This finding would be consistent with less experience in decision-making.

USE AND EVALUATION OF COMMUNICATION. If the essential difference was decision-making rather than knowledge, there would be fewer discrepancies in media use and evaluation than might otherwise be the case. Our data appeared to support this. There were no differences in use of television, friends, or even in personal experience with world problems. Men, however, did use radio and the press appreciably more than women, but interestingly, they did not provide any more evaluation criteria for the media than women. Thus, there was the suggestion that decision-making was an aspect of the male role in Belgrade culture, even though women were almost as well informed and used media very similarly.

Ljubljana (World Problems)

KNOWLEDGE AND DECISION-MAKING. We expected fewer differences in knowledge and decision-making than in Belgrade. These hypotheses were confirmed. Men did not name more world problems, propose more solutions to them, or propose more reasons for their importance. The only difference was in the greater tendency for men to compare one problem to another, while women perceived world problems as being more personally relevant.

USE AND EVALUATION OF COMMUNICATION. Given the lack of discrepancy in knowledge and problem-solving abilities, we did not expect great differences in the use and evaluation of media. Our expectations were almost wholly confirmed. Women and men employed the same number of sources of information. Within media, there were no differences with respect to television, radio, the press, friendships, or personal experience. The only difference between women and men was a tendency for women to cite family sources of information.

Seattle (World Problems)

Our expectations for Seattle were similar to those we held for Ljubljana, and our data appeared to support these hypotheses.

KNOWLEDGE AND DECISION-MAKING. Men and women in Seattle named the same number of world problems and cited the same number of reasons for their importance. Men, however, proposed more solutions, but the differences were not great. Men tended to compare one problem to another slightly more, and women tended slightly more to perceive the importance of a world problem in personal terms. This was similar to what we observed in Ljubljana and more markedly in Belgrade.

USE AND EVALUATION OF MEDIA AND COMMUNICATION. Given the lack of differences in male and female roles with respect to knowledge and decision-making, we expected few differences in either the use or the evaluation of information sources. These expectations were confirmed. However, women were more likely to cite television, friendships, and the family as sources of information; men were more likely to cite personal experience.

Turning to cross-cultural comparisons, Seattle men and women suggested the greatest number of world problems, followed by Ljubljana and Belgrade. Also, Seattle and Ljubljana men and women proposed the greater number of solutions. In Ljubljana and Belgrade there was a greater tendency to compare world problems as a way of assessing their significance, whereas men and women in Seattle saw them in terms of personal significance. The situational factor of war, perhaps, explained this difference. However, the differences were not attributable to sex roles, which was our major concern. There were no distinctive differences cross-culturally between Seattle and Ljubljana in the use of media as sources of information about world problems, and as noted previously, the differences between Ljubljana and Belgrade were only slight.

Across all three cultures, the *patterns* of media usage to define and solve world problems remained constant; in this respect, differences *within* a culture (Belgrade) were greater than differences *across* cultures (Belgrade, Ljubljana, and Seattle).

The productivity expressed in the interrelationships among our variables suggested that our methodology permitted us not only to examine new variables, but to describe essential processes of knowledge, decision-making, and media use and evaluation cross-culturally. This was made possible by the equivalence achieved in defining problems conceptually rather than substantively (e.g., equivalence across individuals and cultures in terms of the degree of concern expressed with respect to any problem that was important to the individual), and it was made possible by a methodology that permitted new variables to emerge.

REFERENCES

1. Begovic, Bruno. "Inquiry of Yugoslav Periodicals in 1966," *Novinarstvo* 4. Belgrade: Yugoslav Institute of Journalism, 1967.
2. Bosnic, Slobodan. "Demographic, Economic, and Educational Features of Yugoslav Population Which Affect the Distribution of Mass Media," in *Factors and Ways of Expansion of Mass Media in Yugoslavia*. Belgrade: Yugoslav Institute of Journalism, 1969.
3. Carter, R. F. "Communication and Affective Relations," *Journalism Quarterly, 42* (1965), 203–212.
4. Dzinic, Firdus. "Expansion of Political-Informative Effect of Radio, TV and Press in Yugoslavia," in *Utilisation of Public Information*. Belgrade: Yugoslav Institute of Journalism, 1970.
5. Edelstein, Alex S. "Communication and International Conflict," in France Verg (ed.), *Mass Media and International Understanding*. Ljubljana: 1969.

6. ———. "The Public Opinion Polls as a Source of Distortion in the International Flow of News." Paper prepared for XVII International Symposium, International Centre for Higher Education. Strasbourg, December 8–13, 1969.

7. ———. *The Uses of Communication in Decision-Making—A Cross Cultural Study.* New York: Praeger, 1974.

8. Harms, L. S. *Intercultural Communication.* New York: Harper & Row, 1973.

9. Lerner, Daniel. *The Passing of Traditional Society—Modernizing the Middle East.* New York: Free Press, 1964.

10. Majstorović, Stevan. *The Cultural Policy of Yugoslavia.* Belgrade: UNESCO, 1970.

11. Marjanović, Stevan. "Graphic Basis of Yugoslav Periodicals," *Novinarstvo* 1–2. Belgrade: Yugoslav Institute of Journalism, 1968.

12. Plavsić, Prvoslav. "Frequency of Listening to Radio," in *Factors and Ways of Expansion of Mass Media in Yugoslavia.* Belgrade: Yugoslav Institute of Journalism, 1969.

13. Rao, Y. V. Lakshmana. *Communication and Development—A Study of Two Indian Villages.* Minneapolis: University of Minnesota Press, 1969.

14. Rogers, E. M. *Modernization Among Peasants—The Impact of Communication.* New York: Holt, Rinehart & Winston, 1969.

15. Rogers, E. M., and F. F. Shoemaker. *Communication of Innovations.* New York: Free Press, 1971.

16. Samovar, Larry A., and Richard E. Porter. *Intercultural Communication: A Reader.* Belmont, Calif.: Wadsworth, 1972.

17. Stoković, Zivorad. "Radio and TV Subscribers in Yugoslavia in 1966," *Novinarstvo* 4. Belgrade: Yugoslav Institute of Journalism, December, 1966.

18. Vreg, France. *Slovensko Javno Mnenje.* Ljubljana: Center Za Raziskovanje Javnega Mnenja in Mnozicnih Komunikacij, 1969.

CHAPTER 20

The Development of a Socialist Communication Theory

TAMÁS SZECSKŐ

The relatively fast development of communication research in Hungary from the middle of the 1960s is incomprehensible without realizing two basic trends characteristic of Hungary's domestic policy and public life in the 1960s and 1970s: the comprehensive economic reform called "new economic mechanism" and the further development of the country's political and public institutions in the direction of "socialist democratism." Both trends concern basic social relations and, as opposed to the overcentralized political, governmental, and economic system of the 1950s, afford a more extensive field of decision, action, and responsibility for different social and economic units. At the same time, because of the increased social relevance of such actions, both trends involve more social planning, particularly planning of the more complex and long-range varieties.

Under such conditions, the leading political bodies' and social organizations' demands for information have rapidly increased. Furthermore, there has been a structural change within these demands. Besides material information, the particular content of social consciousness is getting more attention. The leadership of the Party and the government have increasingly been encouraging the research of public opinion and mass communication. Consequently, the findings of such research are integrated more and more often into information, cultural, and communication policies on a national level.

The development of communication research has been influenced by advances in Marxist social theory and the integration of the results of empirical methods with social theory. Linguistics also bears on the trends of communication research, and Hungarian linguistics may well be proud of its traditions, especially in historical linguistics. Recently it has started integrating structuralism, generative grammar, and other linguistic approaches and probing adjacent fields such as sociolinguistics and psycholinguistics. Since 1960 scholars in the theory of literature have also been adopting methods of

223

communication research such as the quantitative content and semiotic approaches to art analysis. From the middle of the 1960s there have been contributions from the concepts and logic of cybernetics, information theory, mathematical theory of games, and general systems theory.

BASIC ISSUES

Communication research in Hungary, with its close ties to philosophy and with its rather differentiated background in social theory, was soon to find itself facing the basic issue of how to grasp the social nature and historic character of communication.

There appears to be two ways for researchers to tackle this issue. One is to find out about the substance of social information, as opposed to the information concept of mathematical information theory. One researcher is investigating the "produced" information (namely signs and symbols which are the social character), in keeping with Marx's conception of the production of consciousness (2). Another researcher attempts to approach internal dialectics, and through this the historic nature of social information, by distinguishing between so called "fact-information" and "value-information" (6).

Another group of researchers concentrates on the processes of communication rather than on information itself, and its members tend to contrast human processes with mechanical and animal information transmission. One researcher approaching communicational processes from a sociopsychological point of view, recommends juxtaposing man's objective practices with his relations, the two factors being equally important in the interactions between man and his environment (4). The author of another work points out that communication is connected with the formation of all kinds of social relations and that relations between humans are in any case potentially communicative (8). A recent study dealing with the sociological aspects of communication is even more explicit on this point. Its author argues that the metabolism of society appears to be a materially based unity equally divided between movements of energy and movements of information. Thus, the interactions between man and his environment are doubly mediated—partly by the working tools, partly by communication. It follows that social relations become manifest by being communicated (13).

The above efforts are mainly deductive and tend to consist of model-building. Whether these models are workable can be found out by inductive possibilities created by empirical research. The efforts to match inductive and deductive studies and to render them operational are again suggesting two further aspects characteristic of communication research in Hungary.

The notion of "ordinariness" deriving from social theory—mainly from the works of György Lukács—has fertilized communication research. The effect of Lukács's *Die Eigenart des Aesthetischen* up to now appears to be paradoxical. His references to, and sketchy thoughts on, the nonaesthetic and "ordinary" have had a greater impact on Hungarian social sciences than his more elaborate constructs about the specificity of the aesthetic. Philosophers, aestheticians, and sociologists have recently published writings dealing with the phenomena of everyday (nonaesthetic and nonscientific) communication. The majority of the processes and acts of interpersonal communication are examples of "ordinariness," and most of the authors classify mass communication, public opinion, fashion phenomena, and rumors in this category as well. Everyday communication contains more psychological parameters than other forms and spheres of social communication. Speech in context, metacommunicative signs, the situation in which partners of a conversation find themselves, the perceptions of this situation, the stereotypes of everyday thinking encoded in words or behavioral signs, a quick turnover of mutual definition of roles—all these and their like contain a web of interdependent factors for investigation.

The situations of everyday communication (including mass communication) have four basic elements: text, metatext, environment, and relation. The text explicitly manifests itself in a firmly objectified system of signs, which, in most cases, is in accordance, more or less, with the intention of the communicating parties. The metatext contains implicit, more loosely objectified signs and is much less conscious and intentional in nature. While the text lends meaning, the metatext renders sense to a situation. The exchange of signs, signals, and symbols is taking place through the clusters of text and metatext channels which are embedded in the third element, the social-substantial environment of human beings. The fourth element is the human-social relation generating communication.

In aesthetic communication the four elements play a role in the discourse between the author, his work of art, and the audience, but with the roles undergoing a significant change: In aesthetic (and also in scientific) communication the information channel of the text prevails, and its highly objectified sophisticated system of signs enables it to assume the informative functions of the metatext as well as partly those of its environment. The whole aesthetic impact of a poem or a piece of music is encoded in the 14 lines of a sonnet or the orchestral score, and the recipient, in a traditional situation of enjoying art—and aided by a performer—seems to be capable of relishing it without the qualifying interpreting signs of the metatext or that of the environment. In other words, in highly sophisticated forms of communication this relation is almost exclusively expressed by the text; the metatext and the environment have a very small—if any—role to play. Metatext and environment do not in these cases become autonomous elements of communication, although in everyday situations they have independent, equal, and intersecting functions.

Communication theory in Hungary endeavors to grasp the notion of communication situations while challenging the subjective interpretations of situational interactionalism and existentialism and the mechanical probabilistic situation interpretation of cybernetics and the general system theory (13). This interpretation creates a sociohistorical category of several levels. Starting from broader historical situations and proceeding down to the situational microelements of an act of communication, the category is capable of systematically depicting communication as a socially determined process.

HISTORICAL PERSPECTIVE

Postulating communication to be a substantial human-social attribute renders the Marxist approach to communication theory historic in nature. On a theoretical level this is expressed partly by an interest in the ontogenesis and philogenesis of communication and partly through a questioning of the sociogenesis of the social communication system (12). This interpretation of communication suggests a general correspondence—an isomorphism—between the structure of social relations (i.e., social structure) and that of the communication system of society. However, this isomorphism appears to be rather abstract. By establishing an isomorphism between the two, we have not answered questions such as to what extent the system of communication in a given society or in a certain historical period is to reflect social relations or to obscure their actual structure. Or to what extent the microstructures of communication are to reflect macrostructural relations of a society. Indeed, this seems to be a rich terrain for communication research.

Another manifestation of historicity is the multiplication of empirical research that is concentrating on "blocks" of the social mind, on attitude patterns, and on stereotypes within the everyday consciousness. These phenomena developed along with, and occasionally were hardened by, the historical development of Hungarian society. Probing into them may contribute partly to a theoretical explanation of the movements of social consciousness and partly, to an increase in the efficiency of social communication. These investigations are various in their methods and choice of topic; they range from socioanthropological monographs (7) to surveys exploring the formations of the populations's concepts of history (1).

A third manifestation of historical perspective consists of investigations that endeavor to probe modifications of communications through time either in a genre or a cross-sectional content sample, mainly through the use of content analysis. These include the analysis of the concept of politics, based on the editorials of the central daily of the Party over a 17-year period (15), an investigation in the changes of the way political cartoons picture the world (10), and an investigation into the trends of changes in the program structure of 50 years of radio broadcasting.

Content analyses are rather frequent wherever communication research has passed the stage of the "head-counting" type of audience research, of laboratory propaganda efficiency surveys, and of linguistics using traditional methods. These investigations attempt to do justice to historical analysis by embedding phenomena under study in broader historic movements. To attain this objective they usually adopt a multimethod interdisciplinary approach. For instance, the authors of a study into the hit songs of the past 40 years combined the investigation of their melodies and harmonies with a sociological survey of their texts (9). Another promising multiple-aspect content-analysis is an investigation into the almanac literature of the period of Hungarian capitalism (5). Considering the fact that in Hungary (with peasant population in the majority until 1945) almanacs were a basic and sometimes exclusive means of mass communication for the greater part of peasantry, analysis of the materials of these almanacs from a historical and sociological point of view may not only add important facts to the history of the Hungarian mass communication system but may also explore the historical sources of present day social consciousness.

That communication research in Hungary tends to be historic is understandable, because the researchers are analyzing the characteristics of a society that had undergone revolutionary transformations for the past quarter of a century. The assessment of social aspects in everyday life is automatically conveying a sense of history.

THE MASS COMMUNICATION SYSTEM

The system of mass communication organically adjusts itself partly to the structure of political institutions and partly to the structure of educational-cultural institutions. Its political functions are information agitation and propaganda; its cultural functions are the conveyance of culture, education, and entertainment. The massive system of contents conveyed, the size of its audiences, and its ability to react quickly renders mass communication one of the most efficient political and cultural instruments—and one wielded by the ruling classess as an instrument of power in all developed societies. Owing to its immediate political significance and, furthermore, in view of its important integrative, adaptative, and socializing functions, mass communication is a directed activity in all organized societies. The differences among societies lie mostly in the methods and forms of management.

The differences between the functions of the mass communication system are relative. Information also has agitative and propagandistic aspects, and entertainment can either promote or block the possibilities of conveying culture. Moreover, the two basic groups of functions that influence and cultivate masses are interlocking, too. Public education bears on the possibilities and outcome of political influence, and mass media influence may promote or impair the efficiency of public education.

Because the system of Hungarian mass communication is being formed within a new type of socialist society, it has some structural and functional characteristics that are either new or prevail to a higher degree than in the mass communication systems of nonsocialist societies. Because this society involves the planning of the most important social processes, the mass communication system can be more fully and methodologically integrated with political and cultural institutions. This is due partly to the integrated character of social planning and partly to the fact that no single element of mass communication is privately owned.

In this new type of mass communication system the market forces do not play a determining role. Therefore, the characteristic "lowest-common-denominator" principle of the system can be limited. This is to be seen partly in the fact that the opposition of elite and mass cultures is less prevalent than in traditional mass communication systems and partly in the time orientation that is found in the socialist systems far more than in traditional ones. This type of mass communication has a definitely historical character. Present events are not considered to be of interest in themselves but rather in relation to the past or to the future. Because this is a society in some sense "on the way," whose people are living through revolutionary transformations in which the elements of past and present are combined, mass communication must necessarily play a larger part in the process of socialization—in making the new social values and norms accepted—and in the reflection of the conflicting values of a transitional period, than does the mass communication system of a nonsocialist society.

A COHERENT FRAMEWORK

That scientific research should subsume its two essential macroelements— mass communication and public opinion—in a coherent framework seems obvious. The conclusion appears to be the same for research both in Hungary and in some other socialist countries: Public opinion is a dynamic result of communication process. Therefore, as against more traditional schools of public opinion, the demoscopically accessible "collective judgment" is understood to be not a matter of prime interest; however, the dynamic process in which it is engendered is interesting, and the historical, political, sociological, and psychological determinants and conditioning factors of "collective judgment" are revealing.

This approach has theoretical and practical advantages. It affords an operational link of the different phenomena relating to the process and effects of mass communication with other spheres of social existence and with the whole system of relations in the society. It eliminates the methodological gap between the cultural and political aspects of mass communication. It also contributes to a uniform treatment of political and nonpolitical (moral, taste-forming) aspects of public opinion. Finally, it tends to direct the attention of researchers not only to how mass communication is molding public opinion but also to the way public opinion influences the operation of mass communication within the whole system of social institutions (14).

The efficiency of mass communication is a social-strategical category to be interpreted in comparing the complex and long-range cluster of effects with the system of postulated values and norms of socialist society. Such interpretation is closely connected with the principles of social planning and social regulation. Therefore, we examine the system of mass communication and communicational behavior in the system of organic social relations as interpreted by Antonio Gramschi: To what extent does it help the recipient recognize his social-historic situation? How does it rally people for the aims of a socialist society? To what extent does it contribute to the development of institutions and activities of public life? To what extent does it become a molder of, and forum to, the responsible actions of autonomous citizens (3)?

Another example comes from the so-called "generativity investigations." Sociologists and psychologists investigating the reception of the cultural contents of mass communication found the traditional triad of the arts—creator-mediator-recipient—too simple. They found it both necessary and useful to borrow from linguistics and to introduce the concept of the "faculty of generative creation" as an approach to the creative faculties of recipients. In a study regarding the reception of music, the sociological and cultural-political relevance of this category (filled with experimental data) is revealed in the following survey:

. . . this sort of musical productivity operates like a linguistic faculty of a generative kind which does not repeat complete and fixed forms, only some groups of elements and the rule of their combination. Out of a finite number of elements (vocabulary) and a finite number of rules (grammatical transformations) an infinite number of propositions (sentences) can be "generated." Likewise the generative musical faculty is aware of a rather limited number of elements (tonal system) and finite number of productive rules (musical patterns); however, out of these an infinite number of tunes can be generated again. . . . We think that at this point we are facing an important issue regarding the musical life of the whole society. Namely, it is evident that people find most agreeable the kind of music that they feel they can generate. We listen to pieces of music whose structure appears to be familiar, or which we ourselves could produce in a given class, in quite another way than to those we can only follow, or those that we cannot even follow very well. It is evident that by applying this method, the taste-categories of musical preferences fill up with different sort of content. This is the point of trying to find out about the secret of the obstinate popularity of genres from nineteenth century operettas to the recent pop: They don't surpass the level of their audience's generative musical faculty (11).

We may add that the musical generativity examinations seem to prove that it is the music of major-minor tonality and functional order that is most easily mobilizable in the audiences. However, if we consider the fact (proven by the analysis of the 40 years of Hungarian hits mentioned above) that most of the hit songs are to be characterized by such musicality, we appear to have not only come closer to an understanding of an intriguing problem of mass culture, but we can also see that systems theory and the historical approach in communication research can mutually reinforce each other.

RESEARCH PLANNING

The research regarding generative musical creativity exemplifies how scientific research meeting actual social needs may arrive at genuine theoretical questions and then be able to turn back to social practice enriched by the results. The following cultural-political problem was to be investigated: Do mass communicated radio and TV plays, films, and musical pieces that proved to be popular have any common structural characteristics and, if so, to what extent can these serve as bases for cultural-political and communication-political decisions and planning? A part of the series of investigations that was meant to answer this question arrived at the highly abstracted issue of generativity which already pertains to the sphere of basic research, only to recast the findings in terms of practical policy recommendations.

This instance also reveals another trait of Hungarian mass communication research, namely policy-orientation. At times of preparing for, or following up, a decision, social research is more and more often invited to help political practice. This takes place in an increasingly institutionalized way. In the period 1971–1974, for example, 17 special projects in the domain of social sciences were sponsored on themes deemed to be of primary importance to issues of social praxis. Two of these directly related to communication. One was the examination of the system-like efficiency of mass communication; the other was an analysis of modifications in the structure of the population's leisure-time activity due to the increase of leisure time and to the proliferation of television. There is a third long-range plan in social research that directly concerns communication research; its aim is to investigate changes in social consciousness in the last quarter-century.

Apart from more and more frequent demands on behalf of political decision-making bodies that are acting as sponsors, Hungarian mass-communication researchers consider it imperative to keep close ties with social practice. A new branch of science has to assert itself, and there is no better way to do that than to try to respond to genuine challenges of society. At the core of the social praxis orientation one can discover a characteristic of Marxist social sciences—namely, not only to explain phenomena but also to change them.

In conclusion, I outline the issues constituting the key reference points of Hungarian mass communication policies.

- *Mass orientation and stratum orientation:* to find a dynamic balance between the two in programming, partly with a view to the differentiating demands of the audiences, partly with respect to the expanding technical possibilities of production.

- *Centralization and decentralization:* to work out—parallel with the development of the system of political institutions—a territorial structure of the mass communication system which is decentralized enough to promote and give voice to the democratism of public life on a regional and local level and is at the same time centralized enough to have the whole society's interests asserted.

- *Connections between communication media and institution-systems:* to go beyond technical aspects of multimedia development and try to integrate the institution-systems of political communication, public education, and culture in a way that enables the optimal allocation of intellectual resources and energies for development of the interest in attaining the most important social objectives.

- *Communication policy and social policy:* to create material conditions, partly by means of social policy, partly by economic policy, under which differences between different social strata are gradually eliminated as regards their effective use of mass media potentialities.

- *Fields of tolerance:* contrary to the communication policies that emphasize data of the "head-counting" type of audience research and thus preserve the existing demands and taste levels, to make a more conscious use of those so-called "fields of tolerance" in which cultural content is received favorably by the public but without being a commercial mass-product.

- *Creation of demands:* to create, beyond existing demands and necessities, new, more conscious, and humanized intellectual demands of a higher level within the public.

- *Relaxation, "re-engagement":* to solve the basic dilemma of mass entertainment so that relaxation should not mean an escape from reality. The "light programs" should not block the reception of cultural values, and the intellectual loosening should not suggest that culture could be obtained without efforts.
- *Creation of community:* the communication systems should be consciously applied to support the strengthening of real communities formed by common activities instead of quasi-communities produced by the sheer communication-experience.
- *Stability and conflict:* to reflect events and phenomena of the world in mass communication in a way that presents the steady trends of the development of mankind and society and at the same time shows the conflicts and contradictions of the development as well.
- *Continuity and discontinuity:* to try to make people conscious of historically new traits, values, and norms of the socialist society and at the same time to guarantee that they appreciate, integrate, and pass on the age-old cultural heritage of mankind and of the nation.
- *Value-orientation:* to devise mechanisms within the system of communication so that both the direct messages and the indirect ones (in the meta-text) may globally reflect the system of norms and the hierarchy of values of the new society.
- *News-value:* to reappraise the informative functions of the communication system, reinterpreting the "news-value" concept of journalism, which, in its traditional sense, meant no more than unexpectedness, interest, and rapidity. Now it should be based on the "image-improvement" function of the given information—namely, by helping people to recognize the substantial aspects of objective reality.
- *Need of information:* starting from the objective need of information of groups and strata of society, to guarantee that the communication system regularly supplies for all strata and groups more information about substantial issues, which demand publicity, rather than merely the "subsistence-level" of information, and to ensure that the system teaches the public how to find their own information, how to select consciously, and how to interpret.
- *The unexpectedness and the planned:* to establish an institution of social communication, which in its basic aspects can be planned with scientific accuracy (and thus can be integrated in the system of social planning) but which is flexible enough in its actual operation to adapt itself to the rhythm of unforseeable events and rapid differentiation of social demands.

There is no need to add that this chapter does not pretend to be an operational code of the Hungarian communication system. Nor is it an outline of proclaimed policies. It is a series of unresolved issues. The rapidly transforming communication system of a socialist society is trying to create its own structure, institutions, and mechanisms amid these points of reference. And while these principles are assuming the shapes of communication policies, all those participating in the job—politicians, communicators or researchers—are not only trying to find solutions but have to face new dilemmas and devise new strategies for finding the proper balance between the teleology of social values and the historical and social necessities.

REFERENCES

1. Angelusz, Róbert, Ferenc Békés, and László Váradi. "A magyar lakosság történelmi ismeretei" [The Historical Knowledge of the Hungarian Population], Tanulmányok [Studies]. Budapest: HRT Mass Communication Research Centre, 1974.

2. Balogh, István. "Tanulmány a társadalmi információelmélet filozófiai alapjairól" [Study on the Philosophical Basis of the Social Information Theory], Társadalomtudományi közlemé nyek (1973), 48–82.

3. Barcy, Magdolna, Katalin Gallay, Tamás Szecskő, András Szekfü, Róbert Tardos, and László Váradi. A tömegkommunikáció s eszközök agitációs éspropaganda tevékenységének hatékonysága az egyes társadalmi csoportok körében [The Effectivity of the Agitative and Propaganda Activities of the Mass Media in Various Social Groups]. Budapest: HRT Mass Communication Research Centre, 1974.

4. Garai, László. Személyiségdinamika és társadalmi lét [Personality Dynamics and Social Existence]. Budapest: Akadémiai, 1969.

5. Gelléri-Lázár, Márta. "A kitalizmus koràbeli kalendsrium-irodalom Magyarországon" [Calendars in Capitalistic Hungary]. Unpublished manuscript, 1974.

6. Hankiss, Elemér. "Megismerés és értékelés" [Cognition and Evaluation]. Valóság, 27 (1974), 25–36.

7. Hoppál, Mihály. "Egy falu kommunikás rendszere" [The Communication System of a Village], Sakkönyvtár. Budapest: HRT Mass Communication Research Centre, 1970.

8. Kulosár, Kálmán. Az ember és társadalmi környezete [Man and His Social Environment]. Budapest: Gondolat, 1969.

9. Lévai, Julia and Iván Vitányi. Miből lesz a sláger? Az elmult 40 év slágereinek vizsgálata [What makes a Pop Hit a Hit? An Analysis of Pop Hits of the last 40 years]. Budapest: Zenemükiadó, 1973.

10. Nagy, Márta. "Nők és fiatalok a karikaturában" [Women and Young People in Caricature]. Unpublished manuscript, 1973.

11. Sági, Mária and Iván Vitányi. "A 'generativ' zenie készég vizsgálata" [The Investigation of 'Generative' Musical Abilities]. Magyar Pszichológiai Szemele, 29 (1972), 469–487.

12. Szecskő, Tamás. "Megjegyzések a kommunikáció áitalános elméletéhez" [Some Remarks on the General Theory of Communication]. Nyelv és kommunikáció [Language and Communication], in Tamas Szecsko and Gyorgy Szepe (eds.), Szakkonyvtar 3–4, Vol 1. Budapest: HRT Mass Communication Research Centre, 1969, pp. 3–28.

13. ———. *Kommunikációs rendszer—köznapi kommunikáció* [Communication System—Everyday Communication]. Budapest: Akadémiai, 1971.

14. Szekfü, András (ed.), "Public Opinion and Mass Communication." Working Conference, Budapest, 1971. *Szakkönyvtár* 17. Budapest: HRT Mass Communication Research Centre, 1972.

15. Terestyéni, Tamás. "A politika fogalma a párt központi lapjának három évfolyamában" [The Concept of Politics in Three Years of the Central Paper of the Party]. *Az információtól a közéletig* [From Information to Public Life]. Budapest: Kossuth, 1975, pp. 84–104.

16. Tókei, Ferenc. *A társadalmi formák elméletéhez.* [To the Theory of Social Formations]. Budapest: Kossuth, 1968.

17. ———. *Antikvitás és feudalizmus.* [Antiquity and Feudalism]. Budapest: Kossuth, 1969.

CHAPTER 21

Social Integration as an Organizing Principle

IRVING LEWIS ALLEN

The role of media in functional and normative integration and, following social change, in reintegration for both modern and developing societies are examined in this chapter. For large social systems mass communication is a necessary condition for systemic integration, but it may or may not produce integration depending on the content and the existing level of integration in society. Social integration in mass society, however, *depends* in some part on mass communication.

Olsen (31, pp. 157–158) formally defines social integration as "the process in which the component parts of an organization become united so as to give unity to the total organization." He notes that social integration is a group-level or structural property of an organization as a whole and is not a property of subunits of individual participants. In this connection he cautions on the analytic confusion that can result from not distinguishing organizational integration from individuals' ties of linkages to the organization (p. 158). This latter point is particularly important, for many media integration hypotheses are in fact observations that a "function" of mass media is to provide means by which individuals identify with the larger community or society. When social systems are taken as the unit of analysis, this raises the thorny question of conceptualizing and measuring group-level properties, especially those that are not merely aggregate-level expressions of individual properties. One might argue that normative or consensual integration is nothing more than the aggregation of similar individual attitudes. But insofar as social integration is taken here to denote the structure of relations and the moral bonds *among* participants in social systems, it is not considered reducible to individual traits. However, identifying the various linkages or mechanisms that result in integration is tantamount to identifying the presence of a process and state of integration.

Olse: (pp. 161–163) and others argue that functional normative integration occur together as complementary processes in all large social systems.

Olsen sees functional integration as more important for large complex societies, while normative integration is more important in small homogeneous social groups. Although he notes that even in small groups there is some task specialization, there is not a division of labor elaborate enough for full functional integration (pp. 163–166).

Normative integration in complex societies is a special problem. For normative integration to occur there must be a series of social links—groups, associations, communities and other intermediate organizations—between the individual and society. Olsen notes that most sociologists have disallowed mass media any significant role in the linkage, believing they are too large and impersonal (p. 164). However, the following review would indicate a qualification of this, for media seem to be inextricably a part of this process. Writing on the problem of the integration of American society, Williams (50, pp. 580–619) gives mass communication, to the contrary, a central role in the normative integration process and, moreover, defines integration as a dynamic process involving conflict. Similarly, I argue that functional and normative integration in both large and small social systems are at least facilitated by, and to some degree dependent upon, mass communication, even if not primarily a result of media effects on social systems.

MEDIA AND THE INTEGRATION OF MACROSYSTEMS

The distinction here between a microsystem and a macrosystem denotes whether the system is principally integrated through *primary* relations and *primary* communications or through *secondary* relations and *secondary* communications. In logistical terms, face-to-face or voice-to-voice interaction ceases to be feasible as the main communicative channel in social systems beyond a certain size, probably that of the neighborhood or the small bureaucracy. At some point, most likely at the urban community level or that of the large organization, mass communication and other technological extensions of communication become the main means of coordination and consensus.

A review of discussions and empirical research on mass communication and social integration for large social organizations, such as large urban communities and nations, indicates that most treatments are principally concerned with normative integration, but there are a few significant discussions of functional integration. Wright (51) includes normative integration hypotheses among his manifest and latent functions of mass communication and calls them "cultural transmission." Functional or symbiotic integration is not included in Wright's functional inventory, unless by implication in his "surveillance" or "news" function, wherein he notes that news is essential to the economy and other social institutions. But functional integration hypotheses appear implicitly and explicitly in theory and sometimes together as complementary processes.

The normative integration hypotheses usually refer to the potentially integrating content that provides symbols and messages that reaffirm social norms and values. The media, the arguments run, provide collective representations—the social symbols that promote the cohesion, solidarity, and that degree of consensus or common assent necessary to sustain an integrated social system. Thus, the media are said to generate and maintain value consensus and to promote identification with community and nation. The stereotypical symbols, which are understood by diverse social types, *link* individuals and groups of individuals to a society that otherwise would be more atomized.

The role of media in *social* integration has long been observed. Cooley (6, pp. 75–76, 81–89), writing before 1909, anticipated most varieties of normative integration hypotheses and viewed the prospect of modern communications in an almost entirely positive light. Cooley discussed the integration function of modern communications in terms of "enlargement and animation." Cooley, as had de Tocqueville (47) before him, believed that the press made possible the crystallization of public opinion and the consensus essential to democracy. He believed that modern communications were the basis of the psychology of modern life, promoting a sense of community for the nation and even an "international consciousness," which he hoped would produce an "enlargement of justice and amity." Cooley believed that the press could animate millions in the emulation of common models. He also remarked upon newspapers as "organized gossip" and upon their ability, through the fear of publicity, to enforce a popular morality. Lazarsfeld and Merton (21) later called this function of media "the enforcement of social norms."

Deutsch (7, pp. 86–106) perhaps comes closest to asserting that "communicative" integration is basic to normative and functional integration, rather than vice versa, in his communication model of society, which is based on information theory. Communication of all types, including the mass media, he argues, is basic to the development of nationalism or a national community, which depends on a people being "assimilated" or having a common culture and who are "mobilized" or reached and affected by the mass media. Deutsch elevated his communication model of "community" to the international or supranational level of integration. Yet, as Angell (3) notes, if Deutsch's model is taken as communicative integration, "it must be stressed that communicative integration is only the *capability* of acting together, not the actuality."

Shils (42) similarly sees the modern technologies of transportation and communication as fundamental to consensus in mass society, which he believes to be the most consensual kind of society ever to exist. The mass society, according to him, is integrated in two directions—vertically and horizontally.

"A society is vertically integrated in a hierarchy of power and authority and a status order; it is horizontally integrated by the unity of the elites of the various sectors or subsystems of the society and through the moral consensus of the whole."

Meier (26, pp. 1–44) developed a communications theory of urban growth based on information theory. He features a systemic model of functional integration that he calls "cohesion through complementary functions." His hypothesis resembles Durkheim's organic solidarity, including Durkheim's notion of "moral density" or an intensification of communication and exchange in a social system. Meier goes on to argue that communications are basic to urban social organization and development. Meier's model, as he notes, was influenced by neoclassical human ecology.

There have been a few empirical studies of the role of mass communication in social integration and all examine local communities. Janowitz (16, Ch. 1) suggested an integration hypothesis in his study of the role small weekly neighborhood presses play in the maintenance of metropolitan social structure. Speaking of the mass media in general, he says:

> In the process of urban growth in America the maintenance of consensus has been closely associated with the development of the mass media of communications. Mass media contributed to the growth of urban centers by providing the channels of information and symbolism required for the integration and social solidarity of vast aggregates of population.

The smaller urban community press is described "as one of the social mechanisms through which the individual is integrated into the urban social structure." Janowitz, proceeding from this hypothesis, uses the neighborhood press as an approach to the analysis of urban social organization and social control at the community level.

Larsen and Edelstein (20) replicated Janowitz's study by a sample survey of readers of an urban weekly in residential Seattle. Their purpose was "to examine the social functions of a special form of mass communication to ascertain its ability to counteract the eclipse of community" in the city where classical urban theory held social organization to be in a state of disintegration. They describe it as "a study of the extent to which the urban weekly newspaper is, in a full sociological sense, a *community* press." Following Robert E. Park, they define two conceptual dimensions of "community"—consensus and symbiosis—that they hypothesize to be fostered by the community press. Consensus and symbiosis correspond, of course, to normative and functional integration, respectively. Larsen and Edelstein state:

> Two main tasks must be performed if a symbolic mechanism [the press] is to establish harmonious relations between the consensual and symbiotic bases of community. The first is to *energize* local identification and involvement. The second is to *interpret* this activity so that some meaningful linkage is made between households and the

urbanite's increased commitment to groups extending beyond his own immediate territory.

They found evidence in their data that the "weekly stimulates and reinforces discussion of local news content and local identification." They concluded that their data "support the general hypothesis that the urban weekly newspaper is an effective instrument for developing, reinforcing, and extending communication and involvement." They generalized further that "its basic social function is to provide a means for energizing local activities and elaborating social contacts through which a sense of community can emerge."

In another analysis of the same survey Edelstein and Larsen (11) again found confirmation of the Janowitz thesis and concluded that the weekly "operates as a facilitative agent for 'community.' . . . The newspaper is seen as an instrument which facilitates the integration of the individual and the groups into the community structure."

Several other empirical studies conclude that the press tends to support the status quo. For example, Olien, Donohue, and Tichenor (30). Paletz and Dunn (32) and Paletz, Reichert, and McIntyre (33) showed that biases in reporting by local community presses tend to deemphasize real community conflict and cleavage. Donohue, Tichenor and Olien (10) have reviewed recent literature concerning the gatekeeping function and information control by media.

SOCIAL INTEGRATION IN DEVELOPING SOCIETIES

Preceding the contemporary discussion on the role of media in the process of nation-building, there was a nascent but highly suggestive literature on the role of media in transitional society. Thomas and Znaniecki (46, pp. 1367–1936) wrote of the Polish rural press around and shortly after the turn of the century. The press served to reintegrate Polish peasants into the wider community at a time when the isolation of traditional peasant communities was breaking down and individuals were being incorporated into the emerging political system of the nation. Redfield (38, pp. 1–14) analyzed the role of the press in the social change and modernization processes in a traditional Mexican village. Later Reisman (39, pp. 105–132) commented upon the socializing functions of print in the transition from traditional to inner-directed society. Although these sociologists were not discussing systemic integration effects as such, they did specify the role of media either in fostering identification and accommodation with the emergent mass society or as a process of reintegration necessary for continuity in transitional periods.

A set of well-defined hypotheses on the role of the mass meida in socioeconomic development in the less developed regions of the world has been accumulated. The catalog of hypothesized macrosystemic effects denotes functional and normative integration, specifies linkages of individuals and groups the national society, and is predictably similar to the catalog for modern society. Taken together, these social scientists argue that the mass media facilitate the economic and political coordination necessary to initiate and sustain economic development. The media create the consensus necessary for societal coordination; they create and reinforce collective representations and the development of national heroes and role models; the media aid in the development of a national identify and the assimilation of subgroups into the national consciousness; and they can foster the legitimization of a national government.

Several writers who have conducted empirical studies in particular nations and regions have analyzed in detail the connection between media and development. Lerner's (22, pp. 43–75) study of modernization in the Middle East produced an "empathy" hypothesis of the "mobile" or modern personal style, or "the capacity to see oneself in the other fellow's situation." Lerner's concept of empathy is actually quite close to one use of social integration (cf. Rogers with Svenning, 41, pp. 196–218). Lerner argues that high empathic capacity is the predominant personal style in modern society, which is a participatory society in that it functions by consensus. In such society there is a need for a transpersonal common doctrine made possible by shared secondary symbols.

In his study of communication and development in two Indian villages, Rao (37, pp. 104–109) emphasizes the need for cohesion in rapidly changing social structures where diverse regional, caste, language, and cultural groups are thrown together and potentially destructive forces of factionalism are released. "Communication widens peoples' horizons in gradually increasing circles from village to region to state to nation." According to Rao, mass communication assists in readaptation and in finding and accepting new social norms in situations of rapid change and the fragmentation of traditional social groupings.

Exposure to mass communications is frequently associated with increased knowledge of public affairs. Countless studies in the modern societies make this point. Several empirical studies for a variety of developing societies have also predictably found that exposure to media causes increased information levels, political interest and participation (e.g., Deutschman, 9; Hirabayashi and El Khatib, 15; Menefee and Menefee, 27; Rogers, 40; and others). The speculative implication, of course, is that increased knowledge, awareness and political participation result in, or represent linkages to, the national society that are, in effect, political integration of a higher degree than existed before. Hirabayashi and El Khatib (15) found in Egyptian villages that exposure to mass communication, especially newspapers at that time, not only raised information levels but also increased national consciousness.

Hinicker (14) studied mass-media study groups in the People's Republic of China and concluded that the groups, which under government direction study the national media to achieve consensus on goals and ideological indoctrination, are instrumental in achieving national integration.

They do this . . . by forming the nuclear units of mass organization, run by a disciplined cadre corps, focused around the study of the national press. . . . The study group itself provides a new basis for identification and in doing so helps destroy the monopoly of the family as a unit of identification. . . . But also important in this regard is the study group's inculcation of an ideology which promotes identification beyond the family, beyond the village, beyond the province to the superordinate level of the nation.

Liu (24) made an in-depth analysis of communication and national integration in China. He conceives of national integration in totalitarian societies as occurring in two phases, which he calls "penetration" and "identification." Penetration is essentially an effort at assimilation of subgroups in the society.

The role of the mass media in this phase of integration is to convey political authority to the people and to bring political consciousness or identity to the masses from without. The media then reflect not society but policy. In the meantime, the other integrative forces . . . will help the media gradually diffuse a set of common norms, values and symbols among the population, especially the youth, so that identification, vertically between the ruler and the ruled and horizontally among citizens and groups, can be established (pp. 2–3).

Liu argues, however, that mass media are a necessary but not a sufficient cause of macrosystemic integration—that they are but a tool. National integration is dependent upon the existence of an emergent social infrastructure of modern transportation, a national language, and widespread literacy, and that these elements must precede or accompany national integration (pp. 4–5). He notes that mass media in England and America developed only after all of these elements were present. He adds, moreover, that mass media development occurred only after the social infrastructure had laid the foundations of social integration. The media, according to Liu, did not create national integration, but rather reinforced it and advanced it further.

As voluntary associations are viewed as the stabilizing factor in situations of communal discontinuity, the *ersatz* community generated by mass-communicated and shared symbols may augment that margin of social stability and controlled change essential in the developing nations. Powdermaker (35), for example, noted that radio listening provided "*(1)* an integrating and stabilizing agent between the past and the present; *(2)* a dissemination of information and values from other African tribes and from the Western world . . ." (p. 229). But social structures in the developing nations cannot be described as threaded together and sustained by mass communicated symbols, any more than modern societies. The most viable sources of integration, other than the social infrastructure, remain the extended family, ethnic group, caste, and social network. Mass media, Pye (36) insists, seldom reach beyond the few urban centers and the relatively small literate urban elites. Nonetheless, mass communication as a source of integration in the macrosystem can be expected to play an increasingly important role concomitant with increasing literacy, urbanization, improved transportation, and the introduction of modern media technology, including the very cheap transistor radio.

While there are both "positive" and "negative" hypotheses about the role of the media in developing nations, the "positive" theories have generally been more influential (25, 49). And the so-called "negative" hypotheses are of a different quality than those of the mass-society theorists. Pool (34, pp. 234–253) is among the few who have discussed the potential for the media to produce disintegration in the national system. Pool suggests that the media can create a "demonstration effect"—or rising expectations—at a stage in national development when the economy cannot fulfill these media-produced wants. Frustration, discontent, and alienation result. Lerner (23) notes a similar potential of the media. Pool, however, seems to conclude that media are neutral in that they hold the potential to foster integration or disintegration of the system, depending on the content and systems of controls. Almond and Powell (2, pp. 164–189) likewise note both the unifying and stress-creating potential of media for the system, depending on the political milieu. The few empirical studies (1, 42) of hypothesized relationships between mass communication and political disruption do not support the existence of any general relationship, although there may be individual examples of it.

The macrosystemic integration hypotheses, either for modern or developing societies, have not generally articulated the nature of the interaction and interfacing between the macrosystem and the microsystem. The theory reviewed in this section clearly suggests that some degree of microsystemic social integration comes from, or is at least facilitated at, the macrosystemic level. The catalog of integrative effects constantly alludes to integration among individuals in groups and to the integration of these individuals and groups with the macrosystem. The social-psychological or linkage components of the hypotheses are usually the reference of these allusions, but the concepts are seldom pursued.

MEDIA AND THE INTEGRATION OF MICROSYSTEMS

Microsystems here denote small groups, including primary groups, and relatively small social networks of secondary relations in which the predominant mode of interaction is face-to-face, although other kinds of interpersonal relations may be included. Microsystems, for example, are families, circles of friends, neighbors, work and occupational associates, peers generally, direct participants in formal voluntary associations, and other secondary associations where interaction takes place frequently enough or is critical enough to the task of the group so that interpersonal affect or cohesion must be generated and sustained for the group to survive. Social integration is sometimes called social cohesion or affectual integration (cf. 31, p. 159) and is comparable in many respects to normative or consensual integration at the macrosystemic level.

Implicit in many treatments of macrosystemic integration is a more elementary process of integration for various microsystems, the constituent parts of larger intermediate systems, or the macrosystems of the urban community and nation. The mass society is a myriad of small, often intersecting and overlapping, systems that are linked to larger remote systems by various voluntary or secondary relations. Williams (50, p. 547), for example, describes American society as "millions of small primary groups and millions of secondary associations . . . crisscrossed with incredibly long chains of indirect interaction and permeated with waves and counterwaves of mass communication. . . ." The full role of mass communication in the integration of mass society as a whole can be better characterized by specifying the integration mechanisms in microsystems.

Menzel (28) comments on the artificial dichotomization of societal communication as either mass communication or interpersonal communication and calls attention to many kinds of residual but nonetheless important quasi-mass communications, such as public speeches, missionary activities, luncheon club circuit riders, storefront information centers, and other selective dissemination services—all of which are vital to the organization of society. These communications are institutionally arranged, regularized, and recognized, but intermediate to mass communication and interpersonal communication. Menzel notes that this dichotomization has led mass-communication theory to focus on two kinds of functions: those for the maintenance of society as a whole and those for the individual. Menzel suggests that researchers examine functions of quasi-mass communications in social systems of an intermediate level in mass society, such as social movements. He notes that quasi-mass communications can link together people of similar interests as well as the kinds of people who can play requisite roles in an organization. These particular *functions* are, in essence, normative and functional integration. Menzel's concept of quasi-mass communications and their functions for social systems are relevant examples of the important interface between the two "levels" of society. Quasi-mass communications and the intermediate-level systems that depend on them, we may assume, are as involved with mass communication content and process as are macrosystems and microsystems, which represent only the perimeters of the organization of mass society.

Microsystemic mechanisms of normative integration are similar to those of macrosystems in that they provide access to universes of discourse, sharing of common experiences, increasing repertories of meanings, and extending and strengthening reference-group identifications. As in the case of macrosystemic integration, one must distinguish between mechanisms that *link* individuals to groups and the resultant holistic *process* and *state* of social integration. The linking mechanisms designate how integration may be achieved and sustained without arguing that systemic integration is always the result. Because the linking mechanisms are empirically more accessible, they have, as in the case of macrosystems, been most often taken as indicators to infer integrative *effects* on microsystems.

To summarize, the integrative hypotheses at the microsystemic level assert that some degree of social integration is attained and sustained through the sharing of common mass-media experiences. The content of mass communication gives individuals access to new and extended universes of discourse and enlarges their repertories of significant symbols and categories of meaning. In the processes of interaction and interpersonal relations, integration is induced, sustained, repaired, and deepened. Intragroup norms and consensus are created and strengthened in the process of interaction, using common symbols provided by the mass media. Moreover, the mass-communicated messages extend reference-group identifications, including negative reference groups, that may result in strengthened positive affect and identifications with other reference groups. Again as in the case of macrosystems, consensual conflict with agreed-upon rules and boundaries may also be another kind of integrative result.

Whether mass communication can be said to facilitate functional or symbiotic integration at the microsystemic level is at least problematic. Olsen (31) believes that strong functional integration—unlike normative integration— probably does not develop in small systems, for they lack the complex division of labor necessary for functional integration. However, he notes that some task specialization, such as age and sex roles, often occurs. One could reinterpret many functionalist and uses-and-gratifications hypotheses of how media content, such as popular music and soap operas, reflect, promote adaptation to, and reinforce specialized age and sex roles in the microsystems of peer groups and the family.

In particular, the entertainment content of media often presents characters who become role models for many people. Several studies that deal with the socialization function of media could be interpreted as influencing or reinforcing sex and age roles (e.g., Herzog, 13; Reisman et al., 39, pp. 105–132; Warner and Henry, 48; and many others). In fact, in 1948 Warner and Henry concluded that the primary social function of the "Big Sister" soap opera was to "strengthen and stabilize the basic social structure of our society, the family." The program reinforced traditional sex roles for women and "plays up the importance of the role of the wife and therefore deprecates the role (career woman) the ordinary listener has avoided, or has not been able to take. It helps resolve any conflict she may have within her for not choosing the other role (that once might have been open to her) and reinforces her present position." A few studies have shown how television reflects sex stereotyping, thus reinforcing images of traditional role systems (e.g., Gerbner, 12). Tedesco (45) is one study in a symposium of nine articles that show how mass media reflect sex-role stereotypes of women. This reflection is supportive of the status quo and the existing division of labor between men and women and, moreover, may slow social change in this area of functional or symbiotic integrative relations.

MASS COMMUNICATION PROCESS AND INCREASED INTERACTION

In addition to maintaining existing levels of integration, the mass communication process has yet an additional effect on microsystems—*namely, increasing communicative channels in the system and thereby enlarging and intensifying interaction.* The secondary effects of mass communications on microsystems are to increase the number of channels and the frequency of their use and to increase the number of significant symbols flowing through those channels. Taken together, these effects may more than merely reflect and facilitate an existing level of integration; they may also make an *independent* contribution to integration and reintegration.

This suggests a model of two-way causation in which exposure to media makes possible pleasurable social interaction that, if it is to be sustained, must be fueled by increased media exposure to collect more information. Once a person has the additional information, he has motivation to use it in a pleasurable way by seeking and initiating increased interaction with friends, intimates, and even strangers. Insofar as an individual's interests are broadened in this process, he will, in effect, accumulate new meanings that may be shared only by deepening and extending his circles of social interaction.

More important, these extended and deepened social relations are sources of group sanctions that pressure people, largely through the mechanisms of reference group behavior, to collect data from the media to sustain these interactions. Atkin (4) has reviewed much of the research supporting the hypotheses that people attend to media in anticipation of using the content during social interaction, and he presents two secondary analyses and an experiment to support further that assessment. Although his extensive review obviates the need for one here, several other studies further shore up the research consensus on this point. Suchman (43, pp. 140–180) and Johnstone and Katz (17) found that similar social pressures lead persons to expose themselves to various entertainment content of the media. Klapper (18, pp. 26–30) generalized that the pressures of social relations increased attendance to media. Some people may respond to the constant social pressures to keep well informed on current events and may read newspapers partly for raw material to impress others in conversation. Bauer and Bauer (5) and Lane and Sears (19) assert that some people collect public affairs information as an aggressive weapon against others and, in the case of the academic community, because of a professional and social need to be right.

The process model is thoroughly interactive and interdependent. Certain kinds of group relations cause people to attend to media in anticipation of more relations; the result is sometimes extended and deepened social relations, which we may take as indicative of maintaining and enlarging the processes of integration and reintegration in microsystems.

MICROSYSTEMIC INTEGRATION IN DEVELOPING SOCIETIES

Although there is abundant work on the role of media in the integration of macrosystems in less developed societies, sociologists and anthropologists who study the socioeconomic development process have only recently given attention to the role of mass communication in the *reintegration* of individuals and their groups in the context of the contemporary industrializing and rapidly urbanizing societies. Processes similar or identical to those in modern urban societies are emergent in developing societies, but there are important qualitative and quantitative differences between the individuals' use of media in modern and in developing societies. Access to printed media is, of course, restricted to the literate, except by word of mouth from opinion leaders. The state of technology in the new communication industries and low income levels still restrict the penetration of the electronic media to the cities and the urban elite, but this situation is slowing changing because of the proliferation of inexpensive transistor radios. Eventually, education, rising incomes, and access to media will increase the importance of mass communication experiences in everyday life and conversations in developing countries. For example, Powdermaker (35, p. 229) notes the personal functions of radio listening for African miners as "*(1)* a source of pleasure; *(2)* a catharsis; *(3)* a source of understanding and control over the environment; and *(4)* a means of extending the range of identifications and a way of relating to other people." Admittedly, Powdermaker is writing of linkages of individuals to systems as well as of social integration itself.

There is evidence that media also have a role in small-group functional integration of symbiotic role relations in developing society. Nwoga (29) analyzes the content and themes of Onitsha market literature in Nigeria. This pulp fiction has a large audience and is similar to the familiar popular romance magazines in this country. Much of it deals with relations between the sexes and warns in a titillating way of the dangers of immorality and the unlucky in love. Many of the readers are young people who are experiencing a new urban way of life and a new language. This fiction may be said, as in the case of similar media content in modern society, to teach as yet unfamiliar sex roles and responses to new situations and conditions of life. Generally, they contribute to the structure and restructure of microsystemic functional integration in a transitional society.

Hinicker (14) has analyzed the role and effectiveness of mass media for indoctrination in face-to-face study groups in the People's Republic of China. Not only are study groups instrumental in achieving national integration, but in the process generate greater interpersonal solidarity within each study group. The social-psychological process of generating consensus, such as the acceptance of collectivation by studying the national media under the direction of trained cadres, creates similar affective orientations toward the same social object or event. As a latent effect, participants may overcome animosities and learn to like one another. Almost all of the theoretical and research evidence to support the microsystemic hypothesis, however, is derived from the case of more modern societies.

MEDIA AND INTEGRATION: CONCLUSIONS

Research and theory, which would support systemic integration hypotheses, clearly suggest that media have a definite but highly problematic and various role in the integration of large and small social systems. Sociologists by and large have rejected the more anxious fears of theorists of the persuasible mass society as well as the despair of mass-culture rhetoricians over the debauchment of folk and high culture. Some sociologists, largely without evidence, still regard media effects on social systems as attenuating and as weakening the quality of social relations and community life. There is simply no evidence of such an effect. Certainly mass communication, especially in modern society, has affected the structure and content of social systems, but that is not to say that social systems are any less integrated or that the ties that bind are any more tenuous because of the mass media.

I am impressed by the extent to which theory reminds us that media are not an artificial phenomenon in modern and modernizing societies—something *in* society but not *of* it. Rather, mass communication is identical and basic to the meaning of mass society. Modern society does not only *depend* upon mass communication, but the process almost *defines* the nature of mass society. While there may be a revival of interest in media culture, content analysis, and behavioral effects, such as the concern with media violence, mass communication has yet to take an indispensible role in the theory of modern and modernizing society generally. The potential of the media to stabilize is fundamental, but probably less important than its potential to facilitate change. Mass society is dynamic society, and mass communication should be part of any consideration of social change. Media can foster stability or even reinforce a socially unjust status quo, but media must have the potential to facilitate *some* integration and continuity in a context of change. Social change is going to occur, for better or worse, and we must learn the role of media in that change.

REFERENCES

1. Adelman, Irma, and Cynthia T. Morris. *Society, Politics, and Economic Development: A Quantitative Approach*. Baltimore: Johns Hopkins Press, 1967.
2. Almond, Gabriel A., and G. Bingham Powell, Jr. *Comparative Politics: A Development Approach*. Boston: Little, Brown, 1966.
3. Angell, Robert Cooley. "Social Integration," in *International Encyclopaedia of the Social Sciences*, Vol 7. New York: Macmillan and Free Press, 1968.
4. Atkin, Charles K. "Anticipated Communication and Mass Media Information Seeking," *Public Opinion Quarterly, 36* (Summer 1972), 188–199.
5. Bauer, Raymond A., and Alice Bauer. "America, 'Mass Society' and Mass Media," *Journal of Social Issues, 16* (1960), 3–66.
6. Cooley, Charles Horton. *Social Organization: A Study of the Larger Mind*. New York: Scribner, 1927. Originally published in 1909.
7. Deutsch, Karl W. *Nationalism and Social Communication: An Inquiry into the Foundations of Nationality*, 2nd ed. Cambridge: M.I.T. Press, 1966.
8. ———, et al. *Political Community and the North Atlantic Area: International Organization in the Light of Historical Experience*. Princeton: Princeton University Press, 1957.
9. Deutschman, Paul J. "The Mass Media in an Underdeveloped Village," *Journalism Quarterly, 40* (Winter 1963), 27–35.
10. Donohue, George A., Phillip J. Tichenor, and Clarice N. Olien. "Gatekeeping: Mass Media Systems and Information Control," in F. Gerald Kline and Phillip J. Tichenor (eds.), *Current Perspectives in Mass Communication Research*. Beverly Hills, Calif.: Sage, 1972, pp. 41–69.
11. Edelstein, Alex S., and Otto N. Larsen. "The Weekly Press Contribution to a Sense of Urban Community," *Journalism Quarterly, 37* (October 1960), 489–498.
12. Gerbner, George. "Violence in Television Drama: Trends and Social Functions," in George A. Comstock and Eli A. Rubinstein (eds.), *Television and Social Behavior*, Vol.1, *Media Content and Control*. Washington, D.C.: U.S. Government Printing Office, 1972, pp. 28–187.
13. Herzog, Herta. "What Do We Really Know About Daytime Serial Listeners," in P. F. Lazarsfeld and F. N. Stanton (eds.), *Radio Research, 1942–43*. New York: Duell, Sloan, and Pearce, 1944, pp. 3–33.

14. Hinicker, Paul J. "The Mass Media and Study Groups in Communist China," in *Mass Communication and the Development of Nations*. East Lansing: Michigan State University, International Communication Institute, 1968, pp. VI-1–VI-24.

15. Hirabayashi, Gordon K., and M. Fathalla El Khatib. "Communication and Political Awareness in the Villages of Egypt," *Public Opinion Quarterly, 22* (Fall 1958), 357–363.

16. Janowitz, Morris. *The Community Press in an Urban Setting*. New York: Free Press, 1952.

17. Johnstone, John, and Elihu Katz. "Youth and Popular Music: A Study in the Sociology of Taste," *American Journal of Sociology, 62* (May 1957), 563–568.

18. Klapper, Joseph T. *The Effects of Mass Communication*. New York: Free Press, 1960.

19. Lane, Robert E., and David O. Sears. *Public Opinion*. Englewood Cliffs, N. J.: Prentice-Hall, 1964.

20. Larsen, Otto N., and Alex S. Edelstein. "Communication, Consensus and the Community Involvement of Urban Husbands and Wives." *Acta Sociologica, 5,* 1 (1960), 15–30.

21. Lazarsfeld, Paul F., and Robert K. Merton. "Mass Communication, Popular Taste and Organized Social Action," in Lyman Bryson (ed.), *The Communication of Ideas*. New York: Harper, 1948, pp. 95–118.

22. Lerner, Daniel. *The Passing of Traditional Society: Modernizing the Middle East*. New York: Free Press, 1958.

23. ———. "Toward a Communications Theory of Modernization," in Lucien W. Pye (ed.), *Communications and Political Development*. Princeton, N. J.: Princeton University Press, 1963, pp. 327–350.

24. Liu, Alan P. L. *Communications and National Integration in Communist China*. Berkeley: University of California Press, 1971.

25. McNelly, John T., et al. "Perspectives on the Role of Mass Communication in the Development Process," in *Mass Communication and the Development of Nations*. East Lansing: Michigan State University, International Communication Institute, 1968, pp. I-1–11.

26. Meier, Richard C. *A Communications Theory of Urban Growth*. Cambridge: M.I.T. Press, 1962.

27. Menefee, Selden, and Audrey Menefee. "A Country Weekly Proves Itself in India, " *Journalism Quarterly, 44* (Spring 1967), 114–117.

28. Menzel, Herbert. "Quasi-Mass Communication: A Neglected Area," *Public Opinion Quarterly, 35* (Fall 1971), 406–409.

29. Nwoga, Donatus I. "Onitsha Market Literature," *Transition, 19,* 2 (1965).

30. Olien, Clarice N., George A. Donohue, and William J. Tichenor. "The Community Editor's Power and the Reporting of Conflict," *Journalism Quarterly, 45* (Summer 1968), 243–252.

31. Olsen, Marvin E. *The Process of Social Organization*. New York: Holt, Rinehart & Winston, 1968.

32. Paletz, David L., and Robert Dunn. "Press Coverage of Civil Disorders: A Case Study of Winston-Salem, 1967," *Public Opinion Quarterly, 33* (Fall 1969), 328–345.

33. Paletz, David L., Peggy Reichert, and Barbara McIntyre. "How the Media Support Local Government Authority," *Public Opinion Quarterly, 35* (Spring 1971), 80–92.

34. Pool, Ithiel de Sola. "Mass Media and Politics in the Modernization Process," in Lucien W. Pye (ed.) *Communications and Political Development*. Princeton, N. J.: Princeton University Press, 1963, pp. 234–253.

35. Powdermaker, Hortense. *Coppertown: Changing Africa*. New York: Harper & Row, 1962.

36. Pye, Lucien W. "The Nature of Transitional Politics," in Jason L. Finkle and Richard W. Gables (eds.), *Political Development and Social Change*. New York: Wiley, 1966, pp. 519–530.

37. Rao, Y. V. Lakshmama. *Communication and Development: A Study of Two Indian Villages.* Minneapolis: University of Minnesota Press, 1966.

38. Redfield, Robert. *Tepoztlan: A Mexican Village.* Chicago: The University of Chicago Press, 1930.

39. Reisman, David, Nathan Glazer, and Reull Denney. *The Lonely Crowd: A Study of the Changing American Character.* New York: Doubleday, 1953.

40. Rogers, Everett M. "Mass Media Exposure and Modernization Among Colombian Peasants," *Public Opinion Quarterly, 29* (Winter 1966), 614–625.

41. ———, with Lynne Svenning. *Modernization Among Peasants: The Impact of Communication.* New York: Holt, Rinehart & Winston, 1969.

42. Shils, Edward. "The Theory of Mass Society," *Diogenes, 39* (Fall 1962), 45–66.

43. Suchman, Edward A. "An Invitation to Music: A Study of the Creation of New Music Listeners by the Radio," in Paul F. Lazarsfeld and Frank N. Stanton (eds.), *Radio Research, 1941.* New York: Duell, Sloan, and Pearce, 1941, pp. 140–180.

44. Taylor, Charles Lewis. "Communications Development and Political Stability," *Comparative Political Studies, 1* (January 1969), 557–563.

45. Tedesco, Nancy. "Patterns of Prime Time," *Journal of Communication, 24* (Spring 1974), 119–124.

46. Thomas, W. I., and Florian Znaniecki. *The Polish Peasant,* Vol. 2. New York: Knopf, 1927.

47. Tocqueville, Alexis de. *Democracy in America,* Vol. 2. New York: Knopf, 1948. Originally published in 1840.

48. Warner, W. Lloyd, and William E. Henry. "The Radio Day Time Serial: A Symbolic Analysis," *Genetic Psychology Monographs, 37* (February 1948), 3–71.

49. Wells, Alan. "Communications and Development: The Relevance of Media Content," *The Sociological Quarterly, 12* (Winter 1971), 95–99.

50. Williams, Robin M., Jr. *American Society: A Sociological Interpretation,* 3rd ed. New York: Knopf, 1970.

51. Wright, Charles R. "Functional Analysis and Mass Communication." *Public Opinion Quarterly, 24* (Winter 1960), 605–620.

CHAPTER 22

Mass Media and Political Institutions: The Systems Approach

MICHAEL GUREVITCH and JAY G. BLUMLER

The study of political communication could be enriched by the adoption of a systems outlook. This need not be competitive with other research approaches; it can incorporate them. At this stage limitations of evidence make the elaboration of such an outlook problematic, and different analysts attracted to this kind of approach would probably propound different versions of the notion of a political communication system.* Nevertheless, three benefits could ensue from attempts to place political communication phenomena in a systems framework: Pressure would be generated to link diverse bodies of evidence in broader analytical perspectives; there would be an antidote against the tendency to under- or overemphasize any single element of the political communication system (e.g., the audience); and by drawing attention to systems factors that, in varying across countries, might have macro-level consequences that could be measured and compared, cross-national investigation would be facilitated.

Of course an underlying assumption of such an approach is that the main features of the political communication process may be regarded as if they formed a system, such that variation in one of its components would be associated with variation in the behavior of its other components. Before developing the implications of this assumption positively, however, it may be useful to see how certain existing tendencies in political communication research could be subsumed under a systems perspective.

RECENT RESEARCH DIRECTIONS

Effects Research

A distinct shift of interest—a diminished concern to measure the *persuasive* impact of political messages and a heightened interest in charting their likely

*For other examples, see Deutsch (7) and Tichener et al. (23).

cognitive effects—can be discerned in effects research. This is not just a matter of recording simple information gains, but one of investigating the ability of the mass media "to create images of social reality by which the public may structure their views of the world" (26). Moreover, the propagation of such images is unlikely to influence only the cognitive realm. Dissonance theory would predict, for example, that when an individual's attitudinal orientation conflicts with a view of the world that is consistently being projected by a trusted communication source, the former will eventually be modified to fit the latter (27). This feature of the "new look" in political communication research (1) could be furthered by a systems approach, should there be reason to suppose that the perspectives on social and political reality offered to audience members in communications content depend in turn on other aspects of media organization. Such an assumption would be especially relevant to the many studies now being undertaken of the "agenda-setting function" of the media. This stipulates that the relative frequency of references to given political issues in media content will be reflected in a corresponding set of issue priorities in the minds of readers, viewers, and listeners (14, 15). A systems perspective would attempt to link such questions to media and to political structural conditions that might determine the kinds of issue agendas that mass media outlets present to their audience members.

Exposure Behavior

Recent studies of the communication behavior of audience members have tended to conclude that selective exposure should no longer be taken for granted as the natural mechanism that guides much consumption of media material about political affairs. Reanalysis of past survey evidence has shown that the extent of such selectivity was much less than had been supposed, and a review of experimental evidence has failed to uncover the existence of a "general psychological preference for supportive information" (19). The implication is that selective exposure—once elevated to the dignity of a supposed law—has been downgraded to the status of a *variable*. A systems approach would entertain the possibility that variation in rates of audience selectivity could depend on variation in other components of the political communication system, such as those involving differing relationships between media institutions and political institutions.

Audience Roles

In addition to studying the effects of political messages *on* the audience, some investigators have been exploring the "uses and gratifications" involved in audience members' orientations to political communication—what people seek from the political messages they monitor. Some of the results have recently been translated into notions of a number of alternative roles that audience members may adopt when following civic affairs through the media (1). The concept of "audience roles" provides a way of structuring the audience that differs from the conventional unidimensional continuum of degree of political interest. It also implies the presence, at the receiving end, of expectations about communication that may be systematically connected to corresponding role orientations among those individuals who originate and transmit political messages, such as media personnel and political spokesmen.

Institutional Analysis

Increasing attention, both theoretical and empirical, has recently been paid to the processes by which recurrent content patterns, especially those embedded in news output, are produced. Much of this work has emphasized the operation of mechanisms that strain toward consonance and tend to yield consensus treatments of political topics (3). There have also been penetrating theoretical explorations of the relationships between political and media institutions at this level. Seymour-Ure (20) has considered many sources of variation (such as the features of party systems and the values endorsed by political cultures) in the degree to which individual newspapers are identified with specific political parties. Hoyer et al. (11) have examined evolution of similar relationships over time and identified some of the correlates and consequences of trends away from press-party affiliation and identification. Specifically, they have postulated "conflict-provoking" consequences for systems in which press-party linkages are close and "consensus building" ones for systems in which such associations are relatively loose or nonexistent. This line of analysis is especially conducive to a systems approach, because it suggests that variations in the closeness of relationship between media institutions and certain political institutions may have consequences at other levels—including media contents, audience orientations, and ultimately the degree of consensus or dissensus prevalent in a given society.

ELEMENTS OF A POLITICAL COMMUNICATION SYSTEM

In broad terms the main components of a political communication system may be located in:

1. Political institutions in their communication aspects*
2. Media institutions in their political aspects

---

*Boundary problems arise in defining what counts as the communication aspects of the activity of political institutions and as the political aspects of mass media performance. For one thing, one can argue that *all* actions of political institutions have some communication relevance; that all the relationships central to political organization—power, authority, obedience, interest ag-

3. Audience orientations to political communication
4. Aspects of political culture relevant to communication

Expressed somewhat differently, if we look at a political communication system, what we see is two sets of institutions—political and media organizations—which are involved in the course of message preparation in much horizontal interaction with each other; on a vertical axis, they are separately and jointly engaged in disseminating and processing information and ideas to and from the mass citizenry.

The interactions of the two kinds of institutions are to some extent conditioned by mutual power relationships. This presupposes that both have an independent power base in society, one source of which arises from their respective relations with the audience. The power of political institutions is inherent in their functions as articulators of interest and mobilizers of social power for purposes of political action. The independent power base of media institutions is perhaps less obvious and may even be denied by those who perceive them as essentially secondary bodies; entirely dependent on others for the news and opinions they pass on; and highly constrained in their operation by a number of political, economic, cultural and technological factors. Nevertheless, at least three sources of media power can be identified. They are structural, psychological, and normative in origin.

The *structural* root of the mass media's power springs from their unique capacity to deliver to the politician an audience that in size and composition is unavailable to him by any other means. Indeed, the historical significance of the growing role of mass communication in politics lies, among other things, in the resulting enlargement of the receiver base to such an extent that previous barriers to audience involvement (e.g., low level of education and weak political interest) have been largely overcome. The audience for political communication has become virtually coterminous with membership of society itself.

The *psychological* root of media power stems from the relations of credibility

---

gregation, and so on—imply the existence of a communication function. Similarly, political aspects are so intricately interwoven with all other aspects of the performance of media institutions as to preclude the possibility either of isolating them empirically or even of analytically denoting some part of media content as entirely nonpolitical. Clearly, our definition should not be taken to imply that the communication aspects of the actions of political institutions are separable from other aspects of their behavior or that the political aspects of mass communication are limited solely to the processes involved in the production of manifestly political content. It depends, rather, on "the consequences, actual and potential, that communicatory activity has for the functioning of the political system" (9). Thus, all aspects of the performance of political institutions and of media institutions that are seen or perceived to have such consequences are included in our definition.

and trust that different media organizations have succeeded in developing (albeit to different degrees) with members of their audiences. This bond is based on the fulfillment of audience expectations and the validation of past trust relationships, which in turn are dependent on legitimized and institutionalized routines of information presentation evolved over time by the media.

The combined influence of these structural and psychological sources of strength enable the media to interpose themselves between politicians and the audience and to "intervene" in other political processes as well. This is expressed in the media's ability to restructure the timing and character of political events, such as conventions, demonstrations, and leader appearances; define crisis situations to which politicians are obliged to react; require comment on issues that media personnel have emphasized as important; inject new personalities into the political dialogue, such as television interviewers; and stimulate the growth of new communication agencies, such as public relations firms, opinion poll agencies, and political advertising and campaign management specialists.

Because such forms of intervention may be unwelcome to many politicians, the *normative* root of media power can be crucial at times of conflict. This springs from the respect that is accorded in competitive democracies to tenets of liberal philosophy such as freedom of expression and the need for specialized organs to safeguard citizens against possible abuses of political authority. This tends to legitimate the independent role of media organizations in the political field and to shelter them from overt attempts to bring them under political control.

Political communication flows are not merely the product of a naked power struggle waged between two sets of would-be communicators. On the contrary, the notion that such powers are bound together in a political communication *system* alerts us to the influence of other forces as well. One such influence arises from audience expectations, which both sorts of communicators wish to address effectively. In addition, a systems outlook implies that the interactions of the various actors occur within an overarching framework of organizing principles that are designed to regularize the relationships of media institutions to political institutions.

ENTRY POINTS INTO THE SYSTEM

Any analysis of a system comprising a number of components linked by a network of mutual dependencies is faced with the need to identify a set of relevant conceptual perspectives and to select optimal entry points into the system. In the following discussion we select as points of departure those elements in each of the components of the political communication system that are most conducive to generating propositions that offer a basis for both theoretical advance and empirical research. We present suggestions for analysis of this kind, looking first at the audience, then at certain organizational characteristics of political and media institutions, and finally at the political culture as it is reflected in the principles that organize normative relationships between political and media institutions and have some consequences for relationships between these institutions and the audience.

AUDIENCE ROLES

The concept of audience roles has arisen from attempts to apply the "uses and gratifications" approach to the study of voters' orientations to the political contents of the mass media. Collected evidence supports the implication that different receivers of political information are motivated by different expectations of it, develop different orientations toward it, and may therefore be perceived as playing different roles in the political communication system. Investigating such orientations to political communication in Britain, Blumler (1) has provisionally identified four audience roles that might be applicable to the political communication systems of other competitive democracies. They include the *partisan*, seeking a reinforcement of his existing beliefs; the *liberal citizen*, seeking guidance in deciding how to vote; the *monitor*, seeking information about features of the political environment, such as party policies, current issues, and the qualities of political leaders; and the *spectator*, seeking excitement and other affective satisfactions.

The notion of audience roles undoubtedly requires further development and refinement.* Nevertheless, it offers a point of departure for analysis of political communication systems in two respects. One use of the concept would inquire into the processes that lead people in different societies to take up one or more of the roles available to them. Supposing that the validity of a common repertoire of alternative role possibilities could be established for audience members in a designated set of competitive democracies, some of the sociological and psychological correlates associated with the particular political communication roles that different people adopt could be identified, and we could compare their influence cross-nationally. Sociologically, such an analysis might focus, for example, on age (expected to differentiate partisans from liberal citizens), educational background (expected to differentiate

---

*For example, we still need to test the comprehensiveness of the four-fold typology outlined above, to examine the stability of audience role expectations over time and to explore the interaction of gratifications sought and communication effects.

Table 1   The Complementarity of Roles in a Political Communication System

Audience	Media Personnel[a]	Party Spokesmen
Partisan	Editorial guide	Gladiator
Liberal citizen	Moderator	Rational persuader
Monitor	Watchdog	Information provider
Spectator	Entertainer	Actor/performer

[a]For another, partly similar, attempt to identify the primary functions of the media in relation to government, see 17, pp. 27–28.

monitors from spectators), and early patterns of socialization to politics in the family and elsewhere. Psychologically, it might examine variables such as strength of partisan identity (expected to pinpoint the partisans), interest in politics (expected to place the partisans at one pole and spectators at the other), and political cynicism (as a possible discriminant of spectators from the rest). The results of such a study might help to show how political culture impinges on political communication expectations at the audience level in the countries studied.*

A second line of analysis would pursue the possibility that audience roles are matched by similar orientations among political and professional communicators. The underlying assumption here is that audience members and communicators are linked in a network of mutually shared expectancies (22). Such a correspondence of roles will not necessarily always be perfect. On the contrary, imperfections of feedback, differences of purpose, and especially constraints arising from the disparities of political stratification may all be productive of discrepancies between the orientations of the different participants in the political communication process. Nevertheless, the concept of a "communication role" is at least as applicable to political communicators and to media personnel as it is to audience members. Moreover, the very notion of communication presupposes some degree of compatibility between the orientations of the originators and the receivers of messages. Table 1 presents a set of parallels that may be drawn between them.

The utility of such a paradigm depends on its ability to stimulate speculation about the structure of a political communication system and to suggest hypotheses about linkages between the components of such a system. Attention to the role relationships indicated in Table 1 would open up at least three areas of exploration:

*The approach proposed here is to some extent modeled along lines recently followed by Verba et al. (25) in an attempt to examine the dimensionality of several modes of democratic participation in politics and the correlates thereof in five different countries.

System Integration

The degree of integration of a political communication system might be conceived in terms of the degree of correspondence between its constituent parts. Thus, a highly integrated system would be one with high intercorrelations between role orientations across levels (i.e., where all the participants in the communication process share equivalent orientations and consequently speak on, or are "tuned in" to, similar wave lengths). Conversely, a system with a low level of integration would be one with low intercorrelations between parallel roles, reflecting a situation where the leading elements are at cross-purposes with each other and in which a high degree of communication conflict across levels prevails.

The measurement of system integration by communication role parallelism should not be taken to imply some utopian touchstone of complete complementarity. One-to-one correspondence across levels is likely to be impeded not only by the discrepancies and conflicts that stem from political stratification, but also *via* the multiplicity of orientations available to the audience and the difficulties that a given set of communicators will tend to experience in trying to address them simultaneously. Nevertheless, integration can be regarded as a matter of degree, measured by high or low intercorrelations between orientations across levels. The specification of this dimension does not entail a particular judgment about its value or an assumption that communication works "better" when these roles are complementary. For example, the Kennedy–Nixon debates might be described as a communication form in which the politicians acted as gladiators, the media professionals performed as moderators, and many members of the audience expected to enjoy the contest as spectators. This kind of expectation on the part of some audience members might be revealing because it highlights the similarity, perhaps even the interchangeability of the gladiatorial and the actor/performer roles. However, if system integration can be measured in this way, some of its further consequences should also be traceable—for example, in terms of the prevalence of alienation in the audience or of the efficacy of information transfer.

Interlevel Distancing

The relative distance between the audience and the media system and between the electorate and the political system might be measured by the degree to which audience roles correspond more closely with media personnel roles or with party spokesmen roles. Closeness of correspondence might indicate the relative credibility of the media and the trustworthiness of politicians for the audience, and lack of correspondence might reflect a failure of one or the other set of communicators to address themselves relevantly to the needs of the audience.

Cross-Level Influences

The principles that normatively relate media organizations to political institutions in a particular society may help to shape the role definitions regarded as appropriate by those occupying different positions in the communication system. Various specific hypotheses may be derived from this possibility:

1.   In media systems with a high degree of political autonomy, professional communicators are likely to enjoy considerable freedom to adopt a variety of role orientations. This will leave audience role options wide open as well and tend to oblige political spokesmen to perform in multiple roles. This might not be equally palatable to all politicians (some of whom might have a distaste for the actor/performer role, for example). In such systems we might find more evidence of "role distancing" among politicians and of "typecasting" among newsmen.

2.   Where public service goals prevail in media organization, watchdog functions will be favored by media professionals, and audience members will be encouraged to assume the monitor role; this will exert pressure on politicians to give primacy to the information-provider role. More commercially oriented media might give greater prominence to entertainer roles because of assumptions about audience preferences for the spectator role. Conformity on the part of political spokesmen would lead them to adopt actor/performer roles.

3.   Where political parties control the media, the gladiator role will be adopted more often by political spokesmen and the role of editorial guide will be adopted by media personnel; this will exert pressure on audience members to assume the partisan role.

4.   In systems governed by more authoritative and paternalistic goals, one of two consequences for audience members might prevail: Audience roles could tend to follow those assumed by party and media communicators, involving a greater emphasis on partisan and monitor roles; or audience expectations would be in conflict with the equivalent orientations of message senders, with resulting tendencies to avoid political information, distrust the media, and feel alienated from politics.

POLITICAL INSTITUTIONS VS. MEDIA INSTITUTIONS: NORMS AND STRUCTURES

A second point of entry to the analysis of political communication systems springs initially from the necessary involvement of two kinds of actors—political spokesmen and media personnel—in recurrent patterns of interaction with each other. These can be seen as operating on two planes: boundary maintenance between organizations and message production. In the first case members of the top echelons of both organizations might maintain contacts aimed at regulating the relationships between the two, resolving conflicts where they arise, generally defining the boundaries between them, and maintaining the smooth functioning of the system. But second, of course, the bulk of interaction between professional communicators and politicians usually occurs at somewhat lower levels and is more directly concerned with political output. This takes in both formal contexts, such as press conferences, briefings, interviews, and so on, and informal ones, such as a confidential exchange of views over a drink. The products of these interactions include not only streams of specific messages—on problems of the day, policies evolved to deal with them, arguments for and against alternative positions, the personalities involved in controversy, and so on—but also (and more important) those more abiding ground rules that prescribe the standardized formats through which information is regularly presented to the public (6). The interacting parties on both planes are perpetually caught up in a tension between needs of mutual accommodation and various sources of conflict. Without minimal accommodation, little or no communication would take place and nobody's purposes would be realized. Yet the conflicting functions (and independent power bases of the two sides) ensure that the terms of accommodation will continually be open to renewal and revision.

The conduct of both professional communicators and politicians is often assessed from essentially one-sided standpoints. For example, the political activist might treat media output as a trivialized version of his own more lofty concerns (5), or the journalist may regard politicians as inveterate corrupters of the independent press. A more analytical approach might aim instead to identify the sources of certain more or less constant influences on the behavior of both interacting parties insofar as they subscribe to different codes of conduct and belong to different kinds of organization. Such constant factors may be found in two critical structural dimensions that influence the relationship between the parties concerned—the degree of *professionalization* characteristic of the personnel of media and political institutions and the degree of *bureaucratization* characteristic of the two organizations.

Recent studies of mass media institutions have paid much attention to issues centering on the professionalization of staff communicators (8, 12, 16, 24). Although the degree to which media personnel exhibit all the characteristics usually ascribed to established professions might be debated, the influence of professional norms on their outlook is greater than in the case of politicians (13). Some aspects of this distinction may include the following:

1. *Bases of legitimacy.* These differ for the two sets of actors. Media personnel are legitimated chiefly through their fidelity to professional codes. Politi-

cians derive their legitimacy from the authority of the causes they espouse, the degree of consensus among the interests they articulate, and public acceptance of the procedures by which they have been chosen to represent such interests.

2. *The service function.* The centrality of the service function in the behavior of media professionals is reflected in their claim to be concerned primarily to *serve* the audience members' "right to know." The primary concern of the politician is to *persuade* the audience in the cause of political and partisan goals.

3. *Autonomy.* The work rewards that media men enjoy also derive partly from their professional autonomy. Such an emphasis might clash with the politicians' common view of media personnel as essentially middlemen in the political communication process. This potential conflict becomes yet more acute when politicians, who commonly are disposed toward more idealogical criteria of political truth, are confronted with the tendency of media professionals to adhere to a more empirical, sceptical (perhaps cynical), and many-sided description of political reality.

All this suggests an essential discrepancy between the codes of conduct accepted by political spokesmen and those that regulate the behavior of professional communicators, irrespective of any higher order principles that might be shared by both.

Another set of tensions stems from structural differences between media and political organizations. Many mass media enterprises are formal institutions governed at some level of their organization by bureaucratic norms and procedures. Political parties, however, exist for long periods of time as relatively skeletal organizations, which are fully mobilized only periodically or in crisis situations and have only a rather loose hold over those of their members who are not fully remunerated for their political activity. They are not designed, therefore, to exert full bureaucratic control over politicians and cannot base their modes of operation on purely bureaucratic standards. A consequence of this is that, once appointed, media personnel enjoy relative security and need not be legitimated by the consent of others outside their own employing organization.

The position of the politician is essentially less secure, more bedevilled by uncertainty, and more dependent on a continual renewal of the consent of his supporters. The vulnerability of the politician, in contrast to the bureaucratic security of the professional communicator, is illustrated by the highly visible and readily identified position of individual responsibility that the politician holds, as against the greater diffusion of responsibility that obtains in media organizations. To the politician, then, the protective bureaucratic shells of the media must seem intrinsically difficult to penetrate, provoking frustrations that may be less comprehensible and more irritating to individuals who do not usually operate in a bureaucratic environment and who could also resent bureaucratic challenges to the supremacy of their societal functions.

The potential tensions inherent in these structural differences must be managed and contained, if the interests of both sides are to be accommodated. This suggests that one task in the analysis of political communication systems would involve an examination of the formal and informal mechanisms that span the boundaries between the two kinds of organizations. Apart from the evolution of basic ground rules that regulate the production and dissemination of political communication contents, other areas to be examined might include the establishment of specialized agencies, such as publicity and public relations departments, for coping with the demands of the other side; the development of formal and informal procedures for airing complaints; the founding of various regulatory bodies, such as press councils, broadcasting councils, regulatory commissions, and enquiry commissions that exist to relate the workings of the mass media to certain criteria of the public interest; the appointments of individuals familiar with the values of one sphere in key positions in the organization of the other; and the ostensibly informal mixing of politicians and media personnel in social circles outside work.

POLITICAL CULTURE AS A SOURCE OF REGULATING MECHANISMS

A final analytical point arises from the fact that, apart from the procedures and mechanisms that are evolved by political and media institutions to govern the relationships between them, all political systems generate principles derived from the tenets of their political cultures for regulating the political role of the mass media. Such organizing principles are vital, because the contributions of the mass media to the political process are too important to be left to chance. Thus, communication processes are involved in the legitimation of authority and serve functions of political articulation, mobilization and conflict-management. They set much of the agenda of political debate. They are partly responsible for determining which political demands in society will be aired and which will be relatively muted. They affect the chances of governments and other political actors to secure essential supports. In short, they are so closely intertwined with political processes that they must be regulated in some appropriate and accepted way.

The manner of such attempted regulation is ultimately traceable to the influence of various tenets of political culture. The most basic one is, of course, the degree to which freedom of expression is cherished as a basic political value or, conversely, the degree to which restrictions on it are regarded as necessary and permissible for the sake of other political goals. Closely related is the value placed on ensuring the existence of outlets for voicing a variety of opinions and securing their ability to operate in a fashion unhampered by potential attempts of political actors to influence or dominate them. Political-cultural factors bearing on the structure of prevailing opinions may also play a part. For example, how far are the predominant positions polarized? To what extent do they tend to be expressed in ideological or pragmatic forms? What is the manner of their relationship to underlying bases of social differentiation and cleavage? On another level one might identify the influence of assumptions about the suitability of market mechanisms for advancing society's communication goals: Societies that share the basic tenets of freedom of political expression might differ in their conception of the desirability of subjecting communication outlets to economic constraints and to the pressures of a free market. Finally, political cultures may differ in the degree to which they value the political sphere itself as a dignified and important realm of activity, which deserves to have informed involvement promoted. Although all such tenets are relevant, no one-to-one relationship can be traced between any single strand of political culture and any specific principle designed to govern the role of the mass media in politics. In the end the central issue in the relationship between media and political institutions revolves around the *media's relative degree of autonomy* and to what extent and by what means this is allowed to be constrained. Thus, it is the overall cultural mix in a given society that will tend to fix the position of the media on the subordination-autonomy continuum and determine which constraints are permitted some degree of control over them. At least three main sources of constraints *directly* subordinate the media to political institutions: legal, normative, and structural.

Legal constraints include all rules and regulations that define the rights and obligations of media institutions that are ultimately enforceable by the executive and judicial arms of the state. They primarily define the area within which the media may exercise freedom of expression, circumscribed as the case may be by libel laws, legally protected rights of privacy, restrictions on national security grounds, the imposition of censorship on political comment, and so on.

Normative constraints refer to expectations of political and public service by media organizations for which they may be held socially accountable without falling under the direct control of either state or party machinery. They often arise from a conviction that the normal operation of the market mechanism is either insufficient to promote accepted communication goals or may work against them, and they typically invite attempts to ensure that the existing media dispense both entertaining fare and a full and varied supply of political information and analysis suited to the needs of a conscientious citizenry. Some, by now classic, expressions of such "social responsibility" doctrines, especially as they apply to the press, are to be found in the recommendations of the Commission on Freedom of the Press (4), Rivers and Schramm (18), and in Siebert et al. (21).

Structural constraints concern the degree to which formal or semi-formal linkages may be forged between media institutions and political bodies. Political parties, for example, may be involved in the organization of media enterprises through ownership, financial contributions, or representation on policymaking bodies. Linkages may also be established *via* a tradition of editorial support for the party's goals and policies. The phenomenon of press-party parallelism, comprehensively analyzed by Seymour-Ure (20), obviously belongs to this area of constraint.

Apart from these *direct* sources of political constraints, media organizations labor under a host of other constraints, some of which may be employed by political institutions to gain a measure of *indirect* control and influence over the media.* Prominent among these are economic constraints. These apply not only to commercial media organizations (where advertising revenue might be regulated or taxed directly by the political authorities) but also to noncommercial media institutions whose cash inflows (be they license fees, government or nongovernment subsidies) may be subjected to government approval or influence. Thus, the business and administrative personnel of media organizations, who are charged with their economic and financial viability and well-being, might be especially sensitive to external pressures affecting their organizations' finances and consequently might act as a potential channel for the introduction of political influence on their message outputs. Similarly, political control or regulation focused ostensibly on the technologies of mass communication (such as licensing the use of the airwaves or control of the import or price of newsprint) may be used as a form of leverage to exert influence over media policies. More generally, we may, following Gerbner (10), identify a variety of "power roles" both inside and outside of media institutions that are capable of affecting mass communicators' decisions, consequently inducing them to act as (willing or unwilling) channels of political influence on the media.

The two main media of political communication, broadcasting and the

---

*The distinction between direct and indirect sources of political control over the media constitutes yet another boundary problem. Clearly, some forms of control, such as economic ones, are so inextricably interwoven with political relationships that they may be regarded also as direct controls. Our distinction, however, is based on whether a given constraint can be traced to *direct political relationships* between the media and political institutions or whether it operates via other potential mechanisms of control.

press, tend for historical, economic, and technological reasons to be differently placed with respect to these constraints and to exhibit different degrees of
vulnerability to them. However, these differences are relative rather than
absolute, and some important similarities between them may be identified.
For example, although public service broadcasting immediately comes to
mind as an instance of normative constraint on broadcasting, it has a close
analogue in the "social responsibility theory of the press," with its attendant
codes of journalistic practice and press councils set up to pronounce on instances of their infraction. Similarly, although "parallelism" to political parties may seem more common to the press because of the relative multiplicity
of outlets characteristic of that medium, in some countries at least, separate
broadcasting organizations have been instituted to follow political or other
sociocultural divisions (such as the Dutch system or the system that prevailed
in Chile until the 1973 military coup). In other countries representatives of
political parties are admitted to membership of the governing bodies of
broadcasting organizations on a pluralistic basis (e.g., Austria).

Nevertheless, some crucial differences between these media still exist. In
many democratic countries newspapers have traditionally belonged in the
private sector, whereas the dependence of broadcast transmission on scarce
wavelengths immediately placed first radio and then television in the public
domain. Many consequences have flowed from this distinction. Perhaps the
most important one is the development of a regulatory licensing system for
broadcasting, which was either totally absent or far looser in the case of the
press. A related difference concerns the number of outlets. These are typically
numerous in the case of the press, whereas the relative paucity of broadcasting outlets often results in the monopolistic or duopolistic position of many
broadcasting institutions. Yet another difference might be identified in the
relatively greater vulnerability of the press to market forces, from which
broadcasting organizations have often been more sheltered (with the obvious
exception of commercial broadcasting organizations). As a result, the pre-
sumed power of broadcasting has been enhanced, and consequently means of
controlling or neutralizing its potential rivalry to political institutions have
had to be found. These have emerged in the form of norms requiring impartiality in the handling of controversial issues, noneditorializing, and the
maintenance of a balance between the major political tendencies of the day.

Perhaps these intermedia contrasts are reflected in two main differences so
far as the imposition of constraining principles of organization is concerned.
Newspapers can become involved in political controversy as participants
more easily than as mere referees; from this point of view, variations in
media-party parallelism across countries and time periods—with possibly
major consequences for audience behavior and response—are more likely to
be found in the press field than in broadcasting. Simply because broadcasting

organizations are located in the public sector, they will tend—other factors being equal—to be closer to the subordination pole of the autonomy-subordination continuum than the press system of the same society is likely to be.

Because we conceive of communication processes as forming a system, variations in the regulatory connections between political and media institutions should have definite consequences for other components of the system, including content outputs and audience orientations thereto. Some examples of possible linkages of this kind are presented in the following hypotheses:

1.   Party-tied media systems will produce a higher proportion of one-sided political content, tending as a result to activate partisan role orientations among members of the audience as well as selective exposure mechanisms. They will also tend to produce dissensus rather than consensus issue agendas, giving rise in turn to a higher degree of conflict over issue priorities among electors dependent on the different media outlets.

2.   The more subordinate the media system to the political system, the greater will be the degree of free access to communication outlets for the statements and manisfestos of the political system's spokesmen. This may increase the frequency of partisan and monitor roles.

3.   The greater the autonomy of the media system, the greater will be its tendency to generate "balanced" political information contents (in ways which both *reflect* and *protect* its autonomous status). It will consequently perform primarily "moderator" and "watchdog" functions, which will tend to activate "liberal citizen" and "monitor" role orientations among its audience. Two types of autonomous media systems are likely:

- A commercially supported autonomous media system might favor the presentation of political materials in terms of the conflicts and the political strategies, focusing on personalities at the expense of political issues. This will tend especially to precipitate and cater to a greater frequency of "spectator" roles.
- Noncommercial and semi-commercial media systems that are normatively disposed to public service goals will produce higher proportions of issue-oriented political outputs and will tend to generate a higher incidence of "monitor" role orientations among audience members.

CONCLUSION

The view of political communication presented in this chapter draws upon the concept of a system as a set of input-output relationships that bind its constituent elements in a network of mutual dependencies. Such a model has both theoretical and empirical utilities. It should facilitate a comparative analysis of the political communication systems of different societies, and it has generated hypotheses on the basis of which a series of cross-national investigations could be launched.

Utilization of the main components of the system as analytical entry points provides, moreover, a set of complementary perspectives on the political communication process. From the standpoint of audience roles, this is seen in terms of *mutual orientations* to communication content that link (or fail to link) audience members with media personnel and political spokesmen. The structural/institutional perspective provides a view of the system in terms of *conflicting goals and interests*, ascribing these conflicts to structural differences between media and political institutions. Finally, the regulatory perspective focuses on the processes by which these conflicts are *institutionalized and managed* through the application of normative criteria, to which all participants subscribe to the extent that they share in and recognize the legitimacy of the political culture from which they derive.

The model aims to take account of both consensus and conflict relationships in political communication transactions. At this stage, however, it still awaits validation through a sustained program of empirical research.

REFERENCES

1. Blumler, Jay G. "Audience Roles in Political Communication: Some Reflections on Their Structure, Antecedents and Consequences." Paper presented to the International Political Science Association Congress, Montreal, 1973.

2. Blumler, Jay G., and Jack M. McLeod. "Communication and Voter Turnout in Britain," in Morriss Janowitz (ed.), *Sociological Theory and Survey Research*. Beverly Hills, Calif.: Sage, 1974.

3. Cohen, Stanley, and Jock Young (eds.). *The Manufacture of News*. London: Constable, 1973.

4. Commission on Freedom of the Press. *A Free and Responsible Press*. Chicago: The University of Chicago Press, 1974.

5. Crossman, Richard. "The Politics of Viewing," *New Statesman, 76* (July–December, 1968), 525–530.

6. Dearlove, John. "The BBC and the Politicians," *Index, 3,* 1 (1974), 23–33.

7. Deutsch, Karl. *The Nerves of Government.* New York: Free Press, 1963.

8. Elliott, Philip. *The Making of a Television Series*. London: Constable, 1972.

9. Fagen, Richard. *Politics and Communication.* Boston: Little, Brown, 1966.

10. Gerbner, George. "Institutional Pressures Upon Mass Communicators," in Paul Halmos (ed.), *The Sociology of Mass Communicators*. Keele: University of Keele, 1969.

11. Hoyer, Svennik, Stig Hadenius, and Lennart Weibull. *The Politics and Economics of the Press: A Developmental Perspective,* Contemporary Political Sociology Series. Beverly Hills, Calif.: Sage, 1975.

12. Kumar, Krishan. "Holding the Middle Ground: The BBC, the Public and the Professional Broadcaster," *Sociology, 9,* 1 (1975), 66–88.

13. Lattimore, Dan L., and Oguz B. Nayman. "Professionalism of Colorado's Daily Newsmen: A Communicator Analysis," *Gazette, 20,* 1 (1974), 1–10.

14. McCombs, Maxwell E., and Donald L. Shaw. "The Agenda-Setting Function of the Mass Media," *Public Opinion Quarterly, 36,* 2 (1972), 176–187.

15. McLeod, Jack M., Lee B. Becker, and James E. Byrnes. "Another Look at the Agenda-Setting Function of the Press." Paper presented to the Association for Education in Journalism Conference, Fort Collins, Colorado, 1973.

16. Nayman, Oguz B. "Professional Orientations of Journalists: An Introduction to Communicator Analysis Studies," *Gazette, 19,* 4 (1973), 195–212.

17. Rivers, William L., and Michael J. Nyhan (eds.). *Aspen Notebook on Government and the Media.* New York: Praeger, 1973.

18. Rivers, William L., and Wilbur Schramm. *Responsibility in Mass Communication.* New York: Harper & Row, 1969.

19. Sears, David O., and Jonathan L. Freedman. "Selective Exposure to Communication: A Critical Review," *Public Opinion Quarterly, 31,* 2 (1967), 194–213.

20. Seymour-Ure, Colin. *The Political Impact of Mass Media.* London: Constable, 1974.

21. Siebert, Fred, T. Peterson, and Wilbur Schramm. *Four Theories of the Press.* Urbana: University of Illinois Press, 1956.

22. Tan, Alexis. "A Role Theory: A Dissonance Analysis of Message Content Preferences," *Journalism Quarterly, 50,* 2 (1973), 278–284.

23. Tichenor, Philip J., George A. Donohue, and Clarice N. Olien. "Mass Communication Research: Evolution of a Structural Model," *Journalism Quarterly, 50,* 3 (1973), 419–425.

24. Tunstall, Jeremy. *Journalists at Work.* London: Constable, 1971.

25. Verba, Sidnay, Norman H. Nie, and Jae-On Kim. *The Modes of Democratic Participation: A Cross-National Comparison.* Beverly Hills, Calif.: Sage, 1971.

26. Wade, Serena E. "Media Effects on Changes in Attitude Towards the Rights of Young People," *Journalism Quarterly, 50,* 2 (1973), 229–236, 347.

27. Wamsley, Gary L., and Richard A. Pride. "Television Network News," *Western Political Quarterly, 25* (1972), 434–450.

CHAPTER 23

From Mass Media to
Mass Consciousness

KAARLE NORDENSTRENG

In May 1973 the President of Finland, Dr. Urho Kekkonen, spoke on the international flow of television programs at the University of Tampere.* After dealing with national and international communication policies, he concluded his address with the following remarks:

You might ask why I have spent such a long time on communication phenomena. After all, don't economic factors determine a person's life more than communication? I should like to answer by referring to the prerequisites of democracy.

Studies show that the majority of people in countries with high standards of education—Finland, for example—feel alienated from world problems and even from their own society. One study shows the astonishing fact that only half the respondents of voting age knew that in Finland parliament passes the laws. Wide sections of the population are lacking in the most basic social information and do not have sufficient knowledge to form opinions about society and act as democracy would demand. People can of course learn from experience, and their opportunities to obtain information are growing all the time, but the knowledge they have does not form an organized entity. There is a shortage of information which would give them this cohesive whole and the possibility to connect matters with one another.

But a democracy cannot function properly unless there is original, critical thinking among its citizens. The realization of democracy is not possible if only dominant patterns of behavior and the pressure of public opinion offer content to people's views of the world. In such conditions one cannot speak of the will of the people, but of the people merely echoing the message put across by a small privileged group with control of both power and the channels of influence. When this is the case, a so-called free market economy which claims to offer free choice is in no position to point an accusing finger at societies it considers totalitarian.

The conscious channeling of future development towards democracy requires that

---

*The proceedings of this symposium, including Dr. Kekkonen's speech (slightly abbreviated), are published in Nordenstreng and Varis (15), which also contains results of an international inventory of television program structure and the flow of TV programs between nations.

the vast bulk of the population does not remain in the position of bystanders without initiative. By improving the lot of those in a weaker position, we equalize the opportunities for participation. By directing communication and education to the development of spontaneous thinking and the independent assumption of knowledge we make possible the search for consciousness so much desired for the future.

A careful reading of the points made here by Dr. Kekkonen in fairly general language will reveal that the text implies several significant concepts and approaches that are currently coming to the fore in the communication research being carried out in Scandinavia. In this chapter I make these tendencies explicit by first presenting a few concrete examples of research projects reflecting the new approaches and then listing the central theoretical assumptions that underlie the research orientation, thus summarizing current thinking in Finland and increasingly in the rest of Scandinavia. The features that may be seen to characterize a more global state of the art in the field of mass communication research are listed in the final section of the chapter. Such a worldwide perspective is needed to place the particular Scandinavian phenomena in an appropriate context.

EXAMPLES OF RESEARCH PROJECTS: COMPREHENSION AND EFFECTS OF TELEVISION PROGRAMS, INFORMATIONAL NEEDS AND INFORMATION GAPS IN SOCIETY

A typical feature in Finnish and Swedish broadcasting research since the late-1960s has been an emphasis on comprehension. Several studies have been designed to ascertain the mechanisms by which people receive information or, expressed differently, the degrees and ways of understanding messages used by viewers and listeners (11, p. 261). An example of these studies is the Finnish project that included an intensive analysis of the psychological reception of farmers who viewed a three-part documentary TV program on Soviet collective farming.* The comprehension and influence of the Finnish-produced program "A Collective Farm in Eastern Siberia" was studied jointly by the Finnish Broadcasting Company and University of Tampere, where most of the work has been carried out and reported by a young communication researcher Kauko Pietilä.†

The overall design of the study was quite conventional: a measurement of

---

*A description of the programs and the research project and its preliminary results are provided in English in Yleisradio (25).

†An important theoretical and empirical report by K. Pietilä (16), presented as an academic thesis, is available only in Finnish. Preliminary results of Pietilä's study are included in the English version of Yleisradio's report (25). A follow-up report by K. Pietilä (17) is available in English.

relevant knowledge and opinions before exposure and an after-exposure registration of how these were touched by the programs in question. Interesting but by no means unique was the fact that the topic of the programs was emotionally and politically loaded and that the prevailing opinions on it among the public were known (also verified by the interviews) to be most negative among practically the whole population.* What makes this study different from many other before-and-after exercises is the theoretical framework generated and, to a certain extent, the in-depth interview technique employed.

Pietilä has articulated the theoretical framework of the study around one central concept: the world-view or *Weltanschauung* of the recipient.† As an individual acquires information, the world-view functions as a system of induction governed by two antagonistic principles. The world-view is influenced by the "pressure of objective facts"—that is, an individual's subjective world-view has an inherent tendency to correspond to the objective state of affairs around him. However, there is a tendency toward "stability of world-view" as a consequence of the individual's need for coherence in his already-established belief system; as the latter has been created by the socializing institutions, this "principle of stability" is seen as an aspect of the unifying and hegemonic influence deriving from the overall social structure. Accordingly, the study was to test to what extent each of these two principles influenced the reception of a documentary that provided objective facts against hegemonically determined and largely ignorant conceptions.

The results showed that the process of receiving documentary messages did follow the model constructed when viewers were relatively well informed about the subject to start with; however, an equally systematic process was not found to operate among the most poorly informed viewers. Yet practically all viewers did learn something from the programs. In spite of a tendency to stability the world-view changed: New empirical evidence was accumulating upon the existing cognitive and evaluative structures, which were found to change in certain respects. The changes were by no means radical, and there were clear indications of the way basic values of the world-view re-

---

*A similar case study carried out in the United States has been reported by Smith (20). American students sharing the prevailing anticommunist public opinion were confronted with Soviet overseas broadcasts.

†The concept of world-view was first introduced in the Finnish arena of mass communications (research) by the Program Regulations adopted for Finnish broadcasting in 1967 which defined the tasks and aims of broadcasting in terms of offering to the recipient informational building material for the construction of a personal world-view (12, pp. 25–26). A fundamental theoretical analysis of the concept of world-view was provided by Yrjö Ahmavaara (1), a philosopher and communication researcher who at the time was employed by the Finnish Broadcasting Company and helped to define the long-range policies of broadcasting.

mained untouched or were even accentuated. For instance, even if Finnish farmers were convinced by the programs of the effectiveness and rationality of collective farming in the Soviet Union, the farmers maintained their cognitive balance by rejecting absolutely a generalization of this cognition to their own conditions, and they generated several excuses to "prove" how collective farms were impossible in Finland.

Consequently, the programs favorable to the Soviet system of farming were not proved to have brainwashed the Finnish viewers but only increased their knowledge and understanding of the subject. The "pressure of objective facts" did have an impact on certain areas of the world-view, and the "principle of stability" continued to govern others. By and large the study indicated that there is great potential for informational communication in areas where public ignorance and prejudices prevail and that an individual is ready to adopt a new cognitive map if his present one is proven to deviate from the objective state of affairs. However, that an individual does not allow any changes to take place in his world-view as a consequence of only a few pieces of empirical evidence was equally clear. The evaluative and personality levels of the world-view are quite constant and may change only after long-term accumulation of information and its personal application in everyday practice. Accordingly, the study empirically confirmed that a human individual is a relatively independent factor in the process of mass communication. He is certainly influenced by the messages supplied to him, but his terms of acquiring information are determined by his previous experiences and immediate environment—and not by any omnipotent media manipulators.

To expand the focus of attention beyond the media, their messages, and the psychological reception process of the messages to the social and material living conditions of the people is typical of current Scandinavian communication research.* As Nordenstreng (11) expressed it in listing factors that determine the reception of adult education programs:

> However good the timing policy, however dominant the channel, however close to real-life experiences the programs may be, however easy the language, and however much promotional information and even organizational mobilization may be exercised, nothing helps if a person is seriously deprived in his objective and physical surroundings, and consequently if he is psychologically so apathetic and alienated that the total motivation for improvement and change in his socioeconomic situation is missing (p. 35).

---

*First approaches in this line were some internal reports by researchers of the Finnish Broadcasting Company in the late-1960s, based on unsystematic observations and free in-depth interviews among some audience groups (e.g., Margaretha Starck's "Experiences from a Bicycle Ride" and Pekka Peltola's "Report Beyond the Villages"). These reports had far greater impact on both program-makers and researchers themselves than many major projects with representative samples and statistical elaborations.

Manifestation of concern about this way of thinking is shown by the projects started in the early-1970s and called in Finland "citizens' informational needs" and in Sweden "information gaps in society." Both were initiated and are mainly being carried out within the broadcasting organizations. This is an indication of the social and informational commitment of these mass communication institutions (cf. Chapter 10 in this volume and Nordenstreng, 10).

The points of departure of the Swedish project are stated by the researchers as follows:

Marked differences among social groups with respect to access to and utilization of essential information constitute a problem in our society. ("Essential" information is tentatively defined as information that enables the individual to survey and understand the society he lives in, and allows him to actively influence the conditions of his daily life.) These differences are primarily functions of factors outside the control of mass media, factors such as the structure of society, the social and economic status of various groups and individuals, their personal capabilities, etc. Even so, the roles and potential roles of mass media should not be considered a priori to lack significance. Depending on how they are controlled and utilized—in terms of policy, on planning and production levels—the media may doubtless contribute either to the broadening or to the closing of information gaps (21).

The Finnish project on citizens' informational needs shares these points and stresses the socioeconomically determined mechanisms that accumulate material and mental wealth accompanied by informational activity and material and mental poverty accompanied by informational passivity. The theoretical background report of the project * refers to a government committee on the quality of life which found that because of the accumulation process differences in the overall standard of living become greater than differences in any single component of the standard of living. In analyzing mechanism of social inequality, the committee had further pointed out the functions of segregation in society: Minimization of contacts between the privileged and underprivileged reduces the informational and social fields of operation of both groups, leaving the privileged to enjoy their benefits with good conscience and the underprivileged to remain satisfied with their lot. Social studies and official statistics had until recent years largely supported these same overall tendencies.

Empirical results of a nationwide survey carried out for this project further verified the presence of this vicious circle: Those who were already well informed were most open to new knowledge and most capable of finding relevant knowledge, whereas the ill-informed—that is, socioeconomically underprivileged—were passive and unable to tell where to find relevant

*The project, which is still uncompleted, has been reported only in Finnish as a preliminary project plan (22) and a theoretical background report by Elina Suominen (23) in the Finnish Broadcasting Company.

knowledge; furthermore, the latter group did not regard information and knowledge as particularly important. The road towards an informational and social activization of an underprivileged person is both long and complicated, as illustrated in Figure 1 (according to Suominen, 22, p. 30).

An essential theoretical distinction applied in the project is between subjective and objective informational needs. To carry out an opinion survey and register subjectively perceived informational needs and wishes was not found to be sufficient; an all-around picture of the respondent's objective living conditions and his possibilities for social action was also necessary. The aim was to see an individual's informational behavior (subjective needs) as an integral part of his total living conditions and social environment (objective needs). Objective informational needs are least satisfied among the underprivileged sections of the population, and the greatest difference between the subjective and objective levels of informational need is to be found in the same groups that are left outside the positive accumulation of material and informational wealth in society. The "haves" do not objectively have many informational needs unsatisfied and yet they subjectively have more informational hunger than the "have-nots," whose objective informational needs are burning.

Besides the social segregation referred to above, the socioeconomic system is seen to employ various mechanisms that tend to keep the level of subjective informational needs low. One central concept in this connection is the bourgeois hegemony which may be understood as a filter extending to the personal world-view of an individual and biasing or blocking his process of perceiving reality. The *de facto* function of the bulk of mass media is taken to be an overall support of this hegemony—for example, by means of a long-term indoctrination of certain implicit values and a fragmentation of message supply that prevents rather than helps an individual to construct a holistic view of objective reality.

This project—as well as the corresponding Swedish one—could be classi-

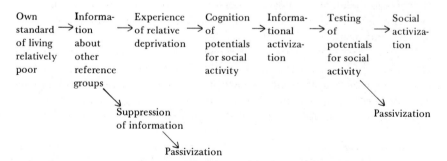

Figure 1   The process of activization of a relatively underprivileged group.

fied as an exercise in political science as easily as a piece of communication research. The problem is to study the actual and potential conditions for social equality and participatory democracy.* In fact, avoidance of a narrow communicologist's point of view is a typical feature of current thinking in Scandinavia. Instead, the perspective is made fairly broad to include a wide range of socioeconomic (objective) factors as well as (subjective) communication phenomena. That the behavior of the receiver is seen to be determined by the material and social conditions of his overall life situation rather than by the messages of mass communication is also characteristic of the present orientation.

CENTRAL THEORETICAL ASSUMPTIONS

The essentials of the kind of thinking exemplified above may be condensed into four categories of conceptual elements and two basic theoretical propositions. These are briefly outlined below to give an analytical account of the current approaches. Naturally these features are not manifest throughout current research, and some of them may not even be implicit in many studies. Much Scandinavian research does not follow this kind of thinking at all but continues to represent the more traditional concepts and theoretical assumptions.†

The first category of conceptual elements characteristic of current thinking is related to the concept of *consciousness*. A derivative of this is the concept of world-view that was found to be central in comprehension studies. As is well known, the concept of consciousness has a long philosophical tradition, including the famous Cartesian reasoning, *"Cogito, ergo sum!"* However, because of the dominant positivist tradition and the consequent behavioral approach such "mentalistic" concepts have not enjoyed a legitimate status in Anglo-Saxon communicology any more than in the Western social sciences in general. Consequently, one may say that the reintroduction of consciousness implies a kind of humanization of the fairly mechanical view of man offered by the behavioral-positivist tradition.

The second category of conceptual elements has a social dimension. The

---

*The conditions of democracy in Finland (called "Tandem"), including the communication component, are being investigated in a project sponsored by the Academy of Finland and led by Juha Partanen.

†In Scandinavia, as elsewhere, a battle between scientific camps, not unrelated to politics within the countries, is a well-known phenomenon. The field of communication research has so far enjoyed a relatively peaceful time in this respect, particularly outside Finland where many kinds of social conflicts tend to become more prominent than in the rest of Scandinavia. These problems of power relations between the current thinking described here and all other orientations have been left completely outside the scope of this chapter.

terms *ideology, hegemony, manipulation,* and so on raise the perspective above the individual consciousness (micro level) to more general cultural phenomena of clearly supra-individual character (macro level). What is involved here is reference to the social institutions that produce and distribute information in society and to a kind of collective consciousness composed of a number of relatively similar units of individual consciousness. The latter is also called "mass consciousness"—a term indicating both the social and the human aspects involved.

Accordingly, the title of this chapter is intended to point out how the perspective of mass communication research in Scandinavia is changing from a narrow and "mechanistic" approach centered around the media (as separated from society) to a wider and "humanistic" approach with the media as no more than integral parts of an overall ideological machinery in society. This machinery, which is an integrated function of all social and cultural institutions with potential effects on peoples' consciousness, is usually understood to have a hegemonistic character—that is, it introduces elements into the individual consciousness that would not spontaneously appear there, but will not be rejected by consciousness because they are so commonly shared in the cultural community.* Thus the term *mass consciousness* is seen not only as a sum or average of a number of individual pieces of consciousness but also as a social phenomenon relatively independent of individuals.

The third category of conceptual elements (clearly seen in the informational needs project) refers to the *material conditions of the individual.* They are seen as critical to determine the individual consciousness. Thus individual consciousness is not understood as a loose intuition but rather as an internal correlate of the material circumstances encountered by the individual—that is, a subjective reflection of an objective state. The term *social position,* which is also used in this connection, implies that an individual has a certain location within the material world and the social relations concretely operating in it. In brief, there is an objective reality seen to extend beyond the individual consciousness.

Consequently, in addition to being humanistic in its approach, the current thinking is at the same time materialistic. It does not elevate the concept of consciousness to such a dominating position that the whole conceptual machinery would be composed of immaterial psychic and social elements. On the contrary, even consciousness itself is understood to be composed of material processes, although most complicated.† Like behaviorism, this mode of

---

*The term *indoctrination* has been suggested by Hemánus (7) and others to denote an influence of the media of which a recipient is not (by definition) conscious; *propaganda* would be a term for such influence taking place when the recipient is conscious about attempts to influence.
†According to materialistic philosophy, human consciousness is the property of a highly differentiated material. An example of a materialistic model of consciousness constructed in the tradition of behaviorism is provided in Nordenstreng (10, pp. 26–27).

thought only approves the existence of biologically determined human phenomena, including a purely materialistic process of communication between individuals; but unlike behaviorism, it does accept the reality of an individual consciousness "inside the black box," including spontaneous thought processes. Yet to call this approach "mentalistic" may not be correct because in many cases the latter term is used to refer to the opposite of materialist approaches, which is certainly not the case here.

The fourth central category also acknowledges material elements, but instead of concepts relating to the individual broader *socioeconomic structures* may be seen to constitute a material correlate to the concepts of social consciousness (the second category). These structures are composed of the material arrangements of production in society—that is, the productive forces and the relations of production, with the corresponding social and economic institutions determining relations between individuals (e.g., ownership conditions). The nature of these structures is materialistic, although in practice they may operate by means of symbolic (and in that sense immaterial) communication.

Consequently, social relations between men are not understood as a communication network operating at the level of consciousness; they are seen to be based on material conditions determining a person's location in the physical reality (mainly process of production). This eliminates, among other things, a conceptual confusion between power relations and the relations of communication—so popular in dominant Western thinking—which tends to reduce the objective power antagonisms to plain linguistic complications (e.g., references to "semantic noise" in industrial relations as an excuse not to further real industrial democracy).* Similarly, the current view does not see political democracy in a typical Western manner as an optimally operating democratic system, because in practice it does not extend to the economic power relations imposed by ownership conditions. In fact, political democracy is understood mainly as a phenomenon to be placed at the ideological level. Politics is being played usually in the consciousness of the masses and only exceptionally—in revolutionary situations—in the real power relations of society.†

Not only are material conditions introduced in addition to phenomena of individual and mass consciousness, they are taken as primary factors in explaining individual and social behavior. Yet the approach is not mechanistically materialistic, because the concepts of individual consciousness and so-

---

*Several Western communication researchers (e.g., Colin Cherry) have such an outlook on social relations as revealed by Jung *et al.* (8).

†The relations of socio-politico-economic power with information and communication phenomena have been studied in Sweden particularly by Cheesman and Hvitfelt (2), Cheesman and Kyhn (3) and Ekecrantz (4, 5). The latter has introduced the concept of "planned ignorance."

cial ideology expand the theoretical framework far beyond what is offered by the conventional behavioristic approach.

Naturally the various concepts listed above are closely interrelated so that what is essential is not the individual conceptual elements involved but the overall theoretical framework or approach provided jointly by all of them. It is not difficult to see how such an overall thinking is perfectly compatible with many modern conceptions of Western communication research, including the idea of media as an integral part of the social system and the new conceptions of the effects of communications as a long-term and often covertly indoctrinating influence. In fact these kinds of "new looks," including a view of the mass media as a dependent rather than an independent variable, are not difficult lessons for current Scandinavian thinking because they already are essential and natural features of it (cf. 18).

The above characterization of the emerging Scandinavian thinking may be further condensed into two basic theoretical propositions: a theory of knowledge and a theory of society. The former starts with the fundamental distinction between objective reality and subjective consciousness and states that subjective consciousness is a reflection of objective reality and that an individual bearing this consciousness is interacting with objective reality through practice.* The latter theoretical proposition places economic production as the primary determinant of social relations between individuals; this theory of society may also be seen to include a historical dimension with consecutive stages of forms of production and the corresponding social structures (cf. Nordenstreng and Varis, 14, pp. 395–398). The two theories are illustrated in Figure 2.

The theoretical assumptions in the kind of thinking described here are in all essential respects identical to the theory of dialectical materialism. Whether the current Scandinavian thinking really represents Marxism-Leninism is a difficult question, because individual researchers—even if they may operate within a common overall framework—usually have different variations in their approaches. Furthermore, there is ground for doubts concerning even the theoretical possibility of generating a Marxist tradition of research in a capitalist society and its institutionally bourgeois climate; the latter may be

---

*A description of such a dialectical materialist theory of knowledge is to be found, for example, in Mao Tso-Tung's essay "Where do correct ideas come from?" (9, pp. 134–144): "At first, knowledge is perceptual. The leap to conceptual knowledge, i.e., to ideas, occurs when sufficient perceptual knowledge is accumulated. This is one process in cognition. It is the first stage in the whole process on cognition, the stage leading from objective matter to subjective consciousness, from existence to ideas. . . . . Man's knowledge makes another leap through the test of practice. This leap is more important than the previous one for it is this alone that can prove the correctness or incorrectness of the first leap, i.e., of the ideas, theories, policies, plans or measures formulated in the course of reflecting the objective external world."

For a more comprehensive presentation, see *Fundamentals of Marxist-Leninist Philosophy* (6).

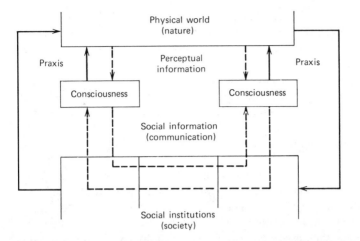

Figure 2 Human information activities within the framework of basic theoretical propositions: the acquisition of knowledge from the physical world (perceptual information—
vertical accompanied by related physical interaction with the objective reality (praxis), and
the exchange of experiences between units of individual consciousness (social information
or communication proper—horizontal). Objective reality = Nature + Society.

seen to eliminate objectively all significant social influence of revolutionary
science no matter how serious the individual (Marxist) researchers might
subjectively be. Consequently, the Scandinavian thinking referred to in this
chapter is dialectico-materialistically oriented.

GLOBAL TRENDS IN COMMUNICATION RESEARCH

What has been presented on Scandinavian thinking is not unrelated to what
is happening on the wider world scene. The reorientation taking place in the
field of mass communication research more or less everywhere in the Western
(capitalist) world is characterized by precisely the same tendencies as the
current Scandinavian thinking. Significant global tendencies may indeed become more visible in Scandinavian circumstances, which provide a kind of
laboratory situation purified from any single dominant cultural tradition and
world-political power commitment, for social developments of advanced capitalism to appear. Consequently, the difference between Scandinavia and
the rest of the Western world may be seen as a matter of degree rather than
of quality. Therefore the global trends reviewed below may be understood as
a "mild version" of Scandinavian thinking.*

*The following paragraphs are based on a paper "Normative Directions for Mass
Communication Research" presented at the first Nordic conference of mass communication
research in Oslo, June 1973, published in the proceedings of the conference (mimeo in Swedish
by the Press Research Institute of the University of Oslo; also in Polish in *Zeszyty Prasoznawcze*,
1974).

The global trends in the field of mass communication research can be expressed in terms of two interrelated tendencies on change: a tendency toward a more *holistic framework* and a tendency toward *policy orientation*. The holistic approach, for its part, may be seen to imply two subaspects: a stressing of the *processual approach* covering simultaneously various stages of the communication process and a stressing of the *contextual approach* tying the particular communication phenomena into wider socio-politico-economic settings.

A rebellion against the positivist-behaviorist tradition is not difficult to trace in these tendencies. In terms of the philosophy of science, this shift from positivism towards antipositivism may be seen as crucial in the present reorientation of communication research as well as in the so-called crisis of Western social sciences in general.

The implications of positivism for policy considerations are particularly important in the present context. The crucial notion of positivism argues that one cannot infer from "how things are," "how they should be." Goals of social activity are understood as something voluntary and subjective; value-bound choices are placed by definition outside the scope of objective knowledge. Consequently, research and politics are sharply separated from each other, and there prevails a relativism of values. Antipositivism, for its part, claims that a study of the objective laws of social processes, in their widest sense, can be derived from social goals grounded on objective facts. This social goal—the "how things should be"—can be inferred, at least to a great extent, from the laws followed by goal-directed social processes, once the latter have been discovered. Consequently, research and politics cannot and should not be sharply separated. As Ahmavaara (1, p. 14) puts it, research into social laws and political decision-making processes "are parts of a unified organism simply violently separated from each other by the Humean guillotine."

At this point one might ask why such a reorientation in the social sciences in general and mass communication research in particular has begun to take place. What are the cultural and social determinants behind this "movement?" In the present analysis only one overall factor will be singled out that seems to be of crucial importance (in analysis of the situation it alone certainly accounts for over 50 percent of the total explanation).

The suggested significant factor is the historical development in Western industrialized societies that has made ideological control over the mass consciousness become increasingly difficult—and hence ever more vital for the socioeconomic system to handle. In spite of the indoctrination influencing individuals throughout all established institutions in society—not least by the mechanism of fragmentation in education and mass communication—large segments of the population remain dissatisfied. Also significant is that new segments, such as students, have become involved in this refusal to digest what is centrally fed to them through socializing institutions, including the mass media.

Accordingly, because the traditional methods of ideological control have proved inadequate, one has been urged forward to search for more effective means to touch the minds of the masses. This is why so much is said today of "comprehension of messages," "audience passivity," and so on; these kinds of new looks into the mass communication process (including the "citizen participation") activists are a must for the established social order if it is going to maintain its mental and material control over the bulk of the population. Similarly, at the level of the social sciences social forces have needed to turn the positivistic tradition into a more holistic approach. It was no longer sufficient to contribute to the manipulative mechanisms by piecemeal studies and theories that bypass many significant features in social developments, particularly those generating dissonance and revolutionary potential.

A more honest assessment of the social reality, including the process of mass communication, in a macroperspective simply became vitally important. This assessment was not to be made for academic convenience but for an emerging socially determined concern for communication policies.* As is well known, systematic policies and long-range planning are another vital response to the objective development of the socioeconomic system ("state-monopoly capitalism"). Consequently, a need for policies and planning in the communication field of society derives from the motives for ideological control and also from a general tendency toward more coherent socioeconomic processes.

In terms of the present analysis, then, the new approach in communication research is no more of a happy chance than boosting interest in communication policies is a social luxury. Both can be seen to reflect the same basic tendency of having the mechanism of the prevailing social order brought up to date and thus supporting the basic tendencies of the status quo. Accordingly, a "progressive" communication researcher finds himself in a paradoxical situation.

REFERENCES

1. Ahmavaara, Yrjö. *Yhteiskuntatieteen kyberneettinen metodologia* [The Cybernetic Methodology of Social Sciences], 2nd ed. Helsinki: Tammi, 1971.

2. Cheesman, Robin, and Hakan Hvitfelt. "Den ideologiska apparaten under kapitalismen" [The Ideological Apparatus under Capitalism]. Institute of Sociology, University of Lund, 1972. Mimeographed.

*For the concept of communication policies, see for example, UNESCO (24) and Pool (19).

3. Cheesman, Robin, and Carsten Kyhn. "Notes on Mass Communication and the Formation of Class Consciousness," in *Der Anteil der Massenmedien bei der Herausbildung des Bewusstseins in der sich wandelnden Welt; Konferenzprotokoll II* [The Role of the Mass Media in the Shaping of Social Consciousness in a Changing World, Conference Proceedings Volume II]. Leipzig: Faculty of Journalism, Karl-Marx University, 1975, pp. 239–267.

4. Ekecrantz, Jan. "Notes Toward Reconceptualizations of the Concepts of Social Control and Communication." Institute of Sociology, University of Stockholm, 1973. Mimeographed.

5. ———. "Mediating Factors in the Production of Systematic Ignorance Under Late Capitalism," in *Der Anteil der Massenmedien bei der Herausbildung des Bewusstseins in der sich wandelnden Welt, Konferenzprotokoll I* [The Role of the Mass Media in the Shaping of Social Consciousness in a Changing World, Conference Proceedings Volume I]. Leipzig: Faculty of Journalism, Karl-Marx University, 1974, pp. 397–406.

6. *Fundamentals of Marxist-Leninist Philosophy.* Moscow: Progress, 1974.

7. Hemánus, Pertti. *Joukkotiedotus piilovaikuttajana* [Mass Communication as an Agent of Indoctrination]. Helsinki: Otava, 1973.

8. Jung, G., H. Poersche, and E. Schultz. *Beitrage zum Begriff der gesellschaftlichen Information* [Contributions to the Concept of Social Information]. Leipzig: Faculty of Journalism, Karl-Marx University, 1970.

9. Mao Tse-Tung. *Four Essays on Philosophy.* Peking: Foreign Languages Press, 1966.

10. Nordenstreng, Kaarle. *Toward Quantification of Meaning.* Annales Academiae Scientiarum Fennica, Series B, *161,* 2. Helsinki: Academia Scientiarum Fennica, 1969.

11. ———. "Broadcasting Research in Scandinavian Countries," in H. Egunchi and H. Ichinohe (eds.), *International Studies of Broadcasting.* Tokyo: NHK Radio and TV Culture Research Institute, 1971, pp. 245–265.

12. ———, (ed.). *Informational Mass Communication.* Helsinki: Tammi, 1973.

13. ———. "Definition of the Audience and How to Increase It." In *Adult Education by Television.* Geneva: European Broadcasting Union, 1973, pp. 31–38.

14. ———, and Tapio Varis. "The Non-homogeneity of the National State and the International Flow of Communication," in George Gerbner, Larry Gross, and William Melody (eds.), *Communication Technology and Social Policy.* New York: Wiley, 1973, pp. 393–412.

15. ———. *Television Traffic—A One-way Street?* Reports and Papers on Mass Communication, *70.* Paris: UNESCO, 1974.

16. Pietilä, Kauko. "Nakiko silma, kuuliko korva" [Did the Eye See and the Ear Hear]. Report Series A 44. University of Tampere, Research Institute for Social Sciences, 1973.

17. ———. "A Study in the Methodology of Consciousness Research." Report Series B 24, University of Tampere, Research Institute for Social Sciences, 1975.

18. Pietilä, Veikko. "Opinion Formation and the Press." Research Reports from the Section for Long-Range Planning, The Finnish Broadcasting Company, *15* (1973).

19. Pool, Ithiel de Sola. "The Rise of Communications Policy Research," *Journal of Communication, 24* (1974), 31–42.

20. Smith, Don. "Radio Moscow's North American Broadcasts: An Exploratory Study," *Journalism Quarterly, 43* (1965), 643–645. (A more elaborated version published in *Public Opinion Quarterly* (Winter 1970–1971), 531–551.)

21. Sveriges Radio (The Swedish Broadcasting Corporation). "Audience and Program Research," *Bulletin 3* (1973).

22. Suominen, Elina. "Tiedon tarve suomalaisessa yhteisdunnassa" [The Need of Information in Finnish Society]. Section for Long-Range Planning, The Finnish Broadcasting Company, 1972. Mimeographed.

23. Suominen, Elina. "Kamsalaisten tiedontarve" [Citizens' Informational Needs]. Section for Long-Range Planning, The Finnish Broadcasting Company, Report Series B, 3 (1973).

24. UNESCO. "Meeting of Experts on Communication Policies and Planning." COM/MD/24, 1972.

25. Yleisradio (The Finnish Broadcasting Company). "A Project on Comprehension and Effects of Mass Communication." Section for Long-Range Planning, Research Report 14 (1972).

INDEX